Henry F. du Pont and Winterthur

Henry F. du Pont
and
Winterthur

A Daughter's Portrait

❧ ☙

Ruth Lord

Foreword by R. W. B. Lewis

Yale University Press   New Haven and London

Frontispiece: Henry F. du Pont at Winterthur in the mid-1960s, with his ever-present notebook.

Except where noted, all photographs courtesy The Winterthur Library: Winterthur Archives.

Copyright © 1999 by Yale University.

All rights reserved.

Designed by James J. Johnson and set in Walbaum Roman typeset by The Composing Room of Michigan, Inc., Grand Rapids, Michigan. Printed in the United States of America by Edwards Brothers, Inc., Ann Arbor, Michigan.

Library of Congress Cataloging-in-Publication Data

Lord, Ruth, 1922–
   Henry F. du Pont and Winterthur: a daughter's portrait/Ruth Lord;
foreword by R. W. B. Lewis.
         p.   cm.
   Includes bibliographical references and index.
   ISBN 0-300-07074-8 (alk. paper)

   1. Du Pont, Henry Francis, 1880–1969.   2. Art—Collectors and collecting—
United States—Biography.   3. Henry Francis du Pont Winterthur Museum.   4. Fathers and
Daughters—United States—Biography.   I. Title.
N5220.D85L67   1998
745'.0974'075—dc21   98-35419

A catalogue record for this book is available from the British Library.

10 9 8 7 6 5 4 3

For
John Grier Holmes
1912–1997

Contents

Foreword

R. W. B. L E W I S

Early in this enchanting and luminous memoir, Ruth Lord tells us that back
in the 1950s she addressed a message to her father, Henry Francis du Pont,
which she called a "love letter to a house." The house was the Golf Cottage,
a compact nineteenth-century building on the vast Winterthur estate near
Wilmington, Delaware. Surrounded by woods and slopes, it had been remodeled into a comfortable one-family home, and Ruth hoped that she
might make it her own; it was so much more intimate than the stately man-
sion her parents occupied, and Ruth felt she could retain her own identity
there when visiting them. Might her father bequeath it to her? The Golf
Cottage is now Ruth Lord's home when, as often, she stays at Winterthur.
But she has also come to realize—and this she confesses in the "After-
thoughts" to her memoir—that her letter about the cottage "was in essence
a plea for a closer relationship" with her father.

The entire memoir—the story of a remarkable man and the fabulous
museum of American decorative arts he established at Winterthur—is a
similar plea. It is a beautifully executed search for the reality of her father,
from his birth in 1880 to his death in 1969, a search for full and permanent
connection between father and daughter. It is a deeply personal book but
at the same time a model of tact and taste. It is also the product of a person
who has for many years been a research associate at the Yale Child Study
Center. As such, it is a work of steady, subtle human perceptiveness.

The book is far from being merely personal. History flows through
these pages, almost two and a half centuries of it, with a parade of historically potent individuals; one of the main attractions of the book is the easy

interplay of the personal and contemporary with the grandly historical. Ruth Lord says in her opening remarks that "the notion of ancestry and family trees quite turned me off," at least until she began work on the memoir. As it is, the ancestry is present in full panoply, beginning with Pierre Samuel du Pont de Nemours (he was the one who added "de Nemours" to the family name, taking it from a town near which he had bought a farm). This Pierre (1739–1817) was a vivid and multitalented figure, a writer whose youthful work was praised by Voltaire, who wrote treatises on philosophy, and who translated Ariosto. He was "ennobled" by King Louis XVI and associated with the economist of genius Anne-Robert-Jacques Turgot and the Revolutionary statesman the Comte de Mirabeau, as well as with the Americans—Franklin and Jefferson.

In particular, Pierre Samuel du Pont was a leading voice among the powerful group known as the physiocrats: a group which held that *soil* was the key element in any national economy and that most people should live on farms, with grain being everywhere distributed free. In a certain perspective, Pierre was a recognizable great-great-grandfather of Henry Francis du Pont, creator of the extraordinary gardens and cultivated farmlands at Winterthur.

Pierre was, in the author's phrase, the "father of us all." He was the father most immediately of Eleuthère Irénée du Pont, who came to America on the first day of 1800, at the age of twenty-eight, bringing with him knowledge of advanced techniques in the making of gunpowder. These he had acquired by working under Antoine-Laurent Lavoisier, the most accomplished scientist of his generation (Franklin enjoyed investigating meteorological phenomena with him). Drawing on this experience, Eleuthère founded E. I. du Pont de Nemours & Company, initiating an "industrial empire," in Ruth Lord's words, "whose future power and wealth no one could have dreamed of."

History continues to color the family narrative. Harry's father, Colonel Henry Algernon du Pont, served with sufficient distinction in the Civil War to earn him a Congressional Medal. In 1866 he was at Fortress Monroe in Virginia, where the recently captured Jefferson Davis was confined. Colonel du Pont served several terms as senator from Delaware. Ruth suspects that in his personal relations, her grandfather may have been an "epic bore," but in her final assessment he appears as strong and honorable—and incurably lonely.

Ruth Wales, our author's mother, grew up in Hyde Park, New York, where her family were friends and neighbors of the Roosevelts, including young Franklin (eight years older than she). Conspicuous at the June 1916 wedding of Ruth Wales and Harry du Pont was Assistant Secretary of the Navy Franklin D. Roosevelt, who brought the two officiating clergymen with him on a naval ship from New York. Even more enjoyable for Ruth Wales was the presence, at the wedding and elsewhere, of her uncle Elihu Root, who had been secretary of state under Theodore Roosevelt and senator from New York. During the New Deal years, Ruth Wales du Pont grew speechless with rage and hatred for her former friend F. D. R., whom she now regarded as an utterly contemptible traitor to his class.

The historical dimension comes to a stirring double climax in the 1960s, when Harry du Pont, in his eighties, helped restore the White House to part of its 1802 American design, at the request of Jacqueline Kennedy and in close collaboration with her, and then managed to keep the Cooper Union Museum in New York, founded in 1897, from being put out of business. Thanks largely to du Pont, Cooper-Hewitt Museum of Design (renamed Cooper-Hewitt, National Design Museum) is now a branch of the Smithsonian Institution.

Out of this welter of historical epochs—from the days of the French and American revolutions to the presidency of John F. Kennedy—there emerges Henry Francis du Pont: frail and indecisive in his early years, especially against all that background; surrounded by death in his childhood (no fewer than five siblings died in early infancy); and then devastated by the death of his mother when he was entering his fourth year at college. With that death, as Ruth Lord says, Harry "had little choice but to begin to define himself on his own terms." It is a not unfamiliar process, and one that illustrates what John Hersey has been heard to say: that people don't really grow up till their mother dies.

In the case of Harry du Pont, he went ahead very much on his own terms to beget one of the great estate combinations in the country: the gardens and the museum at Winterthur. The site itself dates back to the 1830s and was named Winterthur, Door of Winter, by a collateral member of the family after the Swiss town of his birth.

In retrospect, Ruth Lord sees her father as gifted with an "uncanny visual memory, a keen eye for color, a remarkable sense of proportion, an untiring talent for detail." The last-named capacity was represented (see Chapter 14) by the detailed records kept by Harry of every menu served at Winterthur over nearly sixty years and the number of people who sat down to dine. He also knew and recorded to the smallest saucer the fifty-eight sets of china he possessed; and closer yet to his heart, he kept tabs on the flowers adorning the dining room, which normally determined the choice of china.

It is of course acknowledged by our author that, in addition to an estate of twenty-four hundred acres, her father began his career with an "inheritance of seemingly unlimited money." Wealth beyond the need ever to think about it, or even perhaps to understand it, is a main feature of the Harry du Pont story. Not that money or the cost of things could be mentioned in the family household. Colonel du Pont is quoted as intoning that "any allusions . . . to the possession or expenditure of money" were "odious and vulgar." But the atmosphere of "unlimited money" (a phrase my own father used to employ in speaking of the super-wealthy vestrymen in his Philadelphia parish, as though distancing them from us almost metaphysically)—this is palpable at every turn, and it is conveyed to the underinitiated with considerable grace and acumen by Ruth Lord. It could also be entertaining: as when the twenty-one-year-old Harry needed to have a carbuncle removed from his neck prior to his departure for France, whereupon one of the finest surgeons in Boston, his assistant, and a general practitioner promptly reported to the young man's Cambridge apartment to consult about the treatment.

The "eye for color" and the "sense of proportion" that Ruth Lord ascribes to her father became apparent during Harry's college years, when he began to delve into horticulture. They later found expressions in the carefully designed gardens and wooded areas that he laid out, perhaps most dramatically in his azalea plantings. Ruth Lord had her own alertness to the visual charms of nature from her youngest years, and she has the talent to describe it—as in her recollection of coming back to Winterthur from New York, every weekend in her childhood (Chapter 12):

> Driving from the railroad station we would soon reach real country on the other side of the Gatehouse—owl country, fox country—and would speed down the winding mile-long driveway through the enormous woods and up the hill to the house. My first bedroom looked two stories down on a meadow, Holstein cows,

and the Clenny Run stream, whose banks in late spring were crowded with mint, buttercups, and forget-me-nots. Playing outdoors, at first no taller than the turkeys, and before treetops could offer their own hiding places, I was especially aware of the ground and how the trees joined it. The oaks had skirts, and the forked and bulging roots of the beech trees, under low-spreading branches, became mossy rooms. In the fall, nuts were everywhere: beech, hickory, walnuts, acorns, and magical horse chestnuts, shiny rounds of mahogany in tight, thorny cases.

That winning passage, with its easy mix of imagination and physical detail, reflects what Ruth Lord came to realize: that she and her father were "more caught up in the land" than the others in her family, and that this forged one kind of bond between them. The memoir, in this respect, is a final strengthening of that bond.

The bond was expanded later by the shared enjoyment of beautifully designed interiors and, most of all, in the crescendo of Harry's career, of the Henry Francis du Pont Winterthur Museum, which opened at last in 1951. It is, as Ruth Lord aptly calls it in the title of her Chapter 18, "The Masterpiece Within." Readers can discover for themselves, via Ruth Lord's eloquent account, the makeup and contents of this treasury of Americana, a place now of national distinction. They can likewise learn about the graduate program in American Studies begun at the same time in collaboration with the University of Delaware. The graduates, in the phrase of the eminent scholar Wilmarth S. Lewis (and as I can testify), "have a certain nimbus about them."

In the unfolding saga of the museum's creation, the high point is the installation of a spiral staircase. Ruth Lord has long been a central figure in the widely acclaimed Long Wharf Theatre of New Haven, and her presentation of this episode is suitably dramatic.

The staircase, when first installed, was an integral part of the family house (which would be reborn fifteen years later as the museum). Fourteen-year-old Ruth Ellen, her sister, and her parents first saw the staircase in May 1936, on their return from a cruise from New York eastward to San Francisco via Brazil, South Africa, India, and the Orient. Entering their home, they were transfixed by "a spiral staircase of breathtaking beauty, which rose two floors in lightness and grace to the level of our family bedrooms."

A great deal of the memoir is contained in that moment: the adolescent girl with the wonders of exotic travel behind her and the miracle of the spiral staircase facing her and leading up to her bedroom; and standing by, her father, who had kept the whole thing secret and who rejoiced at his family's response to it. With this interior masterpiece, it is suggested, Harry du Pont believed for the moment that his life's work was complete.

Preface

In 1957, prompted by a letter I had written to my father expressing interest in the Golf Cottage, he wrote to me, "I shall be happy to know that someone will see that Winterthur will be run the way I'd like it to be." Actually, since the opening of the Winterthur Museum six years earlier, many people had excelled in doing just that, and they continue to do so. There have been brilliant museum directors, a dedicated staff, and an outstanding board of trustees, among them my sister, Pauline Louise Harrison de Brossard, and other family members.[1] Today Winterthur is alive with activity. I rejoice to think that my father would have approved of the many programs and developments that continue to become realities, and of the countless people who visit and are touched by Winterthur each year. The observations of the museum's second director, Edgar P. Richardson, in part hold true. Seven years before my father's death, Ted Richardson wrote him a memorandum about a "very striking factor":

> the *love of Winterthur*. . . . The people who work here, from top to bottom of the Museum staff, are devoted to Winterthur. More than that, it has a great place in the affections of the community: it exerts a wide influence upon community taste . . . and upon the whole thinking of the community.
>
> By implication you yourself, as founder and creator of this institution, have acquired an affectionate regard and sympathy. You have become a popular and deeply respected figure: remote as you may perhaps feel yourself from the general public.

I salute my father and his high intelligence and energy, which were strongly entwined with intuition. His intuition was trustworthy, and I believe it to have been a key element in his makeup. It informed his judgment of people and human values as soundly as it did his sense of color and harmony of design. Like every mortal, Henry Francis du Pont had bad times, many of despair; surmounting them helped to shape him.[2] He had remarkably good times as well—a happy marriage, the luxury of great wealth, and the time to give expression to his dreams. But above all, he had an extraordinary drive, an urge to create perfection, perhaps a touch of genius. For me to capture it fully in words would be as difficult as painting the wind.

Henry F. du Pont and Winterthur

The Golf Cottage

A T THE START OF the nineteenth century, Eleuthère Irénée du Pont gradually bought several hundred acres of land in northern Delaware. There he raised merino sheep and planted wheat, clover, barley, rye, and experimental millet. Successive generations of the family continued to nurture the farm, later called Winterthur, and added to it—more land, various types of cattle, carriage and riding horses, fruit trees and evergreens.

Winterthur is alive with springs; streams flow across meadows, circle hills both steep and gentle, and border the woods. Many of the trees—tulip poplars, white ash, oaks, hickories, and giant beeches—are now two hundred or more years old. My grandfather was dismayed when lightning struck a distant chestnut, "one of the few remaining relics of the primeval forest." My mother called the flowering dogwood outside her bedroom window "the bride," and at times the ancient maple beside my own Golf Cottage, its trunk and branches marked with holes and crevices, seems to me to be an Arthur Rackham original about to speak. Lovely at every season, it is especially so early in the year when its lacy flower clusters give way to leaves and dissolve into pools of russet dust.

I am challenged by thoughts of Winterthur and the way in which my father, Henry Francis du Pont, brought it to its present state as a gift to the public. I am uncertain when he decided to make a museum of his house there, and also when I decided to write something about him. Happenings in my own family, good and bad, coincided with my discovery of family history in the archives of the Hagley Museum and Library, housed in a nineteenth-century stone building on the banks of the Brandywine River.[1] Learning of events of earlier days, trivial and momentous, gave me perspective on the present and helped to impel this endeavor.

The Brandywine River has always called to me; when I was quite young, on foot or on horseback, alone or with friends, picnicking or canoeing, I grew to know it well. And here, stored in archives on its very banks, my new discovery beguiled me. In case upon case of letters, a host of forebears came suddenly alive. I was drawn first to my father's mother, Pauline Foster du Pont. I had known very little about her, only that she was warm and loving and had died too young. An elderly friend of my parents' remembered being enchanted on first seeing her at Winterthur in a white evening dress with a pale blue satin sash. And that was about all. But now here she was, mostly in letters she wrote to her sister in New York. And with her she brought to life her little boy Harry, my father.

Until I became captive to this project, the notion of ancestors and family trees quite turned me off. Only as I grew older did I begin to want to learn about the past. The self-absorption of youth gave way for me, as it does for many people, to a compelling involvement in the here and now, and for a long time the exploration of earlier generations was far from my thoughts. As I read and learned, however, a new dimension opened to me.

It is bewildering to attempt to understand and describe a human being—that is, to see the person as the end product of myriad inherent potentials, shaped by countless and continuing influences from outside. The wealth of material harbored in the Hagley archives about the generations that preceded Harry du Pont is as nothing compared to the vast repository of lore at Winterthur about the man himself. Perhaps one day someone will write a full-scale biography of him. For now, my hope is to do him justice in a small and personal way.

When I was growing up, I loved my father and also felt a certain timidity toward him, for his was the final authority. It was he, with his wife's full agreement, who set implicit standards of behavior—reasonable expectations of thoughtfulness and "old-fashioned" good manners—for himself and his family, his guests, and his staff. It was he who orchestrated our lives and our elaborate moves and those of the household. He also took over many tasks that were normally the province of wives and mothers: home furnishing, meal planning, and the supervision of what my sister and I wore, even to our party shoes. He took almost complete charge of Christmas, from house and tree decorations to stocking presents, beginning with the kumquat and lady apple in the toe.

My father was busy with a host of projects, and it was hard to corner him. He spoke quickly and rather indistinctly, and conversation with him was minimal. If asked, he would produce snippets of advice: in a train dining car, by all means converse with strangers if you feel all right about it; on the sidewalk, avoid the little dance if you are about to run into someone head on, and "stand perfectly still." Although he was not one for playing with the young, when I was very small and begged him to dance, he would allow me to stand on his shoes while he took a few steps. And seldom did I risk teasing him. Once I hid nearby after leaving an alarming "ink blot" made of tin on his antique bedspread; his composure returned only after my quick reappearance, and I never repeated the trick.

I was quite unaware of the extent or depth of my father's wisdom and knowledge, and for a long time I knew only a fraction of the man himself. I saw him as both lovable and in a way innocent, a man whom I almost always beat at backgammon and at after-dinner word games with my mother and sister. (We shrieked with laughter when he came up with "Pushkin" for an author's name, only later discovering our own ignorance.)

I came to realize that in part my father's reticence—for he volunteered little about his interests or his life, past or present—was born of both shyness and modesty. I imagine that he would not have had answers to many of the questions I now wish that I had put to him. Would he have supposed that the heights of creativity and accomplishment that he attained represented, among other influences, compensation for years of academic near-disaster and social immaturity? I think not, nor do I think he could have explained what brought about his transformation from an inhibited youth and perhaps a borderline dyslexic into a dedicated man, supreme in several fields, who, after a long apprenticeship, would make a difference in the world. Would he have understood the source of his generosity, his desire to share to the fullest extent his gardens and his house and his love of beauty?[2] And what of his insatiability as a collector? Had he recognized it, it is unlikely that he would have connected it to early experiences of insecurity or loss. But I believe that my father was well aware of his indebtedness to a variety of factors in his life—among them the gift of free time, which was essential both for his slow-paced development and for the expression of the restless artistic passion that drove him.

Henry Francis du Pont's love of the land was bred in the bone, handed down by both father and mother, their immediate forebears, and the French, Dutch, and Scottish generations that preceded them. Throughout my father's life, Winterthur was his point of focus. While he was at boarding school, the thought of it both comforted and distracted him. "I have been away from home for so long, I am just wild to get back." One can trace through Harry's life a driven quality, as if, from boyhood on, however subliminally, he was preparing to make of Winterthur something special, accessible, and astonishing.

My father was not articulate about this, at least not to me, but somehow I came by the passion as well. At eight years old, I wrote a *Hiawatha*-inspired verse instantly derided by my sister. It began

> Where's the Land of Heart's Desire?
> Many people often ask me,

and continued, no less fatuously,

> Then I answer slowly, surely
> Delaware of course.

But Winterthur did seem to me to be that land.

From time to time, however, the scale and density of our living quarters there overwhelmed me, and when I was not very old I became aware of my passion for another house, one that seemed to symbolize much of the place I treasured. Alone on a walk by my father's nine-hole golf course, and dreaming of romance and as yet unknown loves, I noticed as if for the first time a narrow, tall stone building with a hill exactly its height on one side and a huge maple tree by the front door. It was the Golf Cottage, untenanted and bare of furniture. It was unlocked, and with great excitement I let myself in. Inside the thick walls I came upon an enormous fireplace and discovered its mate on the floor above, reached by steep and narrow stairs. At this level a Dutch door at the back of the house gave onto a tiny terrace of old brick, overhung by a portico supported on wooden pillars. From here extended a heart-shaped lawn flat as a stage, sheltered on its left side by the hill, which continued as an encircling tree-covered arm. To the right the sharp drop of land was masked by a grove of shrubs—honey locusts, lilacs, mock orange. Straight ahead, seen through the vista, the land gradually fell away, giving over to marsh grasses and a pond; it then became a par five fairway, rising to woods in the distance.

Fifteen or so years later, when our by now monumental house had become a museum, my parents moved to a Regency-style edifice they had built near the Clenny Run bridge at the foot of the hill.[5] Although far smaller than what we had left, the Clenny Run house was quite splendid, with beautiful twin staircases, a conservatory, many bedrooms on unexpected levels, and two elevators. However, as its sartorial and behavioral demands, especially trying for grandchildren, were not diminished, my father consented to my request that when my husband, my children, and I came to visit we might stay in the Golf Cottage. By then this eighteenth-century house had been somewhat enlarged to accommodate the first director of the Winterthur Museum, who had briefly occupied it with his family.

Since my husband and I lived and worked in Connecticut and our children were in school there, our visits to Delaware were infrequent, but the Golf Cottage in all seasons increasingly enchanted me. In marked contrast to the formality almost required by the elegant perfection of the museum a mile away and, to a lesser extent, by its successor house near the bridge, the Golf Cottage had come to represent for me a kind of personal sense of *relatedness*. Its small rooms, most likely first occupied by farmers and their families, suggested an appealing and intimate way of life. I began to brood about the house's future. After much thought, I wrote, put away, slept on, and rewrote several drafts of a letter to my father in which I expressed my attachment to the Golf Cottage and the hope that someday he would leave it to me. I talked about my love for Winterthur and its countryside and my wish to feel that a small part of it could belong to me and to my children.

I had trouble writing this message and was anxious about my father's reactions to it. A reserved and private person, then seventy-six years old, he was not easy to approach on matters of intimacy; he appeared, in fact, to wish to avoid them. This characteristic had been dramatized for me a decade earlier on the death of his great friend Mrs. Harry Horton Benkard. My gregarious mother had observed to me more than once that my father indeed possessed few very close friends, and she now was saddened that he

The Golf Cottage.
Photo by Edith Cann.

had lost one who was entirely irreplaceable. Aware then of the depth of his grief, I wrote a note of condolence for him to find when he returned home late one night. This was never acknowledged, nor did I ever mention it; I respected his silence and did not wish to intrude further on his sorrow.

With trepidation, in October 1956 I mailed my much edited Golf Cottage communication, which began: "Dearest Dads, This is a love letter to a house." Because of the intimacy of its tone, not to mention the nature of its contents, my apprehensions increased during the long silence that followed. I feared that I might have encroached on some forbidden terrain. Weeks passed, and I experienced questions and misgivings: Had my letter, or the reply to it, been lost? Had I overstepped some boundary, made too brash a request, somehow offended my father? At last, on the telephone, uneasiness at a pitch, I was able to ask my mother about it. Yes, the letter had arrived, but all she said was, "It was a lovely letter."

So far so good, but what did it mean? Why had my father sent me no word? I began to suspect that I had thrust too emotional a declaration upon a person of reserve who was reluctant, if not unable, to respond to it. I reflected that a more matter-of-fact approach would have been wiser. It was not until my father and I next met, several months later, maneuvering ourselves over an icy path, that I broached the subject anew. And then he said only, "I'm much too old to change my will."

Now, some forty years later, I still remember that my disappointment at the time was tempered with relief that the charged episode I had perpetrated had come to an end. But the story was not over, for my dear father did in fact change his will. He left the Golf Cottage to me for my lifetime and offered my children the opportunity to rent it from the museum after my death.

From my early adulthood on, dizzying changes shook the world, and of course changes were occurring in my life as well: increasing independence, college, marriage, children, work, psychoanalysis, the deaths, eighteen months apart, of my mother and father, divorce, and a second marriage. During some of these years a not surprising, if delayed, adolescent disenchantment with my parents developed. In any case, my early idolatry of them could never have been sustained.

In order to keep my father company after my mother died, we stayed with him on trips to Winterthur, and the Golf Cottage was put to other purposes. Many years later the cottage again became available to me, and my new spouse and I were often able to use it for days at a time. The magic of the house and its setting became increasingly powerful to me, as in fact did all of Winterthur. The museum itself was undergoing a final phase of building. A two-story wing[4] to provide a proper museum entrance and space for major displays was soon to cover the meadow of my childhood, but it was designed with care, so that Clenny Run, my early stepping-stone stream, could continue its flow underneath it unimpeded.

Again alive with construction, the place hummed with generators, and a cluster of vans occupied an adjoining field. The woods themselves, neglected for a time after my father's death, were being restored to their former beauty. Trimmed paths emphasized the immensity of the trees, as did the lush variety of groundcover that undulated beneath them. Trees and shrubs were carefully and often evocatively labeled: "golden raintree"; "full moon maple." From above the quarry—one of my early haunts, its wet depth now filled with ferns and candelabra primroses—stretched an especially lovely vista of hills, meadows, stream, and woods, and here I rediscovered a sign: "Keep This View Open Forever. H. F. du Pont. 1964."

Harry du Pont "thought big," looked ahead, and was always ready to investigate the progressive and new. In gardening and farming, he was "an innovator and a leader."[5] He cultivated rare plants and experimented with plant propagation. His bold decisions, aided by sophisticated equipment in model dairy barns, revolutionized practices of cattle breeding and milk production. Aware of the need to protect the land from urban encroachment, he was careful to designate hundreds of acres of Winterthur's outer boundaries for well-chosen institutions—a golf course, a museum of natural history—to ensure that its integrity as a "country place museum" would be preserved.[6] This man, in fact, was sui generis, a true original. His experience of the "real world" was limited, and his basic interests were circumscribed. But I see him, over the course of his long life, as both representing the nineteenth century with its Victorian standards and as keenly anticipating the twenty-first century.

In realizing the extent to which my father would have been enthralled with the further developments of Winterthur, I also became aware that something was happening to me. My earlier fascination with him was returning; it had been interrupted by preoccupations in my own life and a resulting distance, in which my affection for him co-existed with a recognition of his feet of clay. I now became possessed with a need to try to understand the man with whom for years I had longed to communicate.

I had often remembered a statement my father made to me in adulthood: he said that he had been so devastated by his mother's death when he was twenty-two years old that then and there he had decided to "give up feeling." This was told to me in answer to a now forgotten question, and I cannot imagine how I failed to pursue the subject. Perhaps I tried to do so but got no further. Or perhaps I was stunned into silence by this shocking revelation from a person usually so leery of intimacy. I find myself still

The brook from the quarry that connects with Clenny Run.

shaken by his statement, or rather by the sense of anguish and vulnerability behind it. The concept leads to unanswerable questions. At age twenty-two, would one already have had to experience great pain to come to such a determination? Had my father, in fact, for sixty some years been able to distance himself from emotional pain? If so, would this diminish any corresponding capacity to experience joy or ecstasy?

As the memory of this avowal of my father's combined with my increasing appreciation of his aesthetic triumphs, with the Golf Cottage as a framework I reexperienced profound love for him. I hoped that if I could begin to learn more about his life, I would have a chance to understand this intriguing creature.

CHAPTER 2

Earlier Generations

H ENRY FRANCIS DU PONT transformed into a museum the house on a hill at Winterthur, Delaware, where two generations of his family had lived before him. It was always a big house, although at first the trees were equal to it. Today, what with the additions made every twenty or so years, the building is undeniably enormous. Beginning in 1928 my father more than doubled the dimensions of his parents' house, and the outline of the Henry Francis du Pont Winterthur Museum began to take shape. Here he assembled, in settings that looked lived-in, the largest collection of Americana in existence. And he was possessed by another passion. He was an extraordinary creator of landscapes, and in understanding the rhythms and retaining the natural wildness of the woods and meadows surrounding the house, he made them even more beautiful.

It is easy to see how the magnetic attraction of the place influenced several successive generations of one family and, in a different capacity, continues to charm visitors today. These fertile acres, over fifteen hundred in my father's childhood and twenty-four hundred in my own, combine hills and valleys, streams and ponds, pasturelands and towering woods, many of which encompass brilliant underplantings. Add to the landscape a big house and widely scattered farmhouses sheltered and masked by trees, and, the oldest structures of all, thirty or so barns built of tile, fieldstone, and wood—pale yellow, red, weathered silver-gray like driftwood, nobly proportioned. Some have open caverns at their base, designed for cattle, sheep, or pigs. Dom Pedro, Eleuthère Irénée du Pont's famous merino ram, who arrived from France in 1812 and founded a new race, very likely had his own lodgings; King of the Ormsbys, the sire of my father's prize-winning Holstein herd about a century later, definitely reigned in a house by himself.

My father's childhood, rooted in the basic values of family and land, has been described as idyllic, and indeed much of it was. His father and mother were both products of close-knit families, some of whose early origins had been in France.[1] Several of his mother's forebears had immigrated to America in the seventeenth century. Harry's paternal ancestors came to this country later, but Pierre Samuel du Pont de Nemours (1739–1817), the father of us all, had long been profoundly inspired by the success of America's struggle for freedom.[2]

Pierre Samuel was the son of a Huguenot watchmaker; his mother was from a noble but impoverished family named Montchanin. At age forty-five he was "ennobled" by King Louis XVI, who was grateful for his role in peace negotiations with Great Britain, and thus became an instant aristocrat, complete with a coat of arms.[3] Perhaps this honor, coupled with the devastating death of his wife, inspired Pierre Samuel to conduct an odd and rather medieval ceremony. Alone in a room with his teenage sons, Victor and Irénée, and close by a bust of their mother, he handed his younger son, Irénée, a sword and enjoined both boys to remember that "no privilege exists that is not inseparably bound to a duty" and to stand together always "to comfort each other in every sorrow, and to help each other . . . in all difficulty & danger."[4]

Pierre Samuel du Pont, whose poetry and an economic treatise written at age twenty-three were praised by Voltaire,[5] was early on accepted by the Parisian intelligentsia and by the Versailles court, where he charmed Mme. de Pompadour, who called him "our young agriculturist."[6] At the court, Pierre Samuel's ideas as a physiocrat—his term for those who advocated labor and commerce based on agriculture rather than mercantilism—resonated with those of the doctor-philosopher Quesnay, the economist Turgot, and the Comte de Mirabeau. Whether in or out of government, at various times he was the editor of two journals and the owner and proprietor of a publishing house, a printing press, and a bookstore.[7] He was always writing—historical or philosophical essays (for example, on deism), political recommendations (as for a new French constitution or a system of pub-

Pierre Samuel du Pont de Nemours (1739–1817);
portrait by Rembrandt Peale.
Courtesy Hagley Museum and Library, Wilmington, Del.

lic education), translations (as of Ariosto's *Orlando Furioso*). He wrote a biography of Turgot and edited the nine volumes of his papers. A Freemason and a liberal nationalist, Pierre Samuel believed in law, order, and a constitutional monarchy. He fought to defend the king in the Tuileries and narrowly escaped death from the mob by hiding in the dome of an astronomy building, where he lived for several weeks on bread and water.[8]

Although he was away from Paris during the Reign of Terror and at the time of the beheading of the king and queen, the exuberant Pierre Samuel could not lie low for long. His whereabouts were discovered, and he was imprisoned for a month. Only because of the arrest of Robespierre did he escape the guillotine—by one day. Three years later he was in prison again, this time because of his diatribes against the new government—to which he himself had been elected. He was rescued by the intervention of his friend Madame de Staël. By now Pierre Samuel realized that he must flee; optimistic as always, in October 1799 he embarked with his sons and their families on what turned into a "horrible and most dangerous" three-month voyage to America, where he hoped—in vain—to create a utopian society based on physiocratic principles.[9]

Pierre Samuel du Pont emerges as a quixotic and fascinating man whose originality, idealism, and intellect made him attractive to learned academies and to such statesmen as Lafayette, Talleyrand, Benjamin Franklin, Thomas Jefferson, and Alexander Hamilton. It is no wonder that his American descendants revered both him and his son Eleuthère Irénée as the founders of their family.

Henry Francis du Pont set off in a direction very different from that of the generations that preceded him. His great-grandfather Eleuthère Irénée du Pont was a man of business. In 1803, when his fledgling company, E. I. du Pont de Nemours, began to manufacture gunpowder and other explosives, Irénée laid the foundation for an industrial empire whose future power and wealth no one could have dreamed of. But despite their dissimilarities, my father and his great-grandfather shared important traits: industriousness, a driving energy, common sense, and a deep reverence for land, with the imagination and resourcefulness to preserve and use it well.[10] And they were both blessed by something beyond the mystery of genes—good luck.

Much good fortune came to Irénée on his arrival in America: his ob-

Eleuthère Irénée du Pont.
Courtesy Hagley Museum and Library, Wilmington, Del.

servation, on a chance hunting trip, of the inferiority of American gun-powder; his discovery and purchase of the ideal Brandywine River site for his powder mills; his father's important friendships in Europe and America. Especially helpful to Irénée's career were the sympathetic new American president, Thomas Jefferson, former ambassador to France, and a Paris-based Swiss banker, Jacques Bidermann, who was an early investor in E. I. du Pont de Nemours & Company. In 1813, Bidermann's decision to send his twenty-four-year-old son to inspect the Delaware plant led to an unexpectedly happy outcome. Not only did James Antoine Bidermann fall

Thomas Jefferson, right, with Eleuthère Irénée du Pont, left. Painting by
Stanley Arthurs. Courtesy Hagley Museum and Library, Wilmington, Del.

in love with and marry Irénée's second daughter, Evelina, but the able
young man soon became his father-in-law's key assistant and sole partner.

Irénée had seven children, three of them born in France. The sixth,
known as "the Boss," or "Henry the Red" because of his fiery beard, was
Harry du Pont's paternal grandfather and would have a significant role in
the family's fortunes. French was the language of their home, Eleutherean
Mills, a house high above the Brandywine River that Irénée had built con-
currently with his powder mills, horse and sheep barns, orchards, and vegetable and flower gardens. Himself a transplant, Irénée was a passionate
horticulturist, and he believed the absence of a garden to be the "greatest

deprivation."[11] Irénée all along bought land as he could afford it. With the addition of the adjacent Hagley Farm he expanded and improved his original Brandywine tract.[12] In part thanks to company profits during the War of 1812, he invested in bigger parcels of land to the northwest, ending up with 445 acres in all at this northern site. Here he raised sheep and pursued his devotion to botany and experimental farming.

Upon Irénée's death in 1834, his seven children together inherited shares of E. I. du Pont de Nemours & Company and the estate in general, but his second son, Henry the Red, who shared his father's love of agriculture, assumed lifelong ownership of Eleutherean Mills. Irénée's son-in-law James Antoine Bidermann for a time continued in a leadership role in the company. On his retirement in 1837, James and Evelina bought the 445 acres from the estate. There by a small creek they built a farmhouse in which they lived while awaiting completion of their main house on the hill above it, a Greek revival structure of stucco-covered stone that they named Winterthur (Door of Winter) for the Swiss town of Bidermann's birth. In true family tradition, and to create a model agricultural establishment, they developed the land, planting an orchard, as well as flower and cutting gardens. They added a gatehouse, a carriage house, stables, a dairy, and a small greenhouse. Evelina died in 1863 at age sixty-seven, and her husband died two years later. Soon after his death, Henry the Red, now president of the company, bought back the property and prepared it as the home for his son Col. Henry Algernon du Pont. The Colonel, a hero of the Civil War, moved to Winterthur with his wife in 1876, two years after their marriage, and in 1889 he inherited the property, now enlarged to 1,135 acres. We will hear more about Henry A., who was to become a senator from Delaware and, later still, my grandfather.

Many changes took place in the fifty-five years between the death of Irénée du Pont and that of his son Henry the Red, whose tenure as president was the longest in the company's history and under whose guidance the company expanded significantly. War—the Civil War, in particular, in which du Ponts were fanatically committed to the Union cause—and the country's growing need for explosives for building railroads and canals, for mining, and for other industrial uses brought huge profits to E. I. du Pont de Nemours & Company. As the only surviving son of its founder, Henry the Red received the lion's share of those profits. While he was growing up,

Harry du Pont doubtless heard, perhaps ad nauseam, a great deal of family history, with probable emphasis on the Civil War heroism of his father and his great-uncle Samuel Francis du Pont, an admiral. Although my father never spoke to me about his family, I imagine that what was drummed into him must have evoked a number of reactions, pride and boredom among them. It also seems likely that he absorbed some of the attitudes of his forebears, including the challenge to make something of himself.

Grandparents and Their Contemporaries

L OUISA GERHARD DU PONT was called by her granddaughter, my aunt Louise, "the kindest person I ever met."[1] She was a spirited gardener who hoped that future generations would carry on the family love of plants and flowers. She need not have worried. Her oldest child, Henry Algernon, Louise and Harry's father, shared these inclinations, as did Pauline Foster, the young woman he was to marry. As it happened, Pauline's background was every bit as agricultural and French as that of her in-laws. Her mother's father, Antoine Lentilhon, was a Parisian who had permanently settled in New York, and her own father was an ardent and distinguished farmer. These credentials did not detract from her charm; she was welcomed by Louisa and Henry the Red as a "perfect sunbeam." The Colonel and Pauline, who lived at Winterthur after their marriage, kept in close touch with the family at Eleutherean Mills, a twenty-minute carriage or pony ride away, and when their children were growing up, they visited their grandparents every day.

As a child, I too went often to Eleutherean Mills, which, having been restored after an explosion,[2] was now occupied in the spring and fall by my aunt Louise and her husband, Francis Boardman Crowninshield. The remnants of the original mills along the river, where black gunpowder was once manufactured and stored, together with the classical columns and statues collected by my uncle for the garden, were ideal for exploration and games of hiding. A child-sized spring house with mossy crevices, like a cave for a tiny oracle, spouted icy water, and the Brandywine itself fascinated me. Changing at every bend—wide, clear, or narrowly rushing, delightful for

Louisa Gerhard du Pont, wife of Henry the Red.

canoeing or for fording on horseback—it has always seemed to me the perfection of a river, the essence, so to speak, of *riverness*.

Since they lived in Delaware year round when they were growing up, Harry and Louise no doubt took these places and surroundings for granted, as well as the activities of daily life. And they were often the center of attention. As the only children in the immediate Delaware family, they were showered by older relatives with presents for birthdays and Christmas and

Henry du Pont, known as Henry the Red, Henry F. du Pont's grandfather.

with valentines and other greeting cards and letters throughout the year. When my father was a boy, his aunts Evelina and Victorine were much in evidence, as was his great-aunt Sophie. This spirited lady, a talented caricaturist and feminist manqué, married a first cousin with the same surname and spent the rest of her life in a house directly across the river from her parents'. Of all her in-laws, I believe that my grandmother Pauline felt closest to the bright and widely read Sophie du Pont. It was in letters to Sophie and to her sister, Anna, that Pauline seemed to reveal her suffering most openly when tragedy struck. When Aunt Sophie died, Pauline wrote to Anna, "I will miss her very much, & no one knows how Henry has felt

Pauline Foster du Pont, Harry's mother.

it, they have been devoted to one another since he was a little boy." She added, "[Aunt Sophie] died as she lived, she will not require any preparation as she was ready to go."

Harry's aunt Lina (Evelina, his father's sister) was also a source of affection and strength for Pauline. A gentle soul, Evelina lived at Eleutherean Mills until her parents died, after which she took up residence in Greenville, about a mile from Winterthur, and, in the summer, in her mother's house in Marblehead, Massachusetts. It was rumored that her beloved had been killed in the Civil War, and although she later again became engaged to marry, she never did.

My father's family on his mother's side was likewise a close one, but with distinct differences, for his mother's parents had both died very young. Her father, Herman Ten Eyck Foster, son of a Scottish father and a mother of Dutch descent, was born in 1822. After graduation from Columbia at the then-standard age of nineteen and one "mercantile" winter in New York, Herman undertook the serious study of agriculture and bought Lakeland, a 260-acre farm on Lake Seneca in upstate New York, where he spent the rest of his life. Harry's love of the land had many sources.

Herman Foster raised crops and livestock, and his farm was more than once recognized for excellence by the New York State Agricultural Society. Herman saw farming not "simply [as] a business . . . [but as a] communion with Nature." A fellow of "gay urbanity," he loved fun and a house "overflowing with guests." A dedicated Christian as well, Herman ran popular prayer meetings and a Sunday School every week throughout his life.[3] Years later, a friend of his daughter Anna remembered him as the "best example [of holiness] he had ever known."

When Herman Foster's brief marriage ended with his twenty-four-year-old wife's death in childbirth, he was left with three small children. Anna Eliza, Antoine Lentilhon, and Mary Pauline were brought up by him "with affection & care" at beautiful Lakeland, as well as in New York by his mother-in-law, the children's devoted Grandma (Eliza Leaycroft) Lentilhon, and a host of other loving relatives there and on Staten Island. Pauline and her siblings, who had lost their mother when so young, were unusually close to one another. After their father's death at age forty-nine, they spent two years traveling throughout Europe and paying long visits to cousins in Paris.

Pauline Foster du Pont with Louise and Harry.
Courtesy Hagley Museum and Library, Wilmington, Del.

In 1874, Pauline Foster, age twenty-five, married thirty-two-year-old Henry Algernon du Pont. Three years later, her brother Lentilhon Foster married Victorine, one of her husband's six younger sisters, a circumstance that drew the families even closer together, especially since the Fosters chose to live in Delaware rather than in New York and established their home, Virieux, in Greenville. This marriage in effect made Lentilhon and Victorine uncle and aunt twice over to Harry and may have been as puzzling to my father in his childhood as it was to me. It also gave them license for gentle criticism that might otherwise not have been expressed, on the ground that it is more acceptable to find fault with one's own family than with one's in-laws.

My own memory of my great-uncle and aunt and their foibles helps me better to visualize a part of Harry's youth, for Lenty and Victorine often provided family members with exasperated amusement. Letters refer to their penchant for making drama or mystery of entirely mundane matters. "Lent & V left for New York [or Newport, or the White Mountains] this morning as usual without announcing their plans until the last moment." Uncle Lenty, described as dashing in his youth, remains in my memory a red-faced, bewhiskered bore, his most notable characteristic a closed-lip laugh that emerged entirely through his nose. He was a master of indecision. To his response to an invitation to dinner that night with "I'll see," Henry Algernon roared back to the butler, "Tell him 'No he won't see, he'll either come here or stay home.'"

Only recently through letters did I learn more about these relatives. In my youth, great-aunts Lina and Vic existed for me chiefly as Duty. In those times, children were up to a point beginning to be heard as well as seen, but they also tended to unswerving obedience. And so it was, at our parents' bidding, that my sister and I, and later I alone, invariably called on these ladies on Winterthur weekends. Aunt Lina, who died at age ninety-nine, had been blind for many years and wore an eyeshade. Swathed always in white to the floor, she seemed bleached, frail as a tiny bird, and quite removed from human bone and flesh. Aunt Vic, younger by seven years, looked every bit as fragile; throughout her six years of widowhood she dressed only in black. That my great-aunts were never away from home seems odd to me now, but long ago their presence was a given; it was inconceivable that they might be elsewhere. What, oh what, to say to them, and how soon could one politely escape them for the refuge of the car?

Surely more fun were the Robinsons, the children of his mother's beloved older sister, Anna. Anna and her doctor husband, Beverley, had two boys and a girl, Beverley, Herman, and Pauline, who were close in age to Louise and Harry, and later a second daughter, named Anna. They lived in New York but paid long visits to Winterthur, usually twice a year. Harry's mother and his aunt Anna were each other's closest confidantes. They wrote letters several times a week, lamenting their geographical separation and the dearth of telephones. The correspondence provides a window on their lives: family and friends, household problems, clothes, gossip, pleasures and sorrows. Especially in the case of Anna, the letters offer a picture of fashionable life in New York and Newport and the beginnings of social consciousness. From both sides the wealth of detail about their children is wonderfully evocative and has given me insight into the mother who was so close to Harry, her son.

Beverley, Herman, and Pauline were certainly more sophisticated than Louise and Harry since they lived in a city and the boys, at least, went to school. Nevertheless, they were all remarkably congenial, and like their mothers they wrote each other many letters, the children's usually in French. When Harry was eleven years old he told his cousin Pauline after the October visit that he wished "something dreadful would happen to the *pipes!!* so that we would all have to come back." And some months later, young Pauline was heard to say to her brother Beverley that "it would be the best thing for him to marry Louise . . . and that she would *marry Harry!* That she knew they could be happy all their lives together!"

Although they had lost their own mother when they were too young to remember her, Pauline and Anna seemed created for motherhood. Sensitive to their children's needs and personalities, they cared for them, played with them, taught them, and wholeheartedly loved them. In the Foster sisters' correspondence, the wish to provide happiness for their children is often expressed, for, as they both knew, "sorrows come soon enough." In 1887 Pauline wrote to her sister, "Does it seem possible that it was 16 years ago that Father died. What joys and trouble and sorrows since then. It seems strange that some people have so many more sorrows than others, but I suppose it must be for the best."

It was not often that Pauline expressed this feeling, but she had reason for doing so. Her first child, Paulinette, had died suddenly before her first birthday, six months after returning with her parents from their long stay in France. This loss darkened the young couple's forthcoming move to Winterthur. Pauline wrote to her aunt Sophie of their first "sad sad visit" to the house after the baby's death, "where before all was so bright. Our darling little Paulinette made sunshine everywhere." Several weeks later, having moved in, Pauline replied to a French cousin's letter of condolence: "Everyone said little Paulinette was a remarkable child. She had said Papa & Maman for a long time, & was commencing to say other words, when she was taken from us so suddenly. We had looked forward with so much pleasure to coming here with her. She would have made our house so bright & happy. But our Heavenly Father saw fit to take her to Himself, & we try to say 'Thy Will Be Done.'"

Another individual touched by the baby's death was Edith Newbold Jones, who later became Edith Wharton. Although thirteen years younger than Pauline, she had known the sisters well in both Newport and New York. In fact, her first extant letter was addressed to "Dear Pauley," my grandmother, then on her wedding trip, and opens with remarks about Anna's engagement to "Doctor Robinson."[4] After the baby's death, Edith Jones, then a precocious fourteen-year-old, wrote a seven-stanza poem for the bereaved mother, which began,

> I saw a fair form standing by
> The death bed of a little maid;
> Divinest pity in his eye
> He bent above her couch and said
> To them that waiteth His reply:
> "She is not dead, but sleepeth"—[5]

Louise was born next, and after her a boy, who died at birth. Then came my father in May 1880, and two years later twin boys. Both twins died, although one, named Paul, lived for seven months. Following his funeral, the minister wrote to my grandmother: "The sight of your grief and tears has deeply moved me. Four times have I followed your dear lambs to their last home. In the present instance how tender & peculiar was the tie binding you to him. In 7 anxious months you have watched over him trusting & hoping for his assured health." Anna Robinson, who herself had lost an infant son, reported that her children, Beverley and Herman, "said 'God wanted little Paul too, he has gone to our little brother.' The sweet faith of children is the only comfort I really think." Pauline, writing to her aunt Sophie of her grief and loneliness, also mentioned the comfort of knowing that the baby was "happy & safe in his Father's arms." My grandmother was, I feel sure, truly religious in a way that I am not, but, having myself lost a five-month-old daughter, I question to what extent belief in the hereafter can mitigate the anguish of such a tragedy. I should add that four years later, on the very bitter loss of her last child, Annette, Pauline was less philosophical in her letter to Aunt Sophie: "The blow was so terrible that I feel almost stunned."

Harry, almost three when Paul died, undoubtedly had some confusing feelings about the baby's death and must in some way have sensed his mother's distress. However, he and Louise had a fine nurse, Phillippine, who was also a source of safety and comfort. But when Harry was four and a half, Phillippine returned to France, apparently for reasons of health. This perhaps confronted Harry with his first tangible loss of a beloved person. Her going was certainly a blow to his over-bereaved mother. Pauline wrote to Anna: "Phillippine has been so entirely a part of the children that it seemed like parting from them all again. She was everything to me, for she was so capable in every way. Of course I can never replace her, & her loss to the children will be dreadful. Harry has asked constantly when she is coming back, & the first night she left he did not want to say his prayers. The house has seemed so deserted & as if there were someone dead. I imagine all the time I hear her."

At the time of this poignant letter, my grandmother was once again pregnant. She had confided the fact to Anna the month before ("that awful nausea etc.") and had revealed her fears ("even if it should all go right in the end, which I think is very doubtful"). This was again a difficult time for her. Along with severe headaches and other discomforts, she was also depressed and lonely. "It has been dreadful to have Henry away so much now." Although happy occasions are reported during these months, such as a birthday celebration—"a great event, a cake with 36 candles & a complete surprise"—Pauline's mood is somber. She laments her helplessness: "If only I could be good for something."

In June 1885, the birth of Anne Victorine Sophie, called Annette, ushered in the kind of family life for which my grandmother yearned—"We are all flourishing here"——and the rest of the year seemed to proceed smoothly. Thanksgiving and Christmas brought their attendant emotions: hopes that "the butcher will not fail"; the children's thrill at helping to choose the tree. Harry gave the baby a red table and a "little Santa Claus on horseback which he bought himself."

Although Annette from birth was a delight, plump and smiling, her mother could not rid herself of forebodings. "The baby lamb is as saint-like as ever, but I always feel uncertain about its lasting." This intuition proved accurate, for Annette died suddenly at eight months old. The new sorrow seemed unendurable. "What a dear little baby she was. I felt all the time that I must have her in my arms, she seemed too sweet & good for this earth. What a sad, sad life this is."

Pauline du Pont, having lost five children in ten years, plunged into a depression. Her new freedom was strange and unwelcome; she wanted most of all to be alone. "I cannot bear to go anywhere," she wrote to her sister. "I am sick in bed & you will think me an awful grumbler." "I have a splitting headache as I have been crying all day." For several years, in fact, Pauline had suffered headaches, often for a week or so at a time, which she had in part attributed to worry and sorrow. When Harry was eight years old, his mother had an illness that lasted two months; the symptoms included extreme weakness, deafness, and recurrent styes. A nurse was required; the coachman, Chapple, among other "escorts," carried the invalid up and down stairs.

All along, Anna Robinson had written letters to my grandmother that expressed understanding and empathy and offered advice about her reclusive life. "Do come to New York. I really think you need the change. I don't believe it is good for anyone to be always in one place, even if it is charming." "Nothing will cure your cough as well as a change of air." "I see now that you feel too wretchedly to write. I hope you don't think me unsympathetic in urging you to come here." A change of scene was looked on as the ultimate panacea. In a letter several months after Annette's death, Anna wrote, "You have quite enough seclusion, what you want is to see people in spite of yourself. I am delighted that you acknowledge that you were *not well* before. Is that not proof enough that you need a change of air & scene? I give you full permission to be quite as insolent & meddling to me as I have been to you."

Far from resenting these words, Pauline could acknowledge their truth and agree with her sister that it is a "bad thing for people always to live in the country."

Anna and Pauline had had a happy and frivolous time growing up in Lakeland and New York. Bright, vivacious, and pretty, they loved people, music, parties, dances, and clothes. Anna later wrote of an evening where "only 3 girls had what we would have called a good time. All the others seemed perfectly contented to sit there & perhaps dance 2 or 3 times in the whole evening, which certainly you & I would have thought very stupid."

During her first twelve years at Winterthur, Pauline could manage only rare visits to New York, usually in order to be of help to her grandmother and other relatives, but she stayed with her sister whenever possible. She depended on Anna to send her various items: material for children's clothes, which she sometimes made herself, including kilts for Harry; books, often in French, for the lessons she taught; toys; cornucopias for the Christmas tree and other things "not available in our much abused Wilmington."

But far more than the shopping, Pauline missed the atmosphere and cultural aspects of the city. On encountering a "very agreeable" woman at a dinner party, she wrote, "It was like having a glimpse of New York again." Although she enjoyed meetings of the Wilmington Shakespeare Club or a magic lantern show or a lecture on crested birds, they were not a patch on former recreations like New York's Thursday Evening Club or the Sewing Class with old friends. Her delight in the city expressed in a letter to her husband in December 1888 is almost palpable: "We went last night to see Mary Andersen, she was really beautiful in the *Winter's Tale*. Anna has tickets tonight for the Mendelssohn, I am so glad as I have not been since before I was married, or did we go once after. I only wish you were here to go with us. Beverley is trying for tickets for the Opera tomorrow."

Having been pregnant for almost half of her married life, and in mourning for much longer, it is revealing that my grandmother did not succumb to bitterness or self-pity. Certainly envy, especially of her sister, would have been easy to understand, but "I envied you the Opera" and "With all your fine dinners, [duck] must be an everyday occurrence to you" are the only examples of it I have found, and mild enough at that. Great wistfulness is there, however: "How nice it must be always to have a large-

Louise du Pont at about age 13.
Courtesy Hagley Museum and Library, Wilmington, Del.

Henry F. du Pont at about age 11.

family" or "It would be so nice to have you to talk to." But expressions of what I take to be genuine admiration and love prevail. "I was so delighted to hear of your fine effect at the Opera & only wish I could have seen you." "I am so glad you decided to wear your white dress, no doubt B found you most charming in it." Her ability to visualize, a trait later expertly developed by Harry, seemed to provide her with real pleasure.

I do not want to suggest that my grandmother was never angry or irritable. She appeared so, and often, in connection with efforts to secure a permanent staff to help her run a big house, or to find the ideal governess, a paragon who would enable Louise and Harry to achieve mastery of Latin and German, not to mention French. Not every applicant clamored for the job or remained in it once there, doubtless feeling, as did their mistress on occasion, that life far from a big city had its drawbacks.

An appealing attribute of my grandmother was her lack of pretension. She wrote of the president's wife: "Mrs. Cleveland is really very pretty but her great charm is being so perfectly simple & unaffected." My grandmother's basic good humor and common sense helped her to find contentment and amusement in many situations: love for her family, young and old; love of country life, and especially Winterthur with all it offered; and love for the church and her work in it. Her faith was deep and sustaining. She seemed able to transcend hardships and to give and receive a good deal of joy.

Soon after the death of Annette, my grandmother described a frightening scene to her sister: "Louise [then 9] was choking with the croup. I rushed to the medicine chest & managed to get as far as the hall, where I was completely unnerved, & Henry had to drag me over to the sofa. Before, I have always been able to do everything until all was over, but last night was more than I could bear at first. A year ago—how well I felt repaid for all my waiting when our dear little baby was here, but now———" Fortunately, Louise recovered without incident, but Pauline's reaction to the episode showed the stress produced by a series of tragedies.

Henry Algernon's role in this occurrence is characteristic, for he was indeed a man of action. The eldest of eight children, he had evidently succeeded at almost every undertaking. His tutor described him, at age fourteen, as the "best historian I ever met with, [who] speaks of every king as of acquaintances, so familiar is he with their histories." The boy and girl cousins who made up the rest of the class are described as "*spoilt* bad children . . . 10 of the worst children it has ever been my lot to know."[6] After four years as a boarder at a "classical school" run by the Reverend James Gilborne Lyons at West Haverford, Pennsylvania, and a year at the University of Pennsylvania, Henry A. went to West Point, graduating in 1861 with the highest grades in his class of forty-five cadets. He saw active combat in the Civil War and was promoted to lieutenant colonel for "most distinguished gallantry."[7]

While courting his bride-to-be, Henry A. was back at West Point, collaborating on studies of cavalry, artillery, and infantry tactics, which were subsequently published. His father and a cousin persuaded him to abandon the idea of making a career of the army, and Pauline's letters make it clear that she was pleased with his decision. Although she "should have felt dreadful to think you did it entirely on my account," she is sure that had her father been alive, "he would never have consented to let me marry in the Army." In any case, Henry Algernon's fascination with military and naval history persisted throughout his life, as did his other strong interests: farming and horticulture, railroads, government, politics, and real estate.

After returning to civilian life, the Colonel first worked as a sales agent in the powder company with his father. Then he served as president and general manager of the twelve-mile-long Wilmington and Northern Railroad. Before his marriage, Henry A. had acquired several acres of land halfway between Eleutherean Mills and Winterthur, on which he built a small railroad station[8] and living quarters for farm and mill workers; he named this cluster of buildings Montchanin in honor of his great-great-grandmother, Anne Alexandrine de Montchanin, wife of Samuel du Pont, mother of Pierre Samuel. The Colonel appears to have been avid for land, for by his mid-fifties he had not only extended the boundaries of Winterthur by nine hundred acres but had also bought four large blocks of Chicago real estate, some with river frontage, from the Du Pont Company. At the time the property was worth about half a million dollars. (These investments would be of immeasurable importance to Harry du Pont in the century that followed.)

Henry Algernon du Pont emerges as a complex figure. Several months before his marriage, he wrote his fiancée, "I am fully conscious that you are 50 times more sweet-tempered & better in every way than I am," and in fact this seems to have been only slightly exaggerated. Henry A. had a prickly nature. He described an acquaintance's overdue letter, "characteristically dated 'on the train,'" as a "rude & underbred piece of business." He instructed his wife never again to speak to an ill-mannered cousin, an order that she immediately dismissed as "absurd." Pauline's light touch contrasted with Henry's heavy-handed formality. Speedy mail delivery prompted him to write: "The results are a signal tribute to the great cause of civil service reform!" He begged her to "pardon my dereliction" for not saying goodbye to her. Although Henry A. was undoubtedly busy, he is somehow reminiscent of Chaucer's man-of-law: "And yet he semed busier than he was." However, his complaints of fatigue, overwork, and being "altogether . . . [not] in very good shape, physically & mentally," suggest a disposition that would cause problems in years to come.

My grandfather was often away in Philadelphia, Washington, New York, Chicago, or on an occasional shooting trip. Pauline continually wrote that she and the children missed him, but she expressed other feelings more strongly on the rare occasions when she was the one who was away from home. Her remorse is striking: "It seems dreadful to leave you so very alone. Somehow all the way I felt that I ought not to have left. I do hope [the staff] will take good care of you, & that someone will ask you out to dine. It seems a shame to have left you, but you will have some compensation in the morning, such a peaceful time to dress, no chatterbox to disturb you." Or, "I wish you knew how to play solitaire so that you could amuse yourself in the evening. . . I do hope all will be well at home, I suppose there is no real reason why I should not have come on, but somehow I cannot help but feel that I ought not to have."

One wonders at the reasons for her excessive guilt other than awareness that she was more popular than her spouse, but the Colonel of course did miss her. He wrote: "It is a pleasure to think how much you must be enjoying yourself [in New York], & we must not selfishly dwell upon the extent to which the children & I miss you here."

Once, when Pauline was at the seashore, an annual fortnight holiday planned for the children, she wrote to her husband, "There is no one here [for us] to know." Henry A., however, made plain his preference for remaining at Winterthur, in the "quietness & repose of our beautiful home." Considering how often Pauline expressed her regret at the brevity of the

Colonel's visits to the summer resort, one suspects that beach life was not for him. An aunt of Pauline's probably got it right: "How did Henry enjoy his stay with you, no doubt he found the beach stupid."

Nonetheless, both Henry A. and Pauline gave much of themselves to their children; they evidently saw eye to eye on the subject of child rearing and tried never to be away at the same time when Louise and Harry were young. More than many fathers today, Henry A. took a lively interest in his children's welfare and progress. He apparently enjoyed the occasional wild game of cache-cache (hide and seek) or word games before dinner, in which nine-year-old Harry at least once happily excelled. Henry A. invariably joined his wife in countless interviews in the search for the perfect governess, and, partly at my grandmother's request, it was he who supervised the books Louise read.

Pauline understood her husband's depth of feeling and, in a letter to Anna, defended his reticence. "Henry I am sure did not speak of [baby Annette's death] the other night because he could not, he cannot bear to speak of it, it has always been that way with all the children." Whether or not they spoke of these feelings together, their shared suffering was surely a bond. Years later, when Harry was nineteen and Louise already married, the Colonel wrote to his wife: "This is a sad anniversary for us, dear Pauline, & my heart is very full. Though 23 years have passed by since our darling first born was taken from us, I can never, never forget her!"

Henry Francis du Pont, the only son to survive of the seven children born to Pauline and Henry A., had much invested in him from the start. He was born to parents who needed children not only to cherish and nurture but in order to uphold deep-seated traditions and values, which in turn would be transmitted to generations to come. The atmosphere that surrounded my father from the time of his birth was one of both love and anxiety. Two infants had already died; the twins were born when Harry was three, and Annette followed in death the longer-surviving twin. It is impossible to assess what effect these events, as well as his mother's immobilizations and depression, may have had on him. But it can be surmised that Harry du Pont set out in life with not only large advantages but also their opposites.

CHAPTER 4

The Colonel

THE library at Winterthur has always been my grandfather's room. It was added to the house as part of the new east wing in 1902, a year of great significance for Colonel du Pont. Early that year, in the thick of battling for the nomination to the Senate, he turned down the offer of the presidency of the now booming Du Pont Company, a position that he would have jumped at (as will be seen) thirteen years before; and in September he lost his beloved wife.

For my grandfather and my father, the completion of the east wing of the house, as well as the addition of a new front wall with a porte-cochère, cannot have been a source of immediate pleasure, so closely involved were they with Pauline's illness and death. She had of course heard a great deal about the marble staircase and hall, the living room of red damask that extended from the hall, and the big rooms (in the three-story addition) to the east—the squash court, billiard room, and library—one on top of the other. That she did not live to see them finished must have diminished their charms for her survivors. My grandfather surely played squash and billiards, but I never knew my father to do so. Years later, after the Colonel's death, the library was used only one day a year, on Christmas afternoon. It was in this room that my parents and their houseguests opened their stockings, stuffed well in advance by my father, and the presents that awaited us all in carefully arranged and labeled baskets.[1]

But since the library was quite forgotten on every other day, I secretly appropriated it. A dark and quiet place, remote from the rest of the house, it was ideal for reading, studying, staring into the fire, and even occasional

Portrait of Henry A. du Pont in 1906 by Ellen Emmet

trysting. Lined from floor to ceiling with books—military, naval, genealogical, many in French, many with "f" for "s," smelling of delicious
musk and times long past—the library epitomized the essence of my
grandfather. Then as now, his marble bust dominated the entrance to the
room, as did his portrait above the fireplace at the far end, in partial profile,
dressed in morning coat and striped trousers. His slightly supercilious expression in both representations caused my mother to observe, "He sure
does hate himself!" The Colonel's sword, sabre, and Medal of Honor are
displayed on the wall in a glass case.[2]

The portrait, painted in 1906, when the Colonel was sixty-eight years
old, and signed "Ellen Emmet," was joined eight years later by an oil paint-

The porte-cochère at Winterthur after 1902.

ing of my father at thirty-four, handsome and tall, dark butterscotch-colored hair parted in the middle, this one signed "Ellen Emmet Rand" (p. 103).[3] The painter, a student of John Singer Sargent (and a much cherished relative of William and Henry James), expertly captured the likenesses of father and son. When the Colonel and Harry, at sixty-four and twenty-two, respectively, lost the "bright presence ... gracious and fascinating manners & [high] intelligence" of wife and mother,[4] this library would have been one of the spaces in which the two men began reshaping their lives. And it was where the crusty old man spent a great deal of time late in his life, living in his reflected glory.

Henry Algernon du Pont was the oldest of eight children. He was seventeen when William, his only brother and the last child, was born. Little was said about my father's uncle William when I was growing up, but since I had no first cousins in any direction (and, I believed, no du Pont second cousins), my interest was limited. When in time I heard my great-uncle referred to as "dirty Willie," I surmised for no good reason that this quaint sobriquet stemmed from the fact of his divorce. Only years later did I discover a far deeper cause for the hostility between Henry A. and William and found that they had not spoken to each other in decades.

Different as these brothers may have been, my grandfather and his son were in many ways even less alike. Henry Algernon, an excellent student and horseman, at first followed the lead of his own father, Henry the Red, who had attended a military boarding school before going to West Point and had abandoned an army career at the request of his father, Irénée, that he return to the family business. In 1850, when Henry A. was twelve years old, his father became chief executive officer of the Du Pont Company. Thus Henry A., well aware of the business so close to the house, must have early on acquired the tacit belief that he himself, as the oldest child, would one day assume this role.

My grandfather's admission to West Point was in no way guaranteed. At sixteen, a sophomore at the University of Pennsylvania, he was "well advanced in his studies" and his "character & conduct [were] all that could be desired." But competition for West Point was fierce, and appointments from the small state of Delaware were necessarily limited. Relatives of Henry A.'s mother, Louisa, made overtures to members of President Franklin Pierce's Cabinet, emphasizing the Du Pont Company's importance to the United States and the incomparable training that West Point could offer to one "of the right name and nature for the army [who was] destined to succeed his father" as head of the firm. The admiral-to-be Samuel Francis du Pont, Henry A.'s first cousin once removed and uncle by marriage, approached Jefferson Davis, then secretary of war, reminding him that Thomas Jefferson had once so esteemed the company as to procure for it machinery at that time available only in Europe. He further noted that Henry A.'s father, head of the "unrivalled" gun powder establishment, wanted the same educational advantages for his son that he himself had received at West Point. (Six years would bring a dramatic change in the relationship between Jefferson Davis and cadet Henry A. du Pont.)

In 1861, at the start of the Civil War, Second Lieutenant Henry Algernon du Pont graduated first in his class from West Point;[5] he later would refer to these years as the "turning point of my life."[6] After several months in an artillery regiment, he was ordered, to his dismay, to return to a teaching post at West Point. He appealed both to his commanding officer and to

his navy uncle. "To see service with troops . . . is an essential thing."[7] Only
after a change of orders two years later did Henry A.'s immersion in real
war finally begin. His service in the field began in July 1863; the next year,
as chief of artillery, Army of West Virginia, and now promoted to captain,
he took part in five months of skirmishes and battles in the Shenandoah
Valley campaign, including those at New Market, Winchester, Fisher's
Hill, and Cedar Creek.

Colorful accounts of these times exist in the form of my grandfather's
contemporaneous or retrospective letters or in reports about him from both
Confederate and friendly sources. Here are excerpts from Henry A.'s letters to his parents in 1864:

> *June 8 Staunton, Virginia.* We made terrible havoc with the enemy. . . . We are
> campaigning with a vengeance—no tents & the soldiers living on flour and fresh
> beef . . . Our power of mischief [has] greatly increased.

> *Sept. 21 Cedar Creek.* I never was under a hotter fire both of infantry & artillery
> than . . . when I was riding along the infantry line & encouraging it to advance.
> My favorite black horse, Joe, was shot under me; a minie ball struck him in the
> leg . . . though it did not break the bone will lame him permanently, I fear. . . . I
> had the ball extracted yesterday.

> *Oct. 21.* I had a splendid chance to use artillery during the final . . . part of the bat-
> tle & . . . took advantage of it to the utmost. . . . Although I lost a lot of personal
> property, both of my private horses are safe. I write on Rebel paper, captured in
> their train.

Henry A. was no end exhilarated by the battle of Cedar Creek, and for
his "distinguished services" he was promoted to the brevet rank of lieutenant colonel. However, general recognition of his courage and his zeal for
combat was from some sides slow in coming.

Of key significance was the fact that Major General David Hunter, for
whom Henry A. had been chief of artillery, mysteriously omitted his name
from every report about the campaign of 1864. Henry A. ascribed this
slight, probably correctly, to Hunter's "bad relations" with his uncle, Admiral Samuel F. du Pont, in the battle for Charleston Harbor the year before. But this explanation did not mitigate his bitterness. His performance
had also earned the praise of at least two Confederate officers, one of whom
wrote of the "unforeseen and almost unparalleled efficiency of Du Pont's
artillery," and another who referred to him as a "gallant commander."

A Union officer at Cedar Creek later remembered him riding "under a withering infantry and artillery fire . . . on a gray horse [conspicuously alone]. . . . I expected to see him fall at every instant . . . [but for his] heroic bearing & distinguished gallantry at the critical moment . . . when all seemed lost . . . nearly the whole of Crook's Corps would have been captured."[8] However, these words in no way eradicated Henry A.'s deep resentment at the injustice done him by Hunter. The Colonel was tormented by yet another slight years later, this time from a Lieutenant Bush, who in *A Short History of the 5th Artillery* entirely failed to mention him, not even identifying him as the one "who galloped forward to the firing line." Henry A. was furious at this omission of the "most brilliant event of my whole military career." Whatever the reason for Bush's neglect, the omission fed Henry A.'s disappointment at not having received the Medal of Honor. The oversight rankled for some thirty years, and in 1894, if not sooner, he set about trying to rectify it.

Three eyewitness accounts of his actions at Cedar Creek produced no immediate results from the war secretary's office, but further correspondence with the secretary and Governor McKinley of Ohio, who had served with Henry A. in Virginia, ultimately resulted in his being awarded the coveted medal for "most distinguished gallantry & voluntary exposure to the enemy's fire at a critical moment" in the Battle of Cedar Creek (October 19, 1864).[9]

Henry A.'s experiences during the Civil War and especially in the Shenandoah campaign represented one of the pinnacles of his life and confirmed his courage, high sense of honor, and compassion. He deplored General Hunter's order to burn down the library and other nonmilitary buildings of the Virginia Military Institute at Lexington and several days later bravely persuaded Hunter not to destroy the White Sulphur Springs Hotel and its adjoining cottages, an act that he believed would have violated the "rules of civilized warfare."[10] Years later in the Senate, Henry A. saw through the passage of a bill that compensated the military college for severe damages perpetrated by the Union Army.

In 1865, at the end of the war, he was stationed at Fortress Monroe, where Jefferson Davis, the deposed president of the Confederacy and his erstwhile West Point sponsor, was imprisoned. Arriving there a year later, for her first visit, Mrs. Davis wrote, "It was comforting to hear that our

young friend, Colonel Henry A. Dupont was on duty . . . for of him I expect
every gentlemanly concession and observance. . . . [He] and other gentlemen among the officers, were kind and courteous to us, and . . . their con-
siderate conduct has been a constant memory."[11] Henry A. severely condemned the behavior of the presiding general toward Mrs. Davis as
"offensive, ungentlemanly, & needlessly harsh" and would forever value
his affectionate relationship with her—"a very old and very good friend
whom I have known since I was a cadet."

Throughout his life, Henry A. continued to reflect on and embroider
his war experiences. They served as a magnetic force, a point of reference,
and often (and at times irrelevantly) asserted themselves. In his first letter
to Harry, homesick at boarding school, his father observed that the date was
the anniversary of the Battle of Cedar Creek, "one of the most important
episodes of my life." Thirty years later, during a contentious correspondence in which Henry A. informed his cousin Alfred that, after his 1906
election to the U.S. Senate, he had transferred his Du Pont Company hold-
ings to his son, then age twenty-six, he could not resist adding, "I could not
help remembering that at 26 I had fully exercised important commands in
battle & been repeatedly called upon to face war-time responsibilities in-
comparably greater than those which were involved in the ownership of
stock in the E. I. du Pont Powder Co." With this statement Henry Algernon managed both to disparage his son and to blow his own horn.

The lasting impact of the Civil War on the Colonel's life, with its personal glories and disappointments, is evident in two books he published
shortly before his death.[12] Both books focus on strategies of war but also reveal something about Henry A.'s personality. Even at the end of his life he
was unable to let go of the memories of injustices done both to him and to
his uncle by General Hunter, an often irrational and fanatical man who was
universally disliked.[13] Henry A. also hotly—and it would appear justifiably—
defended the admiral against the criticism of Lincoln's secretary of the navy,
Gideon Welles.[14] These two books have merit for military and naval historians, and for the Colonel they must also have been a catharsis. But the repeti-
tiveness of their content and detail suggests that the author, until the end of
his life, somehow needed to nourish and exaggerate painful issues.

In 1889, when Henry Algernon was fifty-one years old, he suffered a
major professional setback. The death of his father, itself a sad personal

loss, brought dire consequences. Henry A. and his brother William at that time owned four-fifths of the shares of the Du Pont Company; therefore either, if supported by the other, could have taken control of it. William had no desire for the presidency of the company, but neither did he want this position for his overbearing older brother. Henry A., who had worked for the company in some capacity ever since his marriage, did indeed both want and expect to be named its president, and he felt sure that this was also his father's ambition for him. Since no such idea had been expressed either publicly or in writing, however, Henry A. was powerless in the face of William's failure to support him. Because of this betrayal, and later the near-scandal of divorce, William was for years ostracized by Henry A. and other members of the immediate family.

In 1896, Henry A. suffered another blow. He had the year before been chosen a U.S. senator by a one-vote margin in the Delaware legislature, but the Senate now contested the vote, and in the end, again by a one-vote margin, his appointment was rejected.

During his wife's lifetime (and therefore Harry's youth), the Colonel was subjected to a good share of disappointment. His private life had also been far from free of suffering; although it was difficult for him to speak of personal pain, only two months before his own death he wrote to his cousin-in-law Rodney Sharp, whose ten-year-old son had recently died: "Some people think that the death of a child, with whom one's associations are necessarily of but a few years standing, is a less serious calamity than the decease of an older person, but . . . the fact remains that the taking away of a little child is a terrible blow to the parents. Personally I have experienced this sorrow several times and know how to feel for you."

Although he was often thoughtful and generous, Henry A. was not light-hearted by nature, and letters to his wife repeatedly refer to insomnia, "mental & bodily fatigue or more properly exhaustion," and his "avalanche of cares & duties." He often felt "completely used up," and he took himself very seriously indeed.

I can only wonder if during these years his outlook was not to some extent affected by disappointment in his only son. That Harry was not bold, outgoing, or athletic was early apparent. We have evidence of the Colonel's scorn at the young boy's preference for music lessons to riding, although, as his peacekeeping wife observed, "l'un n'empêche pas l'autre" ("one shouldn't prevent the other"). Harry's lackluster school performance added to the "many cares & anxieties" of his scholarly father; his parents' hope for "pleasure & pride" should he "attain a high place in the form" was not to be realized. Despite the Colonel's belief that West Point offered the best education for young men, there is a suggestion that early on he gave up the aspiration that Harry consider this course.[15] The fact that it would have been hard to find any traits whatever in his son that were suited to the military was quite likely all to the good; Harry's mother surely would have opted for Harvard in any case. Yet, in fairness to the Colonel, an affectionate letter to Harry in his third year at college suggests that he was able to accept his son for what he was; he was gratified by Harry's improvement in trap shooting (of all things), and he valued his suggestions to the architect about changes in the Winterthur house.

It is likely that the Colonel found his daughter's temperament more congenial than her brother's. Louise, an enterprising young adult and mature for her years, by age twenty-three had been involved for some time in teaching a group of underprivileged children; she had many friends, had weathered a broken engagement, and was happily married. Henry A.'s empathy with her had all along been profound; in connection with Louise's unfortunate first engagement, he "cannot help thinking all the time about our Louise & her disappointments." He was "awfully sorry & distressed about her."

Henry A.'s relationship with his wife was more problematic. At the time of their marriage they were undeniably much in love. My grandmother's letters are coquettish and frivolous: "Your conceit would be unbounded if you had heard half the things that have been told me about you. Of course, I can't agree with them"; "I have always been the baby of the family and am accustomed to being spoiled . . . so I am giving you carte blanche to do with me whatever you please"; "It is your bounden duty to go instantly and have a photograph taken. Of course, to hear is to obey, so I expect one by return of mail"; "When doing your best to spoil me on the sofa . . . I believe I like it just a little, & would not mind having a repetition today"; "It never seemed to trouble your conscience when you disarranged [my quite respectable] hair, nor mine either."

She could also be serious. She mentioned a hint that had come her way, expressed by some of Henry's friends at West Point, "that I would not be good enough for you, which is just about the case my darling. I love you so much and only wish you were here." "Sometimes when I think how much more you may expect that I can do, but darling I will do my best, and then you know you must help me."

And Henry A.'s letters, often written twice daily, as were hers, show that he was every bit as smitten. "I knew that I was desperately, irretrievably in love with you," he wrote describing a time early in their relationship. "I think of you constantly." "I only wish I could be with you and pet you this minute, my own dearest Pauline. The more I see of you ... the more I love you ... though I did not believe I could love you more than I have for ever so long." However, her replies tell us that duty as well as love was on his mind: "I suppose you are right to feel happy to be unselfish & to do one's duty, but I cannot say that I do as I want to see you so much my darling & grudge every minute that separates us."

In one letter Henry A. assured Pauline that what she had last written was both "charming and interesting." They exchanged views on what they were reading: for Henry A., letters written by his grandfather's friend Thomas Jefferson and accounts by Schliemann on the recent discovery of Troy; for Pauline, romantic novels. "If I had read it last year ... I would have been blue ... to have no one who really cared for or loved me." Unlike her fiancé, she delighted in Dickens. How was it that Henry A. could not like *Bleak House*?

But as their marriage progressed, the content and tone of their letters changed, and preoccupation with children, illness, the weather, and politics took over. Henry A.'s 1874 signatures, "I love you with all my heart" and "I love you very dearly & am always yours, most Devotedly Henry," a decade later had become "With fond love, Your aff't husband H. A. duP." In turn, my grandmother's amorous engagement letters—"So goodnight dearie ... With any number of kisses and all my love" and "Love ye dearie, Your own Pauline"—of early married years had turned into "Always affectionately, Pauline." Surely the loss of five children took a heavy emotional toll on both parents during the first half of their life together. Furthermore, the feud with William, the loss of the company presidency, and the Senate fiasco were themselves severe blows. President McKinley's offer in 1897 that Henry become Minister to Russia, which he turned down, may have helped to mitigate his bitterness, as surely as did the Congres-

Colonel Henry A. du Pont.

sional Medal awarded to him the following year, although too late by more than three decades, in his opinion.

During twenty-eight years of marriage, my grandmother's ardor for her husband dimmed, although she remained at all times loyal to him. She encouraged him, quoting a friend on his "very swell appearance," and maintained that "the least the President could do would be to make you Secretary of War." To read her occasional scolding is refreshing: "The idea of your telegraphing me about a chaperone. I think I know who is proper quite as well as you & Victorine." Short-tempered, Henry A. was quick to criticize his wife for her lack of "prudence," or Anna for her "mania on the subject of coolness & ventilation [which] has had a good deal to do with [all the sickness] at her house this winter." Henry A.'s self-importance could quite overtake him, as suggested by the following communication to a minister in Wilmington whose new secretary had innocently misaddressed a letter: "Referring to your letter, I am very much surprised to find that you address me at Chester Co., Pennsylvania. I beg to call your special attention to the fact that I was born in the State of Delaware and have always lived here. . . . Had I been a resident of Pennsylvania as you suppose, you would have had not occasion to write your letter to me."

Such high-handedness elicited precisely the reaction it deserved. The minister, not wishing to put his reply in writing, exploded to Henry A.'s secretary on the telephone, saying that he considered the letter "wholly uncalled for and ungentlemanly" and that although he realized that the Colonel's "feelings of self-importance had been hurt," he felt that an apology was due him. The Colonel, with his oft expressed (but far from true) opinion that "Harry has no sense of humor," had aptly described himself.

My grandmother's greater resiliency and her ability to share her feelings helped her in the long run; the Colonel's inability to speak openly or to express his grief was a handicap. Pauline also had the advantage of wholehearted enthusiasms. Her religion class for young women, to which she drove one evening a week despite bad weather or fatigue, seemed to recharge her spirit, as did her sense of fun and her interest in people.

Pauline was able to gloss over many of Henry's bouts of irritability; on one vacation, writing to Louise, she reported on the "doleful" appearance at dinner of Uncle Lenty and Papa, but added, "Papa looked much the more lugubrious." All things considered, however, Henry A. and Pauline's life together seemed a satisfactory one. Pauline understood her spouse, admired much about him, and tried to forgive him his pomposities. It is clear that she appreciated her freedom in later years to spend time in Boston with friends or with her grown children. During her final illness the Colonel's concern and devotion grew increasingly apparent, and his letters returned to their early expressions of love. "Good bye, my Darling, always Your loving H A dP." On the envelope of Pauline's final letter to her husband, dated September 3, 1902, Henry wrote, "My sweet loving Pauline's *last* letter to me." There was no question about the depth of his sorrow.

⇒ · CHAPTER 5 · ⇐

Early Childhood

GROWING up at Winterthur, Harry and Louise had the run of the place. Their mother told them, "Play anywhere. Play in the meadow," and so they did—in snow and ice, in leaves, hay, and mud. Their corner of the fertile Brandywine Valley teemed with possibilities—the stable and barn below the big house, the barnyard with turkeys, chickens, and ducks. And there was fun away from home as well. Annual visits to the seashore meant sandcastles and crabbing, bowling and croquet, and the occasional juggler or ventriloquist at the hotel. These summer holidays also provided the children with playmates their own age, apparently in short supply at home, and playmates with whom, for a change, they spoke English.

When the children were small, French was the language used for both everyday conversation and correspondence. Harry, writing to his parents from college about the Groton School's sixteenth birthday party, described the school's "eldest grandchild," age four, who emerged from a "huge cake. He cannot speak a word of English just the way I used to be." We do not know when Harry became bilingual, but his background on both sides of the family was unmistakably French. The Colonel, evidently supported by his wife and her sister, was eager that all the children be fluent in the language; consequently, at least in his own household, good spoken French was a must for the governess and nurses and probably for the butler and other staff as well.

We have a fine account of Christmas dictated—in French, of course— by six-year-old Harry, in which he described at length to his Robinson cousins a variety of presents, although an attempted translation of his mother's handwriting makes censored wartime letters look tame.[1] We can decipher references to a badminton set, sachets for handkerchiefs, cologne, a *magnifique* horn, along with a monkey on a tricycle, but how about the "pretty little _____ painted by Aunt Victorine," or the "_____ with pretty red flowers on each side," or the "_____ all with new ribbon," the "pretty _____ of paper with an *echarpe* of pretty blue lace," or the "hat of _____ of gold." Nevertheless, as evidenced by his repeated use of the adjective "joli," Harry even then delighted in colors and objects. He liked familiar animals as well; he described a lake with frogs and wading cows and a water-shy rooster who rode on a duck's back.

Young Harry's life was a happy one, but it also was laced with apprehension. Perhaps inevitably, given the family's early history, illness and the fear of it loomed large. Anna's physician husband, called in because of Harry's bronchial pneumonia, wrote to Pauline: "I know how anxious you feel, & appreciate the reason for it fully." Dr. Robinson was much in demand, and the du Ponts compensated him for his time and skill both in cash—"This could send Anna & me on a spree to Chicago"—and in commodities like terrapin and cases of wine and champagne. As Colonel du Pont wrote to his wife, this "pays our debt in one sense."

My grandmother's letters are full of worries: "The snow is so wet I am afraid the children will take cold"; travel is postponed as "I fear [the heat] will make them ill." Even though such alarm was often realistic a century ago, and pneumonia was an ever-present danger, more than normal anxiety reigned in the Henry A. du Pont household. September 1884: "We have had a regular hospital here." April 1885: "We are like nickels in the well. Harry was with fever again yesterday, & in the night Louise had a bilious attack." Virtually every one of Pauline's letters includes at least one allusion to a malady of family or staff. My grandfather seemed unduly afflicted with rheum or gout, and Pauline herself was often unwell. Incapacitated during her last pregnancy, she observed to her sister, "Last year [the children] were not sick a day" (far from true) "& this year because I am sick in bed they must be sick all the time."

My father's continuing health-consciousness, which often approached heights worthy of Molière, must have been inculcated in him from the start. Prematurely born at four and one-half pounds (in actuality, he weighed more at birth than did Louise and their twin brothers), he was always considered delicate. At age one he sustained a frightening illness, and later he experienced the usual childhood colds, earaches, and toothaches, for which he was variously dosed with "tonic," "drops," cod liver oil, licorice, blackberry cordial, quinine, and apple jack, the last two sometimes taken together. At four years old he was described as "so thin & pale & [seeming] so weak." References abound to "dear little Harry" or "poor little Harry," with hopes that sea bathing or cooler weather or a trip to the mountains will help him to be "strong & well" or to gain "flesh & strength & appetite." When he was not quite five, days spent in bed with his mother, "to have him where I could get at him," must have also been heady compensation for illness. Overreaction to his various ailments would hardly have instilled in him the sense of becoming the hoped for "strong boy."

Along with his general sense that his health was frail, my father's fear of illness lasted throughout his life, and he gave a wide berth to anyone, family members included, suffering from an ailment that could be construed as remotely contagious. Doctors often attended his head colds. One day, on boarding a train in New York bound for Florida, he felt unwell, and the ever-ready thermometer registered a slight fever. Alarms were triggered. A secretary in Wilmington was instructed to contact Johns Hopkins Hospital so that a desired doctor might join the train at Baltimore. The board-certified physician appeared on cue, positioned his stethoscope, and disembarked in Washington, having pronounced my father fit to continue on his journey.

Harry was less adventurous than his sister. Seven-year-old Louise was "delighted by the trained horses, but Harry was overawed by the people, light, music, etc." Harry's parents, his father in particular, expressed concern about their son's development. An early indication of this appeared in the context of riding. Often the tearful Harry would ride his pony only when cajoled by his mother. Pauline reported to her sister the Colonel's telling reaction to five-year-old Harry's wish for music lessons: "Said he, 'Ah-hah, by taking music lessons he cannot ride on horseback.'" The scorn of the accomplished horseman cannot have escaped Harry's notice, and to please his parents, the boy did continue to ride. His mother wrote, "After persuadings & tears I induced Harry [then aged 10] to go on his pony, & from his account he enjoyed the ride & went on a trot. But I am not sure how much trotting he did."

Harry du Pont in childhood, a "most charming boy."

Like many other girls, I fell in love with horses at about this age, and for several years I rode in hunts and horse shows, although my riding skills may have been as questionable as my father's. He later confessed to me that, as a young adult, after being rolled in the Brandywine, he never ventured on a horse again. Harry's timorousness extended also to other sports like swimming and ice and roller skating.

Although as a child Harry cried easily, Louise habitually defended her brother and on at least one occasion announced that other boys had also cried. Harry's shyness with children other than his Robinson cousins was a cause for concern; observed at a birthday party when he was three, this characteristic continued as a theme in his parents' letters and may well have been accentuated by his relative unfamiliarity with English. My grandmother wrote hopefully from the seashore that perhaps Harry, now nine, "will be induced to play with" the other children, but "as soon as he gets the worst of anything, he wants to stop, or cry." "I have done my best to make him play with boys, but have not succeeded, he is so terribly bashful. There really seem to be some nice little fellows here, but they all seem to know each other—but of course, Harry could have known them if he had chosen." "Harry doesn't play like other boys, there is no denying it."

Colonel du Pont wrote back expressing his hope that Harry was not "still standing aloof from all the other boys," but in another letter he seemed better able to understand that his son's aloofness was a matter not so much of choice as of temperament.

> Sept. 3, 1889
> It distresses me very much . . . to hear that Harry is so shy & that he will not have anything to do with other boys who are suitable companions. This is bad for him in every way & will make his life a very unhappy one when he goes to school. At times I feel very uneasy & anxious about his future & think that so far as the governess is concerned, his lessons & intellectual development are of more importance than those of Louise. For, although he has plenty of natural intelligence, he is much more backward for his age than his sister is, & this very fact will serve to increase his reserve when he is forced to come in contact with other lads of his years.

Colonel du Pont's concerns about Harry's immaturity and troubles with lessons were well founded. A hint of my father's dismal scholastic future appeared during his fifth year. As his mother wrote to Anna, "Harry shows no more fondness for his letters than before & it is pretty uphill work." And uphill was to be its course. Although at the age of six he was "commencing to read quite nicely," he continued to do so only "if he *wishes*." And he had been known to complain of a worsened earache at lesson time.

Reserved and never gregarious, Harry was appreciated more by adults than by other children. At four he was described as "cunning" and "looking like a little man," and later as a "most charming boy" with "beautiful manners." No Fauntleroy, however, he could be stubborn and tearful, although in the end he apparently yielded to requests by his tactful mother and would wear the white flannels or ride the pony or go to the dance. He was not above making a scene at the dentist's or when he was not included in an invitation received by Louise. He and his sister were good playmates, and her age and precocity helped her to be protective of him.

Harry was extremely jealous of the baby, Annette, born one month after his fifth birthday. My father told me this in a rare burst of confidentiality and intimated his vast (and of course secret) relief when Annette died. Whether or not his parents were aware of their son's all too human feelings I do not know, but some years later, when I reopened the subject, perhaps in connection with my own children, my father hotly denied ever having felt or said any such thing. Such are the vagaries of age and memory.

A strange scene was described by my grandmother to her sister: "November 1887. As I expected the children were disgusted with the nurse. Harry said, 'Je n'ai jamais vu une *chose* si horrible de ma vie,' as if she had been some kind of wild animal!" In the absence of any clue, I am at a loss to comprehend the meaning of the "so horrible thing" for this seven-and-a-half-year-old boy other than that "as expected," he had picked up his mother's "disgust."

Harry du Pont comes across as a pleasant, vulnerable, and at times sickly and shy little boy, whose childhood does not seem remarkable for someone of his background except for the emphasis on French. Although he was exposed to his mother's suffering early on and later became the object of parental concern (and sometimes his father's disapproval, if not contempt), he was also seen as "well & happy" and contented with generally noncompetitive activities—playing with his dog, singing "so sweetly," collecting stamps and birds' eggs. The fact that he was not an athlete did not seem troublesome. And he had robust enthusiasms. At a family wedding, which he called "magnifique," he filled up on croquettes and cream puffs.

Groton

P RIVATE boarding schools for boys began to sprout in earnest in the United States after the Civil War, influenced by, among other factors, the expansion of private fortunes and the rapid growth of cities. Such schools answered the needs of families who, with the decline of rural academies, aspired to better college preparation for their sons than was available in local high schools. Groton was the eighth such school to open.

Given Harry's temperament and upbringing, it is unlikely that he would have thrived in any boarding school, but in keeping with family tradition, in 1893 off he went to Groton.[1] The school, in Groton, Massachusetts, thirty-four miles northwest of Boston, was founded in 1884 by the Reverend Endicott Peabody, a young Episcopal minister filled with zeal and a first-hand knowledge of English public education.[2] The small church school was probably as good a choice for thirteen-year-old Harry as any would have been, and it offered him a few congenial prospects. He responded to the beauty of its setting and to its religious orientation (which included daily chapel and evening prayers), and he would forever revere Mrs. Peabody, who helped make his school life bearable, as he later observed more than once. But in two crucial aspects, Groton was not for him. As a nonathlete, ill equipped for the much esteemed sports program, he certainly would have been ranked as "inconsequential," and as an indifferent student he did not begin to live up to Mr. Peabody's ideal that Groton students take "college exams as a matter of course without definite preparation."[3] Far from it!

An applicant for admission to Groton, according to the brochure of 1893, "must be able to pass an examination in writing, spelling, geography, the elementary portions of arithmetic, Latin grammar and easy Latin composition." I wonder, as I read his letters, how my father came to be accepted, for the fledgling institution had had a waiting list ever since it opened. The cosmopolitan background of Harry's charming mother, his father's brilliant Civil War record, and the likelihood that the $600 annual tuition charges could be met probably combined to persuade Mr. Peabody to accept him as one of the twenty-two boys in the class of 1899.

Harry's introduction to Groton School was not helped by his father's participation, for, as my mother told it, the Colonel marched him in with the stentorian announcement: "Voici mon fils Harry du Pont," and continued to speak in French. This incongruous scene surely occasioned enormous mirth and would lose nothing in the retelling by masters and students, but any version of the reality must have been horrendous for Harry, who carried more than the usual load of homesickness and anxiety. Many other first formers were doubtless also frightened and shy, but most came from Boston or New York, Philadelphia or Baltimore, where they would have known some of the other boys and quite likely had attended a day school. The timid and awkward youth from Delaware, educated at home chiefly by governesses and now launched by a pompous military father who did not see fit to speak English, would surely have been an irresistible target.

Harry's first months at school were miserable indeed. Letters, both written and received, were his best antidote to homesickness, a state of mind that he did not attempt to disguise from his parents although in letters to others he kept up a "brave & manly" front, for which his parents commended him. His first thirty or so surviving letters to them were in French. This one, blotched, smeared, and replete with misspellings, was in part a reaction to his father's cancellation of a planned visit.

> Je suis si homesick maintenant que je ne sais pas que faire, il ne faut pas montre cette a personne . . . si qu'elqun ne vient pas me voir bientot je mourais de chagrin. S'ilteplait vien me voir je pleurs temps que je ne pepas ecrire.
>   Aurevoir cher Papa et Maman votre petit
>
> >   Harry
>
>   J'ai embrassee tous les pages[4]

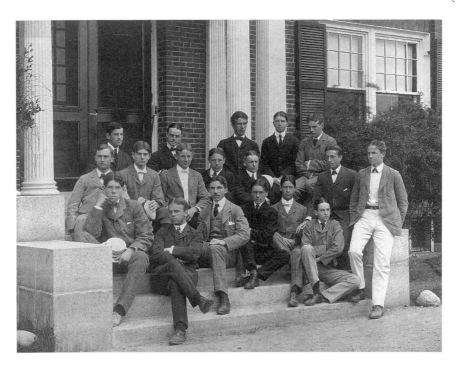

Groton, sixth form, 1899. Back row, from left: C. Brown, H. Whitridge,
R. Derby, H. F. du Pont, J. R. Roosevelt, Jr. Middle row: W. Wharton,
A. Swann, E. Bowditch, A. C. Lord, A. M. Brown. Front row: F. Riggs,
J. Waterbury, W. Hadden, H. Krumbhaar, J. Peabody, G. Draper, F. Alsop.
Courtesy Groton School, Groton, Mass.

Harry's record of homesickness, which persisted intermittently through
his fourth form year, reads like a medical chart. "I am homesick only during the day"; "I am not at all homesick this morning"; "You know I am not
homesick all the time, it only comes on from time to time." On Easter
morning, a month before his fifteenth birthday, having opened his presents
(among them "a big Egg, a Nooga egg . . . a book called Lilies for Easter
Tide"), said some prayers, and read a chapter from St. John, he wrote: "It
is now 20 minutes past 9, you must be finishing breakfast. . . . I am not exactly homesick but I have a longing for home."

From the beginning Harry's parents had tried to cheer him up. The
Colonel "thoroughly" appreciated his feelings and wished it were in his
"power to make [him] feel immediately happy & comfortable." He re-

minded him that both he himself and Harry's grandfather had gone away
to school, the latter at age ten, information that is not likely to have brought
cheer to the homesick boy. His mother's first letter, chattier and in French,
promised to send him some clothes, tennis balls, and bulbs to plant and rec-
ommended that he take a bath every morning before 7 o'clock. "Je t'embrasse de tout coeur et mille fois." The love and appreciation of both
parents for their son were unmistakable, but following their advice—to
temper his misery through academic achievement and the forming of
friendships—was not in his power.

Harry's early consolations other than letters were also rooted in connections to home; he kept a garden and raised hens. (Evidently other boys
were also permitted these hobbies.) Then too he had his stamp collection,
and he was comforted by presents of gingersnaps, boiled chestnuts, and
raspberry vinegar. He gradually found small pleasures, such as in singing
a "pretty anthem about the son of God" in which he must "hold a high note
for a long time." Snowshoeing, skating, canoeing, golf, and whist were also
fun, or so he said. Through these activities he formed tentative relationships, one of which, with John Dix, the son of a New York clergyman, became a real friendship. Unfortunately, this boy left the school halfway
through second form. Harry's response to Dix's severe illness was an early
instance of his reaching out to another person. "I never knew how much I
liked him before now." The school prayed for his recovery, and Harry
brought him violets.

Harry often expressed himself best through flowers—both as presents
for others and for himself. In early days at school, he placed pots of violets
or daffodils close to the photographs of his parents, and the first thing he
did one Easter morning was to take a "long sniff at my daffodils." His garden, flourishing with pansies, carnations, and spirea, had given him great
pleasure, but he abandoned it at sixteen as "too much trouble & very few
of the bigger boys have them." But throughout his Groton years he was
drawn to visit a Mr. Huebner's garden center as a kind of refuge from loneliness during the long Massachusetts winters.

Harry not only bought flowers from Mr. Huebner but was permitted
to use part of a greenhouse for his own sweet peas, arbutus, and other flowers. He wrote of the "gardiner's" fine violets with sixteen-inch stems and
superb cyclamen, a "lovely dark claret a very unusual color . . . [with] 12

flowers and any amount of buds," whose bulb he would later send home. Harry and his mother often exchanged flowers. When sending narcissus or lilies-of-the-valley packed in sphagnum moss to Mrs. Peabody, his mother would send some to Harry as well, and throughout his life the lily-of-the-valley remained his favorite flower.

Harry understood the fulfillment he found in flowers and plants during his Groton years. He wrote home of a "nosegay of sweet peas plucked in the garden" and of waterlilies collected from the river. ("I am wearing one now.") He seemed in no way embarrassed about his love of flowers, although at a school like Groton one might suppose that such interests invited a good deal of teasing. One February day, with Richard Derby, another second former, Harry went "up to the gardiners, & I bought a button hole of lilies of the vally. I guess you must think that I am very extravacant but really this is very important."[5]

Groton School aimed "to cultivate manly Christian character, having regard to moral and physical, as well as intellectual development."[6] In Harry's first winter at the school, at least two occurrences pointed to the need to polish up his manly morals. In one instance, having been involved in after-hours horseplay in the dormitory, he pretended to have been asleep in order to avoid the black marks issued to the other miscreants. The next morning, conscience, doubtless supplemented by peer pressure, brought him to admit his deception, and he too was awarded black marks. But this was Groton. "Mr Peabody after dinner called me & asked me why I hadn't spoken up the same evening. When I told him, he scolded me very hard."

Soon after this episode there was another. In order to lower his French teacher's expectations, Harry denied that his family spoke French at home and dutifully reported the "lie" to his parents. The Colonel responded to this confession with outrage, never suspecting that his son may also have been attempting to lessen the stigma of his own dreadful introduction in French when Harry arrived at the school. "I am very much pained to hear of your statement to Mr. Gladwin. Although I am very glad indeed that you had the courage to tell your mother & me about it, this is not enough. Dear boy, I want you to go to Mr. Gladwin as soon as possible . . . and tell him that you are very sorry that you did not tell him the exact truth. As soon as you can, after having the conversation, write & tell me all about it." Whatever behavior the boy further reported, we do not know, but it is hard to believe that it warranted the severity of this reprimand:

> I have been thinking about your letter all day long and will say in the first place that I am most seriously concerned about your conduct. If you do not behave better you will be sent away from school which would be a terrible misfortune and cause the greatest possible distress to your mother and me! Think of the shame and disgrace, my dear child, and for your own sake and for that of your parents and family as well, keep scrupulously the promises you make in your letter that such bad behavior will not again occur . . . Goodnight, dear, dear child. I love you most tenderly and devotedly. You must be worthy of the name you bear.

Although Harry had done wrong, his conscience had helped to bring about these chastisements, which in turn, playing into Groton's moral code, had probably deepened his sense of fairness. Two years later, writing home about a classmate who claimed to have won a nonexistent toss of a coin, Harry said, "It makes me so mad as I know that we did not do anything of the kind."

Soon before Harry's fifteenth birthday, his mother visited Groton and heard about her son from an especially sympathetic master. The Reverend Sherrard Billings's assessment was remarkably similar to the concerns expressed by the Colonel and his wife some six years earlier. Pauline wrote to her husband: "Mr. Billings asked me if Harry went into anything, work or play, with a will or rather whole souled, & I really could not say that he did. He thought he seemed young for his age (which he is) & so very shy, the most shy boy he had ever met, for he said that hardly any boy was shy with him. Mr. Billings thought that Harry spent too much time with his stamps, & is anxious for him to play ball as he thinks that will develop him in other ways." And so it was that in the fall of 1895 Harry du Pont began, without notable enthusiasm, to participate in the game of football. His letters home are revealing.

> Oct. 15, 1895 [postcard]
> My dear Mama
> I have decided to play football. I suppose you will let me do it. If you don't want me to write & tell me.

No such prohibition having arrived, five days later Harry elaborated:

> Oct 20
> Dear Mama & Papa
> The reason I am playing football is that all the boys play it, & if I dont play there isent hardly anything to do, & everybody said I ought to try it, & the mas-

ters try to make every body play, any-how I tried it & I like it quite well in fact very well, another reason is that some of the boys thought that I was afraid. And I am very glad you gave me permission. I will not play to excess.

The five reasons Harry gave for taking up the game (along with the fact that football at Groton was all but required) suggest his hesitation, freely translated as terror, which it would not do to admit to anyone, perhaps especially a warrior father.

The third form in other ways marked a turning point for Harry, as in his election to the debating society. (Debating, a required activity, was short-lived for my father; when I knew him, he would no more have entered a debate than a training program for astronauts.) More important, Harry's confirmation took place that winter, a rite that he and his mother had often discussed and took extremely seriously. He wrote home: "I can't describe the feeling when I walked up the isle & when I was confirmed, it was very solemn & impressed me very much. I was confirmed between Jack Minturn & Richard Derby."

It was typical of Harry to see to it that his parents were aware of his exact placement vis à vis his schoolmates, whether at meals, study hall, or in chapel. He was likewise quick to report on clothes as well as grades, describing Bill Emmons's "bright yellow cravat with red & green spots on it" and "Dan Draper's golf stockings . . . of the most glaring colour." He also mentioned boys in other connections: a walk on which he and John Dix found a robin's nest with one egg; a canoe trip with "Rosy" (James Roosevelt?); an invitation to spend Thanksgiving with Joe Grew, which he declined. (When Joseph Grew was Ambassador to Japan, five years before Pearl Harbor, my parents, my sister, and I dined with him at the embassy at Tokyo, but I had no inkling that we were there because my father had first known him when he was fourteen years old.) Harry of course longed for acceptance, and he learned about ways not to behave. When he was a second former, his parents acquiesced to his request that they not speak to him in French on their next visit. That Easter, after a classmate had produced a box of candy for the dormitory, he decided not to share his smaller chocolate egg, feeling that, by contrast, "it would not be appreciated."

The theme of illness runs through the correspondence, but it was more pronounced in letters from home; at school Harry seemed to have been remarkably healthy most of the time. However, before his first Christmas vacation, he was one of many who succumbed to what was probably an acute viral infection. His illness was so severe that his mother rushed to Groton via two trains, only to find him better. The following day, mother and son joined the Colonel, who had come as far as Boston, and together the three returned to Winterthur on Christmas Eve, after stopping overnight in New York to avoid the risk of exposing Harry to the "night air."

The foregoing episode might be thought of as an example of appropriate parental concern, but overprotectiveness was often glaringly apparent. Harry's immaturity seems to have been unwittingly prolonged by members of his family. He counted the weeks and days before the start of every vacation and often seemed determined not to settle into school life— to think of himself, rather, as an exile from home. The time and length of parental visits assumed paramount importance. "Two more Sundays & you will be here. I hope you will be able to come up on Thursday before the St. Marks game & stay till Monday for if you come up Friday you will be here only Saturday & Sunday, & I wont see much of you on Saturday as we march in the morning it being Decoration Day & in the afternoon is the game of course." Unlike many adolescents who seek to loosen or even sever family ties, Harry throughout his school years continued to rely on his family for primary support and companionship. In his first desperate month at Groton, he called his New York cousin Pauline Robinson a "rayon de soleil" in a storm and sent her violets and two coveted stamps by special delivery. Although in the course of time he began to notice other pretty girls who came to visit at the school, he never invited anyone but Pauline and his sister Louise to a festivity there.

In letters home, Harry shared astonishing detail. While "silking" his teeth he lost a gold filling "from the upper right hand side of my mouth . . . it is the 5th tooth back counting the right hand side front tooth." Clothes in general, underwear included, were a big topic in his letters and continued as such even throughout his college years. "About my close shall I send back my summer ones when the winter ones come. I wont have room for both. I wish you would tell me what to do." Harry had his mother on the go, and evidently she did not complain. "Please have [my white cravat] cleaned as soon as possible"; buy some "turned down collars of the kind I got at X Mass the size is $14\frac{1}{2}$ as you know the kind I want it would be better to get them now." He would like from home a "necktie that is not orange," his white trousers, another pair of slippers, his coat and "west kit" and his silver cuff buttons.

The most elaborate of Harry's Christmas lists dates from December of his second form year:

1. A cherry handled black silk umbrella
2. A tennis racquet & case
3. 2 Photograph frames
4. A perl stick pin
5. An English leather belt, not yellow, kind of brown & not as broad as my last one
6. In stead of a silver key chain I want a leather one to match my belt. They are the fashion.
7. A pocket chess board you can get them at Spauldings. The men are made of paper & it folds up like a book.
8. Gold links
9. Silver pencil I have told you what kind I want
10. A pocket book not to swell not to large small convenient to carry and so forth

"I will let you know if there is anything else," he then added, thoughtfully.

And after Christmas, indeed there was: two bantam hens—one black, one yellow—and a sack of wheat for them; sealing wax and cold cream; a particular issue of stamps. "Get them right away because the longer you wait, the harder it will be to find them. Remember I want the ones without the triangles in the corners." A strain of familial imperiousness can here be detected. A shorter list for Harry's fifteenth birthday included a "waterbury watch" and three gold stud buttons, and again the kindly afterthought, "I will write the rest some other time."

At seventeen, Harry seemed not much less acquisitive. He asked for nail scissors, a comb, and a clothes brush, all with silver tops, and a "silver case to carry your money in," along with a pocket "Kodak," with case and strap; waterproof cushions for his canoe, not "swell, just plain cushions"; and from his Aunt Anna, then abroad, "some fashionable English paper with my initials on it." The following year, he requested an "ever ready electric light."

Harry's most intense exchanges with his parents at this time occurred in the context of schoolwork. Although Groton students were told their overall academic average every month, grades for each subject were sent home. Harry du Pont was therefore in a fever of apprehension, "on pins & kneadles," seven times a year, as he awaited the usually abysmal news, for he showed no more academic prowess than he had as a little boy. He also seems to have been a model procrastinator. After one unusually poor showing, he wrote, "Have not gone up to the gardiners yet, but I expect to go today when I have written my seven letters. . . . I am beginning to feel like studying & I hope it will last."

Another time, "mental weakness" forced him to postpone finishing a paper. He had been studying "much harder" for exams and also playing golf "morning & afternoon for 2 days so it has cleared my mind tremendously." One wonders about the accuracy of his observation later that year: "If my average isent better it wont be through lack of studying." Harry was an optimist; he wrote about having "past" this or that exam. He flunked math and "lattin" but it will be "all right." He was not discouraged by a "C" in Greek. "I dont think I have done any worse than anyone else." Harry's chief motive for studying appeared to be the hope for a passing grade. Although on occasion he referred to novels he was reading—*Lorna Doone, Ben-Hur*—and called *Les Précieuses Ridicules* "so very interesting," he seemed to have had no lust for learning whatsoever. Still worse, there was minimal respite in sight, since vacations were devoted to tutoring. When not tutored at home, Harry went into steamy Wilmington every summer for this purpose, studied madly during most of one Christmas vacation, and at Groton often took private lessons as well.

The Groton ledgers record Harry's marks for all six years with dismal monotony. The French and Sacred Studies columns reveal an occasionally acceptable score, but those of other subjects, encased in horrid little boxes for all forty-eight months, are chilling.[7] Furthermore, as he grew older, his marks got worse. Mr. Peabody remarked of Harry as a fourth former that, "despite studying faithfully, it is very difficult for him to grasp a subject." The boy's English teacher the next year observed, "Harry simply cannot express himself, he does not know how to write English." About this comment my grandmother remarked to her husband, "I wish we had suggested to Mr. Nutter that it might be well to teach him."

Colonel du Pont took notice of Harry's poor grades in several early letters—*"Are you working hard . . . and are you doing your very best?* Tell me frankly & fully all about it." "Never forget that the du Ponts are not accus-

tomed to take back seats. That you have a family reputation to maintain."
It is surprising, however, that the Colonel was not more outspoken on the
subject. It may be that his letters have not survived, or that politics, with
his contested election to the Senate, preoccupied him, or that the topic was
altogether too dreary. Harry's mother also fell increasingly silent about it,
although on at least one occasion she spoke up: "The marks (4th form) came
yesterday. Mr. Peabody wrote 'very fair,' but I think some of them pretty
bad. You had 'D' for two things, but I will copy them all & send them." Her
husband finally blew the whistle after years of reading Harry's "knead,"
"kned," and "nead" for "close." Harry replied, "Dear Mama & Papa, Your
letter came last night. I don't think I *need* my winter *clothes* yet (please see
how correctly these words are spelt)."

Because of Harry's worsening grades, in the winter term of his fifth
form year Mr. Peabody threatened not to allow him to take the prerequi-
site examinations for Harvard unless he studied for them at home. This
threat, tantamount to suspension, created a crisis that sharpened the family's focus and perhaps brought about a surge of development for Harry.
The year, except for academics, had nonetheless begun well, despite
Harry's observation that his "genius does not lie in the football line." He
was elected to his first and only school office, that of Tennis Court Manager, of which he wrote with pathetic accuracy, "Of course it is hardly nothing at all . . . but still I felt gratified." Consequently, the possibility of having to leave Groton came as a severe shock and precipitated an unusually
revealing letter to his parents, one that, in fact, suggests the beginning of
what was to become a forceful and eloquent writing style. Having mentioned the options presented by Mr. Peabody, including that of repeating
the year, Harry continued

> If I should go down to the IV form, I would not go to college until I was 20, which
> would be very old, and anyhow the fourth formers are much younger than I am,
> which would not be good for me, and beside the few friends I have are in the V
> form, & I think most of the boys in our form like me more or less, which I know
> the IV formers do not, so that I really do not think that I could go down a form. I
> have not been very happy here as a whole, but nevertheless I like it, & the boys are
> nicer to me as they know me. But still I think I will have to leave at Easter, if I am
> going to college in '99. I know you will not like it, but if you knew what a great
> difference it made with whom you go to college I am sure you will finally consent
> to it. Doubtless Mr. Peabody will tell you that I would soon become acquainted

with the other boys, but I know very well that I could not. I know that I am stupid, but I think that if I had a tutor to myself I could pass my preliminaries. . . . I know that you will feal very badly about this but I have been trying very hard. I feal in fact that I am doing too much. Please do not think of letting me go down to the IV form, for I really could not do it, before you write to Mr. Peabody let me know. I do not think it would do any good for you to come up, for there is nothing to be done.

This situation, so distressing to Harry, created a rallying point for the whole family and produced offers of visits from his father and cousins. However, again thanks to Mr. Billings, the rector changed his mind, in spite of describing Harry to his mother as "behind & undeveloped in every way." Harry next wrote to his parents, "I cannot tell you how relieved I feal because I would have felt very badly if I had had to leave. . . . I hope you will forget the first letter as I wrote when I was kind of queer."

Abashed at having shared his distress with his parents, Harry also showed that he was beginning to gain a sense of self, including the ability to identify some strengths and weaknesses and to make practical choices. He was leery of turning eighteen and having to "feel so much more responsible. . . . I feel so old I do not know what to do." But he repeated his need for a private tutor. And in fact, in an unusual occurrence, the school arranged for such a person, who arrived at Groton in the spring term and remained with him throughout the summer at Winterthur. As Harry had requested, they worked in a special room in a farmhouse, "as I would like to have my books & everything fixed before I begin."

The intensive tutoring enabled him to pass the essential Harvard preliminary examinations. His mother praised him, and his father went further: "You are now rewarded for your conscientious labours last summer, and I want you to know how deeply gratified I was to note the energy and perseverance with which you worked and to feel that you had the true du Pont grit in your makings. Adieu, mon cher, cher enfant. Je te presse contre mon coeur et t'embrasse mille fois!"

But his final fall term was again studded with disasters—in Greek, English, "lattin," and "geometery." In this sixth form year, Harry ranked last in his class of sixteen three times, and second or third to last three times. The question again arose as to whether he should leave school, but the wise Mr. Billings continued to counsel that Harry stay. The tutor returned, and Harry again squeaked through.

But other aspects of his life improved for Harry in the sixth form; one of the masters told his mother that "the boys seemed so fond of him." The school play provided additional camaraderie, and Harry wrote home, "Acting is great fun. If I make the part [of a young girl] I have very touching love scenes." Although failing to get the part—he surmised it was because he was not "small & pretty"—he claimed satisfaction with the lesser role of a meddlesome housekeeper. The *Grotonian* reported that "with his shrugs, grimaces, and Scotch accent, he delighted the audience."[8] His mother described his performance as "capital" and wrote to her husband that she was "so glad for him to have done something before leaving school."

At the end of boarding school, then, Harry du Pont was an immature nineteen-year-old in a time of transition. He was making small gestures toward independence: he requested an allowance for his expenses, and he undertook to buy his own railroad tickets. Certain interests were beginning to occupy his attention during his Groton years, music among them. He wrote of Mr. Codman's "splendid baritone voice singing an aria from Faust" and of Mr. Gladwin's phonograph, which played the "ouverture to Tanhauser beautifully there is not a single note left out." As a sixth former he was "extremely interested" in his singing lessons. Harry's delight in the outdoors continued and broadened beyond his initial love of flowers. He wrote of a shining mass of trees in an ice storm; the moonlight during a "slay" ride; a spring day when "everything is leaved." Harry was enchanted with a new acquisition at home, a cabinet for his collection of birds' eggs.

In later life, Harry often spoke of the importance of color to him, and some of his school letters have a lyrical quality. "The country is beautiful now the trees are so lovely with their different shades of red and yellow"; "when the sun came out the trees & grass were like silver & the mountains were simply beautiful in the bleu sky." His observations included indoor settings: a "very pretty" curtain in the chancel; "the school saloon has been painted dark green . . . & looks very well"; the rector preached in the town hall before "a curtain with the most gaudy colors." People's appearances—especially in terms of color—were never lost on him: Mrs. Carey's hair "first was a light yellow, the second time auburn, no doubt this time it will be black." With his "eagle eye" he observed and often commented on women's clothes, not excluding those belonging to the women of his own family. Harry requested that on their next visit his mother please not "wear the old green dress which I think has had its day" and Louise leave behind the "bleu waist from Aunt Anna."

Insecurities continued to plague him, many typical of adolescence, such as nervousness about a party or clothes, including a fear of being "unable to manage my tails skillfully." Harry's courses and grades were all too realistic a source of worry, as were his plans for Harvard. The decision as to which living quarters to apply for and whether to choose a double or single room in turn depended on finding somebody to room with—"but . . . I cant find the somebody." In the end, Harry wound up with his second cousin Eugene E. du Pont, an arrangement made by the boys' fathers. Louise had recently become engaged, and Harry's agitation about writing to her fiancé points to an unusual lack of self-confidence. "I never had such a letter to write in my life & I hope I never shall. Is it all right to call him by his first name, it seems almost impossible that he is to be my relative." (Impossible it proved to be—Louise subsequently broke the engagement.) And two days later: "I hope he will like my letter. I am thankful it is the only one of the kind I will have to write in my life." This fuss would seem humorous had it not been so painful to him.

Harry's surviving communications from boarding school days can only suggest aspects of his personality. He doubtless kept his deepest hopes, fears, and fantasies to himself, or perhaps he shared them with his closest friend, Joe Oglesby. Joe went to a different school, Taft, and Harry spent time with him every summer. At Groton he did not forget the departed John Dix, whom he missed "dreadfully, as he always went out in the river with me." Only rarely did he actually describe other boys: one whose "terrible nightmare" kept them all awake, one who "had a fit in church & kicked viciously," and a newcomer to the fourth form who was "very homesick, & seems too old for his age. He is very small & dark and looks like a Jew, was Mr. Biddle a Jew?" Harry took particular notice of those with more difficulties than his own and wrote of a classmate whose mother had died. "It will be so sad for Hermann who looks rather badly. [He] stands it very pluckily."

Aside from Oglesby, Harry's closest relationships continued to be with his parents, especially his mother. He was of course interested in his father: "Does Pappa wear a nightshirt?" "Is Pappa elected to the Senate or not?" "Was Pappa in the artillery or cavalary, I always forget?" Harry requested a West Point catalogue on behalf of a schoolmate and professed interest in it himself, but this never seemed a serious matter. He was sorry that the Colonel was not coming to the school play but doubted that he would enjoy it. The more important bond was with his mother, and his letters and postcards were increasingly addressed only to her.

Harry advised his mother at length about golf clubs—the merits of a driver versus a brassie, for example. He was glad that her sprained ankle would not prevent her from visiting him, but then he apologized for his "very selfish view." Their exchange of birthday and Easter letters in the spring of 1899 suggests the closeness between mother and son (and her letter of May 25 perhaps points to an unwitting tendency to perpetuate his dependence on her).

April 18, 1899
Dear Mamma

Before I do anything else, I want to wish you a very very happy birthday. I have nothing as yet to send you except a great deal of love. . . . I had an awfully nice holiday. I really think I have the nicest home of anyone I know.

April 18
My dear Harry

I am so afraid you will not receive this for Easter, with my loving wishes & feelings—but you know they are nonetheless fervent for you dear boy, with every blessing that can be given.

May 25
My dear Harry

I want to send you dear boy my very best love and every good wish for your birthday and the coming year. It will mean a great period in your life for now you will really seem to be grown up. Now that you are leaving school and going to be a College *Man* & so much your own Master. You have always been so sweet & loving to me, and all I ask is that you may always be the same & never keep anything from me. Always feel that you can make me your confidant & come to me in every trouble as well as joy. I only wish I had you here to give some good hugs & kisses, provided of course you have not the mumps.

May 27
Dear Mamma

Thank you so much for the clothes brush, it is a beauty. I am much obliged for the dates and candy. Your telegram, your letter and Papa's all came this morn-

ing It almost made me think I was home I cant realize you are having strawber-
ries while we are freezing. I recieved a nice letter and a book, called When all the
Grasses are Green, by Dr. Weir Mitchell from Melle this morning. . . . Dear Mama
Thank you so much for the telegram letter present and good wishes all of which
gave me great pleasure
Your loving son
Harry
This letter seems very cold, but I cant express it as I want

Harry still had a lifetime of growing up ahead of him. Could his masters or even dear Mrs. Peabody, not to mention his parents, have imagined
that this inept youth, not "whole souled" about anything, would some day
have passions that would bring him distinction in not one but three different fields?

Could he himself have imagined it?

CHAPTER 7

Harvard

H AD today's formidable admissions requirements existed at
Harvard at the turn of the century, Henry F. du Pont would
certainly not have been accepted. During the presidency of
Charles W. Eliot (1861–1909) the survival of Harvard, owing
to its meager endowment, depended to a great extent on attracting young
men who could pay the tuition. Those who had attended a private boarding school were especially welcome, and in the late 1800s they constituted
about 80 percent of the undergraduate body.[1] This may help to explain why
the Reverend Endicott Peabody ultimately allowed Harry du Pont to apply
for Harvard and why, despite his appalling entrance scores (two C's, seven
D's), Harvard accepted him.

If the three hundred or so letters that Harry wrote home from Harvard, mostly to his mother, are to be believed, his academic life there was
almost as joyless as it had been at Groton. Although he expressed a rare op-
timism that history or geology would prove "interesting," and he described
Slavic 4 as "very entertaining so far," these rays of hope were fleeting.
Courses once begun turned into monsters that only a passing final grade
could vanquish.

The elective system of the time required no major field of study, so in
his three years at Harvard Harry undertook a variety of subjects, including English, French, German, European history, and history of art.[2] About
one course he wrote, "Philosophy is very hard to understand, I think," and
added that he was "more than glad" to get a C in chemistry. He seems never
to have been aware of the intellectual giants then on the Harvard faculty,

such as George Santayana and William James, nor was he apparently attuned to possibilities for fruitful exchanges with classmates. As suggested by earlier evidence (as well as letters written during history lectures), Harry's frequent reports of "studying like the mischief" are open to question, although his heavy course load probably kept him busy. Again, intense private tutoring was his salvation and helped to raise his final year's average to a C.

Harry participated very little in college life. His mother gently prodded him:

> You never mention Hermann. I would go to his room as much as possible. He is such a nice boy, & all these nice Philadelphia boys are his friends.
>   I suppose all the Groton boys will have an eating club together, don't they usually do that.

In the fall of Harry's sophomore year, Pauline gave him a further nudge: "Don't you think it would be a good idea for you to see as much of the boys as possible when you first go back and be friendly with them, for if you show a disposition in that way, it would make a good deal of difference. So don't shut yourself up and expect them to make all the advances." That this was well accepted is evident in Harry's reply. "Dear Mamma, Your letter has just come & I think your advice is very good. I have been as agreeable as possible to everyone." From then on he made a greater effort to be sociable: he gave several "successful" tea parties in his sitting room and wrote that he had "conversed affably" with a group of girls. For exercise, he walked a great deal, several times as far as Groton, thirty-four miles away. On occasion he played squash and took fencing lessons. In the spring of his sophomore year he was elected to Harvard's Institute of 1770 and to DKE, which automatically followed. His delight was touching. "Lots of fellows came in to congratulate me I was so excited that I did not sleep till 5. I have been congratulated by lots of nice fellows today & they all seem glad that I made it. I am awfully glad as it gives me something in common with a lot of other nice fellows. Then if I had not been taken on I would have been the only boy except [one] in our Groton form who did not make it."

Election to DKE, with a membership of seventy or eighty, was considered by many undergraduates a mere stepping-stone to one of the smaller and more prestigious clubs, such as Porcellian or A. D., the "apex of the social pyramid at Harvard."[3] That Harry was not invited to join such a club probably did not surprise him—the feelings of inadequacy expressed in the Groton letter were still with him. He wrote a matter-of-fact note about it to his mother, pride doubtless preventing him from admitting what must have been real disappointment.

Nonetheless, despite the "archetypal tragedy" for a boy of Harry's background not to be admitted to a club, his social life became increasingly active. Thanks to his mother's Boston friends and the proximity of the recently married Louise, as well as to his own good manners, good looks, and shy charm, Harry received many invitations.[4] He also began to show increasing interest in girls. He was chagrined that "as usual, my partner at the Saturday evening last night was unable to come" and that plans for two houseparties at Winterthur fell through. Always aware of aberrant peer behavior, he described a theater party for a Miss X who was "hopeless as usual. Her mother has suddenly decided to skip the dances & take her abroad for the winter. I am not surprised her courage failed her." Nevertheless, although he seems to have often resorted to such denunciations as a means of coping with his own social uneasiness, Harry was acquiring savoir faire, and his mother wrote her husband that he "would have been pleased to see how well he did as an usher at a Boston dance. He did not seem the least embarrassed & brought in all the boys & girls in a very graceful way. It is too funny & yet with boys he is so shy." Evening clothes and ceremony were more easily mastered than personal relationships.

In fact, Harry had begun to accept the demands of the social whirl, and (apparently with the same people every time) he went to private and subscription gatherings of various kinds in Boston and New York—sleighing, skating, and theater parties; tea, dinner, and supper dances. He described many of them as "very good fun," and he attended concerts, operas, and plays with boundless enthusiasm. "*Gotterdammerung* and *Carmen* were fine," *Figaro* "lovely," *Cyrano* "wonderful." Despite the poor acting in *Ben-Hur*, "the staging was wonderful and beautiful." In an unusual expression of feeling, he wrote his mother of a production of *Camille:* "I never expect to see anything as wonderful again as long as I live. Bernhart was simply marvelous. She really looks like a young girl, her clothes & jewels were stunning, and her French! But her acting is the best of all. Every look, every gesture was realistic. Half the audience was weeping I am not

Harry driving a carriage at Aunt Lina's house in about 1908.

surprised." He also observed that Mr. and Mrs. Tom Thumb were in the audience.

Although Harry was branching out in many ways, his prime interests continued to be off the beaten path and connected to those he developed at Winterthur. These included an awareness of interior color and design. At Groton, as mentioned, he had been unusually observant of decorative details, and on moving to his Cambridge lodgings at 13 Randolph Hall, with his mother's help he found furniture, rugs, and pictures to go with the green fleur-de-lys wallpaper. Caught up in helping Louise and Frank with their Boston apartment, he described in several letters the exact locations of a mirror and several watercolors and etchings that they had distributed among the parlor, library, spare room, and hall. "The outside curtains . . . make the [parlor] look much better. . . . The bookcase is nice but the afect is spoiled by having two shelves instead of one on either side as I suggested." Harry's interest in the 1902 remodeling of the Winterthur house was intense. He was wild to get home to study the plans, and his suggestions about the back staircase, squash court, and a connecting door for the pink and green rooms were adopted as first rate.

Harry had other matters on his mind as well, matters that also stemmed from his Winterthur childhood. He was devoted to his wire-

Harry with fox terrier puppies at Winterthur in about 1904.

haired fox terriers and wrote explicit instructions about them—including the care of their skin, their dewclaws, and their living conditions. He was vehement on the subject of the doghouse. "I do not think you understand that I am going to raise dogs, and puppies must have heat in the winter." He allowed himself rare expressions of irritation with his parents: "I really think you might have the heat put in. I shall not have a moment's rest ... my nerves are already on edge." Should a puppy die, he had arranged for an autopsy with his "kennel friend at Wellesley." Harry was an avid follower of dog shows but thought his animals not yet ready for such competition. He also found time for poultry shows and horse shows and wondered about the ducks and hens at home and about whether the colt had been broken. For a course in landscape design he wrote a thesis on Virieux, the Greenville home of his aunt and uncle, Victorine and Lentilhon Foster. And, as always, he thought about flowers. The Boston botanical gardens and flower show were superb, and the lilies-of-the-valley that his mother sent him were "as perfect as ever." In turn, the primrose that he had sent her was "Primula obconica" and should be planted at once. Harry and a girl cousin spent an October weekend in Marblehead "robbing all the gardens" after the summer residents had left, and "in consequence [Aunt Lina's house] is full of flowers. It is so nice to be able to pick flowers again."

Soon after his twenty-first birthday Harry went abroad for the first time, to join his parents, Louise, and Frank in France and Switzerland.[5] His departure was delayed by a hospitalization for the removal of a carbuncle on his neck. To me, the most striking feature of the experience, which Harry evidently handled well, was an elaborate house call, in which three doctors—"one of the best surgeons in Boston," the surgeon's assistant, and a general practitioner—converged in his Cambridge apartment. Such a meeting, arranged by his physician uncle, strains credulity a century later but seemed entirely normal to Harry. After all, did not doctors and even dentists repeatedly descend on Winterthur in person?

Along with Harry's general immaturity, the illness may have contributed to his lackluster behavior on the ship and his lassitude in London, where he began his trip, evidently for the purpose of having his father's tailor make him a coat. Few young men in these circumstances, convalescent or not, would be so lacking in curiosity and the spirit of adventure, and it is particularly hard so to imagine my father, for he would one day become a fiend for sightseeing. However, in June 1901 he wrote that he could not wait to catch up with his family, either in Aix-en-Provence or Geneva. "London is fascinating but I think it would be rather stupid to stay here long alone.... I'm afraid I shall not do much sightseeing as it is so hopeless to find your way." There is little information about this summer abroad, since the letter writers were for the most part traveling together. However, during a side trip Harry and his mother took to Zermatt, Pauline wrote her husband, "The scenery from Viège is superb as it follows the river all the way & it is a mountain torrent.... This hotel directly faces the Matterhorn. About 50 cows all with bells were coming down the mountain path single file. After dinner we heard all the bells tinkling down in the valley.... Harry is delighted & so pleased we came."

This trip gave Harry a developmental push, and in the fall term of his third year at Harvard, he had a kind of revelation: he embarked on the serious study of horticulture. He wrote his mother of his "sudden resolution . . . the outcome of my great desire to really know something about flowers & to give me some real interest this winter & next. College life is nice enough but I want something more than it can give me. In fact flowers etc. are the only real interests I have . . . My mind has been more or less dormant since my examinations." As a result, Harry enrolled in the Bussey Institution, a relatively new department at Harvard situated on four hundred acres southwest of Boston, which offered practical instruction in agriculture and horticulture. He had learned of Bussey from Marian Coffin, a young family friend and a landscape architect-to-be, whom he thought was "much to be admired." His letter continued, "I do not think I am impulsive I hope not at least. I merely think it is the smouldering of latent thought which has burst into flame."

At the Bussey, to which Harry commuted by train three times a week, instruction in Horticulture I and II emphasized both the scientific and the practical in such matters as soil preparation, planting procedures, cultivation of shrubs and trees, flower and kitchen gardens, and greenhouse maintenance. Laboratory sessions included work in the nearby Arnold Arboretum and in the field. After studying techniques of pruning, Harry wrote his mother, "We heard all about the treatment of grape vines & I thought of our poor straggling ones." Simultaneously with horticulture (which, despite voluminous note-taking, he barely squeaked through) he audited another Bussey course on hardy and ornamental plants, including wildflowers, ferns, and grasses. Harry's third course in this subject, offered by Harvard proper, included the study of fine gardens in England, France, and Renaissance Italy. For this he received his best mark, a triumphant B minus. At last he had found an academic field that called to him, but this hard-earned grade did not exactly foretell his triumphs to come.[6]

As the "revelation" letter suggests, Harry's level of development at this time did not permit him to take advantage of many college opportunities. Since he lacked intellectual curiosity and any dedication to books, academics certainly held no appeal for him, nor evidently did the interchange of ideas with either fellow undergraduates or faculty members. Although he met with Groton classmates in the newly opened and spacious Harvard Union, membership in DKE, which also offered lunch, seems to have been his chief extracurricular activity. It was not enormously rewarding—no bull sessions, no general carousing, no girlfriends. Despite his pleasure in the Groton play and in singing lessons, he did not try out for either the Harvard Glee Club or the Hasty Pudding, an organization that presented light-hearted musicals. Perhaps it was shyness or fear of rejection that held him back. Nor did Harry emulate his sister, mother, or maternal grandfather by participating in religious or charitable activities. However, he always went to church. "Sunday will be all taken up with church." Although at times he visited the Harvard chapel (compulsory attendance had been abolished), he more often sought various churches on his own. He said of the Church of the Advent, "too much bowing and scraping & chanting"; he found a Congregational church "awful." Football games probably represented his closest involvement with college life, and securing good seats was a major priority. Harvard's performance aroused real excitement in him, as had Groton's; when his team lost, he called it "perfectly disgusting."

To return again to the "revelation" letter, how can one interpret Harry's statement that "flowers, etc." were his only "real interests"? First, it can be said that this "real interest," which was to become an abiding one, could point to the crystallization of an important aspect of his sense of identity. It also suggests that this young man, showing no trace of self-consciousness at what might seem a highly constricted view of life, was entirely without guile. One wonders about the extent to which his sexual impulses were repressed and is tempted to read a good deal into the importantly added "etc." In the *Camille* letter Harry had given evidence of passion. His recognition of the need to get more out of life through the study of flowers seemed to open a peephole into another world, perhaps a world of aesthetics in which he could find a unique place but of which he was now only dimly aware.

Harry's years at Harvard in no way prepared him for the realities of life. Neither his studies nor his contact with other students seemed to influence his conservative outlook. Although his parents had repeatedly urged him toward academic success, the recurrent family sentiments that he must make something of himself, stirring as they often were, came across in writing as the blandest of abstractions. On Harry's sixteenth birthday his paternal grandmother had wished him happiness and expressed the hope that he would "grow in goodness and usefulness." The next year his father expressed similar thoughts, with the exhortation that he be a "good, useful, honorable man, appreciating the duty he owes to the community . . . and to his fellow men." On his twenty-first birthday Harry's mother hoped for nothing more than that he would always follow the example of his father and grandfather. "You must be worthy of the name you bear."

Harry's parents deeply loved him but did not seem ambitious for him in any practical or specific way. That his maintenance of their values and customs took precedence over new ideas and originality and that college failed to bring about a change of pace or direction in his thinking of course says something about Harry himself. How ashamed he was at having to escort three hatless girls a few blocks to the theater! "I thought I would die. Fortunately, I did not meet many people I knew."

Harry and his mother loved many of the same things. The sheer number of letters they exchanged, sometimes writing daily, points to the delight that characterized their devoted relationship. Before Easter of Harry's twenty-second year, in 1902, he wrote, "I went all the way down town to get you a fascinating fluffy little duck made of silk . . . but alas they had all been sold out. So I shall only send you my best love." Harry, who had once advised his mother about golf clubs, was now pleased to assume a more proprietary tone. "Did I not tell you there was money in chickens if you had the right kind?" or "Don't you want to consult me about some feature of the new addition?"

Harry du Pont at his graduation from Harvard in 1903.

Pauline du Pont fell ill that summer, while she was visiting the Crown-inshields in Marblehead. An attack of pain in July subsided only to return. She wrote home less often, but, given the frequency of illness in the family, neither the Colonel nor Harry was at first unduly alarmed. (During this time, they had been staying by turns at Winterthur to oversee the addition to the house.) However, the tone of Harry's letters became increasingly tender and anxious. "Don't get too tired"; "Do be careful & not too energetic"; "The beach is entirely too far for you to walk to." As the summer wore on, hopes rose and fell as telegrams brought good and then bad news. Silences became ominous. The Colonel, now in Marblehead, wrote Harry that an X-ray had revealed an enlarged liver. "Your mother suffered a great deal today but is as brave as possible & wonderfully cheerful." Pauline was moved to Aunt Lina's house, where she died, presumably of cancer, on September 20.

Throughout his life, Harry's mother had been the person closest to his heart. As he grew older, his everyday reliance on her was perhaps not as pressing, but even at college he sought her opinion on such matters as how often to go to the opera and whether to wear yellow rather than low black shoes in the summer. His love for his mother and for Winterthur were intertwined. Of his last spring vacation with her, Harry wrote, with reverberations of Groton homesickness, "I had a lovely time when I was home & I am living in the memories of the past & the hopes of my next visit." His mother was at the core of his emotional life, and he felt that some of it died with her. His letters to her seemed to provide a validity or a completeness to his experience, and he himself later questioned whether he had ever come to terms with her death.

Harry du Pont lost his mother after having lived out only a quarter of his life. At twenty-two he was ill prepared to deal with any catastrophe, least of all this one. I am again awed to remember what he told me about his pain. Little information is available about the next few years other than that, granted a leave of absence from Harvard, he abandoned the idea of graduate study, stayed on at Randolph Hall, and traveled every weekend to Winterthur.[7] Fortunately, he had already completed his required courses, and he graduated as planned, in June 1903, with a bachelor of arts degree. He had life with his father ahead of him, but the light had gone out.

≈ᶘ · CHAPTER 8 · ᶗ≈

Finding Himself

POST–CIVIL WAR AMERICA was alive with anticipation and
change. The country's sense of a new nationalism as well as of
its role in world affairs was surging, as was the population, on the
move from farm to city and swelled by a vast and steady influx
of foreigners. An expanding economy and greater affluence had led to the
growth of the middle class and to new cultural patterns. Large-scale buildings sprang up—opera houses, museums, hospitals, hotels, and, in Chicago,
the first skyscraper. Most immediately affecting everyday life at the turn of
the century was the expansion of technology, which brought electricity, the
telephone, telegraph, typewriter, camera, and other marvels of invention
within the reach of many. The automobile and faster trains and steamships
revolutionized travel, and in 1903 the Wright brothers began the mastery
of the air.

In this era of change, Harry du Pont was born into a family entrenched
in the values of continuity and convention. The assassination of two pres-
idents rocked the country during his early lifetime, but it was his mother's
death in 1902 that brought personal devastation. This misfortune stripped
him of his major source of inspiration and support and catapulted him into
a less protected world, a world where he had little choice but to begin to define himself on his own terms, to take up the tasks of adolescence that
might otherwise have been indefinitely postponed. It was a long, slow journey, but it was also steady.

In that first winter, the Winterthur house was a lonely one, now bigger still, extended by the marble hall with its two-story staircase and the

high-beamed pseudo-Renaissance red living room. Father and son, the
wide black bands of mourning on their left sleeves, were together on
weekends at Winterthur, and adaptation to their new relationship must
have been difficult indeed. What did they talk about? When they were
alone at night, did they cry? It is painful to imagine the rhythms of their
life. Harry, on leave of absence from Harvard, continued to spend the
midweek in Cambridge; his friend and former schoolmate William Hadden asked if he were not "rather tired of your weekly trips of travelling
up & down." But in the depth of his grief, it is likely that the arrangement suited him well enough, especially since he knew that his mother
would have approved.

A year later Louise wrote to her brother, who had by then moved back
to Winterthur, "I am much excited about your new position, do you have a
salary? And why do you want it to be a secret?" Louise's questions presumably referred to Harry's new undertaking, that of managing his father's
house. The assignment had much to recommend it for someone in deep
mourning: by taking over his mother's household duties, Harry could further identify with her, acquire much needed structure in his life, and gain
as well the opportunity to lose himself in detail that, more often than not,
gave expression to his aesthetic needs.

The management of the Winterthur house included supervision of the
staff, and in these duties the dress code was no small matter. As he undertook to select uniforms for his father's male employees, in a correspondence
of at least 150 letters in nine years, Harry consulted Brooks Brothers, the
old New York store, on every point imaginable, from the butler's garb at
various times of day to the coachmen's costumes for the stable and beyond
(silk and rain top hats, matching lap robes, gloves of coon or pigskin). The
Colonel's election to the Senate in 1906 and his establishment of a second
household in Washington, along with his purchase of an automobile, enlarged my father's assignment. Brooks Brothers again to the rescue! Although Harry soon learned about chauffeurs' clothes—double-breasted
braided greatcoat with blazed velvet collar, overcoat of beaver or whip-
cord—he was uncertain about the footman on a motorcar—whether "leggings or plain black trousers, & how much shorter should [his] coat be than
for the chauffeur?" "With [dark blue livery] do you think I had better have
gilt or silver buttons?"

These letters highlight two basic characteristics of my father—practicality and impatience with carelessness. The clothes were made to order, and my father insisted that "plenty of extra material" be left in each suit so that it could be adjusted for the next wearer. As had been true the year before, "Joseph Benoit's coat & vest do not fit at all. It seems to me that you should have made a note & saved me further annoyance. He has a very long neck." "It seems to me that you have not made much of a success of our liveries this fall."

Harry was in charge of numerous other orders for Winterthur and for Washington (to be sent, respectively, to Colonel or to Senator Henry A. du Pont). These ranged from the mundane—prescriptions from a Philadelphia pharmacy, a clothes wringer, a knife-cleaning machine—to pink, white, and blue "chop frills," sherry and brandy glasses, and a dinner party record book in red morocco with a gilt stripe. Many items were made to order: "complete bedroom drinking water sets, including tray, of our regular cream & gold pattern"; a silver-plated centerpiece to match the existing silver platter; a Lowestoft pen holder with bronze mounting.

The young man was also in charge of special foods: sixty jars at a time of currant jelly, cases of Novida water, and, at Christmas, artichokes, terrapin, and Camembert cheese. One year he complained to the candy maker Henry Maillard that the caramels "lately have been quite tough" and the Christmas chocolates not the usual ones, "but there is no use wasting time over the matter now."

After Pauline's death Harry and his father tried to continue the tradition of a festive Christmas at Winterthur. The house was decorated with holly, long-needled pines, and other greens, which arrived every December from a company with the pleasing name of Caldwell the Woodsman, in Evergreen, Alabama. For a Christmas party in 1911 the Paris branch of Brentano's provided twenty-four place cards, twelve with Santa Claus holding little potted trees to the left of the card, and twelve to the right.

Out of college as during it, Harry's outward life was anything but noteworthy. One of his fox terriers won a prize in a dog show in Atlantic City, he bred his beagle bitch, sold some Muscovy ducks at $4.50 a pair, and bought white Holland turkey gobblers. He became vice-president of the Water Fowl Club of America and treasurer of Christ Church in nearby Montchanin, where he collected money for a horse for the minister and

fired the organist. He danced at at least one cotillion, attended a masked
ball, and joined the University Club in New York. At age twenty-five, when
he was hospitalized in New York for an unspecified illness, he spurned the
illicit offer of drugs from an orderly who was a "cocaine fiend."

We do not know whether Harry regretted giving up his plan for graduate study in agriculture and horticulture, but he by no means lost his
commitment to it. His mother had encouraged both children to be active
gardeners, and when they were little, she planted a bed of yellow daisies
for them, in anticipation of the wreaths they would make for their grandparents' golden wedding anniversary. Pauline and her children had always
grown vegetables and flowers below the house, and she and Harry had intended to expand the beds. Now on his own, Harry could feel close to his
mother as he redesigned her beloved rose garden and added flower-
bordered terraced lawns. This space, which included a fountain, wisteria-
covered arbors, and a small pool that gleamed with bubbles and waterlilies,

Harry's garden at Winterthur in about 1906. The rose garden,
not shown, is at left.

became one of my favorite childhood playgrounds. Harry was also rebuilding the greenhouses and experimenting with wildflowers and a narcissus grove where he planted fifty varieties of daffodils. The assistant gardener he hired in 1906 was kept busy. Harry continued his mother's practice of sending gifts of flowers to friends and acquaintances near and far. The feeling expressed in one letter of thanks, often to be repeated, "You are so like your mother, dear Harry," must have cheered him.

From 1906 until the start of World War I, father and son went abroad every summer but one. They spent time together in London, Paris, or at a particular inn in a village in the French countryside. (There they regularly rented the lower branches of cherry trees owned by a local farmer, to be sure of a supply of fresh fruit.) But they also went their separate ways. The Colonel would "take the waters" at Aix-en-Provence for his gout, and Harry in the first two years visited a different spa in Puy-de-Dome. He also traveled alone or with friends through England and Wales and to other destinations—among them Trouville, Geneva, Potsdam, the Italian lakes, Venice, and Dalmatia. When they were abroad, father and son made the Langham Hotel in Paris their headquarters. These European ventures were among their most congenial times together.

Harry had benefited from his first trip abroad, and subsequent experiences in Europe of course heightened his growing sense of identity. Travel seemed an entirely natural way of life for the Colonel and his son, who, like many fortunate Americans of the era, sought a change of scene, pace, and culture, and the opportunity to discover or to become reacquainted with European ties. In Harry's case, there was more, for his innumerable visits to gardens, houses, and museums were sharpening and enhancing his inherent gifts, and he remembered everything he saw. Each trip brought a deeper commitment to his already powerful interests in both horticulture and interior design.

During Harry's bachelor years, his tastes in the decorative arts were principally French, and when in France he was on the lookout for objects for Winterthur. In 1908 he sent a chair to Paris to be upholstered as a model for American workmen and ordered others to be made at the same workshop and covered in fabric that matched the dining room curtains at Winterthur. He was now twenty-eight years old, and his attention to detail was striking. "The design will be very much improved when picked out with a little green as you suggest, to fit in well with the tapestry border on the curtains." In his next two years in Paris he ordered 180 yards of toile damask, requesting also "samples of colored cretonnes in shades that were found in the Louis XIV period." Probably this fabric was to be used in a bedroom at Winterthur "which we are refurnishing in the period of Louis XIV. Our aim in our country house is to keep everything as simple as possible [but the present mantelpiece] is so entirely modern that it makes a false note with the old furniture in the room." In this letter Harry was seeking the opinion of a Boston architectural firm about an antique mantelpiece he had considered buying. In eleven communications, he provided blueprints of the room and posed questions about the suitability, size, fit, etc., of the mantel, inquiries that elicited elaborate replies. His terse last letter to the firm almost a year later surely belongs to a department of anticlimax. "I have decided not to carry out the plans we were working on." The reaction of the architects is not recorded.

On his trips abroad Harry stepped up his horticultural pursuits. The beginnings of real scholarship, fueled by his growing excitement in the field, are reflected in extensive notebooks dating from 1903. He began to order plants in numbers that increased exponentially: in 1907, from Somerset and Surrey and Kew in England came delphiniums, fifteen types of phlox, herbaceous peonies, and rock garden plants; and from at least twelve American nurseries and the Arnold Arboretum came azaleas, lilacs, tree peonies, lilies, and hydrangeas. In 1908 there were, among others, orders for one thousand Golden Spur daffodils and five hundred tulips of two varieties. Harry studied books, articles, and catalogues with discipline and intelligence. He congratulated a Boston company as the first in America to offer a large choice of tulips and crocuses: "I think the public should appreciate your enterprise." In 1909, the Colonel, now seventy-one years old and absorbed by his duties in the Senate, recognized his son's vision and judgment by giving him responsibility for the Winterthur grounds. Harry responded with a dramatic surge of activity. He began to plant his "wild" or naturalistic garden, then as today known as the "March bank," for which he ordered an astounding twenty-nine thousand bulbs: snowdrops, squills, windflowers, grape hyacinths, miniature iris, tulips, and daffodils. The next year he ordered thirty-nine thousand more bulbs.

In 1911 and at the height of his zeal, my father fell ill in Paris and was forced to postpone his return to America. As he wrote to Marian Coffin, "I shudder with horror to think that I may not be able to get back to do my wild planting, as no other mortal under the circumstances could carry out my ideas." This was serious; bulbs were arriving by the thousands, with no place to go. In the end, Harry had to depend on another mortal after all. He prevailed upon the good nature and intelligence of Anna, his youngest Robinson cousin, to whom he wrote these peerless instructions:

> All you need to do is to walk over the sloping bank looking for wooden labels corresponding to those on the list, and, in addition, September 1911 written on them. Should there be 4 or five labels with the same name, what you must do is give the package of those bulbs to Nicholas and say, "Here are the bulbs; they must be divided into two, three, or four lots," as the question may be, and then show him where the places are. I find it is not safe to give him one lot until the one previously given him is planted.
>
> After the bulbs are planted I wish you would leave my labels simply as they are, simply tying on another wooden label with "Anna" written on it. If, by some mistake, there should not be enough bulbs to fill the required spaces, simply omit planting one of them, but kindly note the fact on a little label. The bank, of course, in addition to the spaces already marked is full of labels of bulbs that are already planted there, and naturally these must not be disturbed.

Anna's sterling reply reached him some weeks later: "Dearest Harry—I write in triumph to tell you the bulbs are all planted. I have passed sleepless nights . . . & now the relief is intense. . . . However, I have decided one thing & that is flowers in their bulbous state are most confusing and that bank is a maze! My admiration for you who evolved it is unbounded."

Harry's enforced absence also worried him for other reasons. In a letter to John Chapple, now the foreman, he made known his horticultural ideas, as well as his wishes for chicken and duck houses, with hints of disagreements with his father. "I hope the Colonel is not too annoyed with the work I trust you did for me in the garden. . . . Please do not wait too long to have the sash put on the conservatory. . . . Sometimes [the Colonel] does not realize the length of time it takes to put it up, & I do not want to take any risk of having the plants frozen." These assertions demonstrate Harry's new sense of authority as he clearly began to think of himself as the person in charge of the gardens and not merely as his father's agent.

His travels during these years doubtless contributed to his growing self-confidence. Most important for his gardening expertise were the trips he took with his learned friend Marian Coffin and her mother. One highlight of their summer tour of 1909 was a meeting with Gertrude Jekyll, the grande dame of British horticulture, and a visit to her famous garden, Munstead Wood, in Surrey. For Harry to meet this sixty-six-year-old lady, whose books he already knew well, was thrilling indeed, for here at last was a person whose interest in color matched his own.

Harry's sense of color and its subtle uses in the garden are evident in many of his letters and garden notes. At Drayton Hall he admired Lady Sackville's "deep black red snapdragons [which gave] character to pink border." Early one April he described the woods with their tulip poplars as "distinctly green [against] the cream & pale pink tint of oaks, & the deep magenta Judas."

In 1912, Harry again attended the Royal Horticultural Exhibition in London, again traveled with the Coffins, and again visited Gertrude Jekyll. He also met for the first time William Robinson, the influential proponent of the wild garden, as well as Ellen Willmott, another horticulturist and author of great repute, and visited her matchless gardens both in Surrey and in Aix-en-Provence. He wrote to Marian Coffin, who had missed this last adventure, that, after an earlier rebuff by the butler, this time he "brazenly rang the front door bell, sent my card in, & to my great joy & delight, was led up and down the hills." He continued, "Planting quite charming, little side gardens everywhere.... The hills were a mass of colchicum.... After this legible & illuminating letter, I expect many nuggets from you in return."

Harry now had the bit in his teeth, and the huge quantities of flowers he ordered in the next two years—hundreds of different varieties from more than fifty nurseries at home and abroad—were balanced by his scholarly notes about gardens—those he had seen and those still in his imagination. He went to great lengths in pursuit of certain plants. Could a particular nursery track down a purple petunia "without a trace of pink or magenta . . . growing all over Berlin last summer"? Distressed when plants did not survive the journey home—a 1913 shipment from England arrived dead, "having been bandied about from steamer to steamer from 4 to 5 weeks"—he took to carrying certain specimens back with him in his stateroom. These included "12 clumps of Viola 'Maggie Mott' . . . packed in a box with a hinged lid."

In the summer of 1914, in the shadow of World War I, Harry and his father visited a pine forest on an estate in central England which inspired them to plan the Winterthur Pinetum as a joint project. The outbreak of actual fighting thwarted Harry's hope of taking home "in my trunk" many narcissus, 650 incomparabilis Firelight included. But before catching the last possible ship, he requested that Miss Willmott send by special messenger to the Stafford Hotel her "whole set of Autumn crocus . . . 3 additional dozen of Crocus caspius, a pink verbasum and 24 pink alstromeria."[1]

The bond between father and son was strengthened by the Colonel's developing friendship with Charles Sprague Sargent, the first director of the Arnold Arboretum, with whom Harry had already established a mutually beneficial working relationship. Sargent sent many newly discovered plants, unobtainable elsewhere, to Winterthur, partly for experimental purposes, and encouraged the establishment of a truly fine collection of conifers in the fledgling Pinetum, calling it a "patriotic work." The Colonel, who five years earlier had put Harry in charge of the grounds and rewarded his horticultural expertise with the gift of a new camera for color photography, in 1914 turned over to him a bigger assignment, the management of Winterthur Farms, thus acknowledging his son's administrative abilities and his grasp of farming.

As he assumed his new responsibilities, Harry age thirty-four, set out to improve both the quality and the size of the Winterthur herd of cattle.[2] With his father's blessing, he began an intensive search in New Jersey, upstate New York, and the Midwest for the best specimens of Holstein stock available.[3] At the same time he saw to the replacement and expansion of the farm buildings, equipping them with the most modern technical advances. Even at the age of twenty, in the midst of his dismal academic performance at Harvard, he had said in a letter to his parents on the subject of his terriers, "I assure you, I shall never be satisfied till I raise a champion." This aspiration to perfection in something that was important to him was a vital component of his makeup.

In the twelve years since his mother's death Harry had transformed himself from a lonely youth adrift to a determined young man accomplished in the fields of horticulture and farming. But his thoughts in these years were by no means limited to such interests. When the Senate was in session he was often with his father in Washington, and as time passed, he found that his friendship with an entrancing young woman was at last turning into a romance.

Ruth

RUTH WALES was born in Hyde Park, New York, in June 1889, the only child of Edward Howe Wales and Ruth Holmes Hawks Wales. Her father, a graduate of Columbia, was a stockbroker and an associate with his father in patent work. He retired at the age of thirty-nine, apparently rather impulsively, for he had not accumulated enough money to make such a decision practical. He joined the Naval Reserve during World War I, became an aide to Theodore Roosevelt, and achieved the rank of commodore. The Waleses' marriage was not a happy one, and, partly because of Edward's philandering ways, husband and wife often lived apart, Edward mainly in Washington. Money was a constant problem.

Ruth Wales grew up in Hyde Park with her mother, her mother's mother, and—sporadically—her father. Ruth's much-loved grandmother Hawks, called "Denver" because of a sojourn in Colorado, was to me a legendary character. How could it be, I wondered, that the oh-so-ancient person photographed in black headdress and veils and lacking only a witch's wand had at one time been a young divorcée and possibly the subject of a scandal? To complete this ménage, which included a parrot, there was also Miss Margaret Graham, a "trained nurse," as the title then had it, who looked after my mother and also helped with the housework. After my mother's marriage and the birth of her children, Graham joined our family as what might be called "head nurse." As it turned out, however, I was her charge. Whatever my mother's reasons for selecting her—and I must assume that they were charitable—this arthritic soul, hobbling on a stick and crying out in pain at night in the bedroom we sometimes shared, was a poor choice as companion for an active child. But in my mother's youth, Graham was doubtless hale and vigorous, as was Ruth's mother, my beloved grandmother Wales. Widowed soon after I was born, my grandmother became a semi-invalid and a recluse; during my childhood she spent much of her time in bed.

However one understands the Hyde Park chemistry, there is no question that it produced a star in the form of my mother. Her early years were quite a contrast to those of my father. Probably because of her less than ideal home life, when she was twelve years old Ruth was sent as a boarder to Miss Spence's School in New York, where she excelled in her studies and made lifelong friends. Photographs from the time, and her compositions and letters home, with beautiful penmanship and perfect spelling, show that her gifts of intellect, wit, and good looks began to flourish early. At fourteen, with uncharacteristic lack of modesty, she wrote home about her report card, the best in the school. "It is simply *corking*!! I know that you will be wild with joy when you see it!!" One of my mother's outstanding attributes was her sense of humor, and one of her essays, written when she was fifteen, announced the importance of "being able to laugh at the absurdity of some especially trying incident. . . . As for the few poor souls who are hopelessly without [a sense of humor]—let us pity them & keep away."

Throughout her life my grandmother and her daughter were hand in glove, and when they were apart they wrote to each other at least once a day. "I hang on the mail," my forty-year-old mother wrote to my grandmother from Florida; "Louise says I act as if I were engaged!!" Nicknames abounded: my grandmother was at various times "Puss," "Rabet," "Chafor," and "Dove," my grandfather "Weeps" or "Fathure Wales." Mysterious in-jokes often referred to mispronunciations that amused them, such as "ex-pecially" and "it-*salf*"; "write" and "good-bye" became "wroite" and "good boi." The coined "Wraugh!" was a favorite exclamation of distaste.

My mother's letters, several thousand of which survive, were unfailingly tender and solicitous about her mother's health and state of mind. On certain anniversaries, such as her father's birthday, she would sensitively convey an awareness of bittersweet feelings. And she was quick with compliments.

Ruth Wales, Harry's wife-to-be, at Hyde Park, New York.

Mrs. Cushman . . . remembered you as such a beauty in Providence & I said you still were . . . & more fascinating than ever.

Ed & Mame were saying how stunning you were . . . & then the former said, "She is not only beautiful to look at, but she is *good!*"

Ruth's father took her to London and Paris when she was in her early twenties. She described the trip in scholarly diaries and in letters home. Father and daughter were given a tour of the royal stables by Rosa Lewis, a mistress of Edward VII and soon-to-be owner of the fashionable Cavendish Hotel in London.[1] "They keep 150 horses . . . all stallions (oooh!) & are bred '*ex pecially*' for the King. . . . Mrs. Lewis is one of the most fascinating women I have ever met. She started in life as a cook for a rich man [who] left her an awful lot of money. . . . She has a marvellous business head & is now the finest cook in England. . . . She is very good-looking, you would take her anywhere for a swell. She is 45 years old." In the same letter, my mother commended the British concept of rank, which "certainly keeps people in their place [with] no overlapping of the classes." She seemed to be oblivious to the inconsistency between this view and her approval of Rosa Lewis's rise to fortune and fame. Years later, when her old friend Franklin Roosevelt became a national figure, her fury at his politics suggested that there had been little change from these early undemocratic leanings.

My mother took up the piano early in life. She put nursery rhymes to music as a child, began piano lessons at age thirteen, and grew up to have a brief career as an accomplished composer and pianist. When she lived in Washington, she was "writing . . . very hard," and she composed at least one "chorus for a ragtime." She entertained a Belgian guest at the British Embassy by playing "all the rag I knew." The year after her marriage she traveled every week to the Peabody Conservatory in Baltimore. "Musically gifted, industrious, and intelligent,"[2] she was accepted as a student of harmony by Gustave Strube, the founding conductor of the Baltimore Symphony. At first her enthusiasm was boundless: "Had a wonderful lesson. . . . I am to start Canon at once and fugue possibly in the spring. . . . I am thrilled."[3] However, three years into her marriage she wrote to her mother, "I am terribly busy & the thought of my music weighs on me as I cannot give it the proper attention." Two years after that, increasingly burdened with the responsibility of running a big house, the demanding presence of her eighty-three-year-old father-in-law, and the birth of a second daughter, Ruth abandoned her studies. She adored Harry du Pont and wanted to save her best efforts for him. But she did not give up music entirely, and among my happiest family memories are hours with Mother at the piano, playing from sheet music or by ear, belting out old or new, happy or sad songs in music hall fashion, while my father listened contentedly and my sister and I and our friends—and later our children—sang with her.

Before she became engaged to my father, my mother, always popular and with many beaux, had led a very active social life. She took part in amateur theater productions and generally kicked up her heels in Southampton, Bar Harbor, Watch Hill, Providence, and New York. Nevertheless, during this time her moods were in a good deal of flux. She had undergone periods of despondency; a diary entry reads, "Most terrible day all alone . . . never have been more depressed." Her letters were by turns disconsolate—

> I cannot bear to think of going to another dance & it always depresses me to see how happy my engaged friends are

starry-eyed—

> The imagination cannot picture the wonderful dance. . . . I have never in my palmiest days had such a grand time

and amused—

> You bet I am glad not to be going to a dance every night. Bowie told me if he were 10 years younger he would pop the question to me. Thank the Lord for those 10 years.

Perhaps as early as 1908, the Waleses rented a house in Washington so that Ruth's father could be treated for glaucoma by the famous ophthalmologist William Holland Wilmer. Certainly another drawing card was the presence there of the Elihu Roots. Senator Root, who represented New York from 1909 to 1915 and had been secretary of state under Theodore Roosevelt,[4] was married to Clara Wales Root, my grandfather's sister. Clara and Edward were the children of Salem Howe Wales, for many years managing editor of *Scientific American* and one of the founders of the Metropolitan Museum of Art.

As my mother told it, in the early days Harry was unpopular with her Washington friends; the son of a less than beloved senator and not gifted with social chitchat, he was both a misfit and a figure of fun. Being seated next to him at dinner was cause for dismay. But such was the fate of Ruth Wales. As respectively the niece and the son of senators and often the youngest guests at big dinner parties, where protocol reigned, they were both very much "below the salt" and almost invariably seated together. At one point, Ruth wrote to her mother in Hyde Park, "Du Pont called me up about 6 times. I did not go to the 'phone, finally I went & he said he was sorry, he did not intend any rudeness. I told him to let the matter drop, he sounded quite cut up."

The nature of this "matter" is unknown, but as she came to know Harry better, my mother's feelings underwent a radical change: she fell desperately in love with him. An extraordinary series of more than eighty letters that Mother wrote to him before their marriage tracks the course of a most unusual four-year relationship. Although my father's reciprocating letters have not survived, my mother's amply reflect his state of mind as well as her own during this time.

Beginning in 1912, Ruth went to seven Winterthur houseparties, and she also saw Harry in New York, Philadelphia, and Hyde Park, as well as in Washington. That March, on a cruise through the recently completed Panama Canal with a woman friend, Harry, another young man, and a chaperone,[5] Ruth wrote home: "No one could be nicer or more dependable than Henry du Pont. He is a winner 'for fair.' . . . I do not think any trip could have been more fun." As early as 1913, Louise heard that Harry and Ruth were "almost engaged," and the rumors persisted. A propos of them, in February 1915, Mother wrote to him, "Do let us go on as before & be natural, I don't care where or how often I am seen with you, if you don't. I am tremendously fond of you & love to be with you as you must know, & our friendship is a wonderful thing to me, & I can't bear to have it in any way affected by untruths." In March, she called the rumors "terribly funny & I just hope everyone talks until they are exhausted." Asking Harry for a photograph of his portrait, she teased him with the threat of displaying it in the parlor "to give the gossips a treat."

Ruth, to her credit, kept her deep love entirely to herself—but she bought some dresses to aid in the process of "catching" him, and a spring hat, of which she hoped he would approve. Her reply in late March to a letter from Harry marks the beginning of a new phase in the relationship:

Now I want to talk to you about your letter, which I think is one of the very nicest things that has ever happened to me. This is the very first time that you have ever told me anything in regard to yourself or your feelings, that I have not had to drag out of you with wild horses. I know just how you felt when you wrote. It isn't a very pleasant way to feel. It may be difficult for you to do but I want you to try to realize that there are very few experiences through which I have not passed in the last ten years. . . . I don't think I have much to learn in regard to the . . . unrequited part of it. I know every bit about feeling old & lonely & unhappy & discouraged. . . . You have every bit [of sympathy and understanding] that I have to give. I know just how hard it is trying to be a good sport & a good loser, & to do the right thing for right's sake. Virtue has never seemed to me to be tremendously its own reward. Wrong is pretty attractive most of the time I think. However I am going on & do the very best I can, as I know you are doing. . . .

As for your asking me about my affairs, it is so kind & sweet of you, & I appreciate your interest very deeply. It was all wrong of me to have bothered you except that I have been doing it all during my acquaintance with you . . . Perhaps some day I may with your permission take advantage of your kindness to ask you some advice.

During the summer, Ruth continued to respond to Harry's sense of inadequacy, which perhaps he had not revealed to anyone since Groton School days. It now had more to do with adult misgivings, especially about marriage. He dwelt on the realities of his life—filial obligation, absorbing interests, professed selfishness—wondering how he could honestly ask anyone to marry him. Ruth's reply, signed "your true friend," was a masterwork of reassurance. She wrote that any young lady of his choice who "approximates to the majority of your standards . . . would undoubtedly be a wonderful person . . . [who] would give you everything you are most needing now, & . . . your life would become broader & complete. . . . I am sure it would be a joy for the right kind of person to consider your father in every way."

Carefully sticking to her role of affectionate but detached adviser, Ruth maintained that she herself never expected to marry. In one letter to her beloved, she even tried to promote a twenty-eight-year-old acquaintance, Laura Delano, as a prospective bride: "beautiful & . . . very high-bred, a girl of great refinement, intelligence, tact, sweetness, & has a fine sense of humor. . . . I think you would be an *ideal* couple."

Given that this recommendation sounds suspiciously like a self-description, could it have been Ruth's way of calling attention to her own at-

tributes? Or was it a reckless gesture of inordinate selflessness? It is difficult to understand the full complexity of my parents' relationship during
that crucial summer of 1915. Indirect, guarded, vulnerable, they circled
each other, raising and responding to hypothetical questions. Ruth offered
ostensibly objective advice as she attempted to steel herself against the pain
of unrequited love, and Harry tried to protect himself from the potential
danger of an intimate attachment, which carried with it the possibility of
Ruth's turning him down.

However, if self-confidence ever was needed, Ruth was the one to provide it:

> You [could not] help being "desirable" in every way. You tell me you are selfish &
> occasionally cross. I know you fairly well, & I confess that as I see them, those qual-
> ities do not appear in alarming proportions. Seriously, I don't think you ought to
> worry about not being able to offer anyone on this earth, enough. You are too sen-
> sitive & always underestimate yourself, for you really have great beauty of char-
> acter, and besides, you have charm, subtlety, sweetness, & a wonderful sense of hu-
> mor. . . . I hope if you can only find the lady, you will give her the opportunity of
> thinking it over; & if you do, it is my earnest wish that she will accept & will make
> you happy for the rest of your life. I can't tell you how much I hope everything
> will come right for you. . . . You have Youth, & all the world is before you, & I am
> sure Romance should not be far distant if you felt it possible to go a little of the
> way to meet it.

Well into the last phase of this curious courtship, Harry's uncertainties
about marriage continued, dismissed by Ruth as

> chimerical & far-fetched. . . . *Of course* I think your father should come before
> everything else & you ought to consider his pleasure always, but I feel sure that
> your happiness means more to him than anything & that he would never want
> you to give up anything vital on his account. . . . I have not the slightest belief in
> the unselfishness of children to the extent of their giving up their own lives. . . .
>
> You are far too conscientious & you try so hard to do what you feel to be right
> that you become confused as to your objective. . . .
>
> I *do* think you are doing too much, and I hope you may be able to readjust
> things before long so that you will have time to live your own life to a greater ex-
> tent.

Less than a month before Harry's proposal of marriage on May 5, he
still called himself "impossible," and despite Ruth's by now numerous displays of affection—"Do let me hear from you soon"; "Do stop buying cows

The marble stair and hall, installed in 1902 by Henry Algernon du Pont.

& come back here soon"; "It changes the whole day whenever I hear from you"—he claimed to worry, astonishingly enough, that she was about to embark on an "uncongenial alliance." Ruth's equally ludicrous response to this fantasy was that, as she was "so happy at home," she could not "for one second consider marrying anyone."

All along, however, Ruth had been melting in the warmth of Harry's increasing expressions of devotion—invitations to parties and to the ballet, flowers galore. On one occasion he sent a "marvelous bunch of pink tulips. . . . The whole house was decorated, & then he came to see me this p.m. & was furious because he had ordered lilies instead. . . . So tonight what comes up but the most enormous lot of pink lilies you ever dreamt of." The gratitude and love expressed in my mother's letters during the first week of May, presumably in anticipation of Harry's proposal, are enlight-

Portrait of Henry F. du Pont in 1914, by the now married
Ellen Emmet Rand.

ening. Her first long letter to him after the engagement, bursting with joy
and love, tells of the hopes and fears so long unexpressed during her years
of uncertainty.

Hyde Park, Hudson River.
May 9*th*. [1916]

My dearest Harry ... Yesterday was the very happiest day of my life, you
looked so heavenly all in greens; I really think you are the most divine looking boy
I ever imagined, all your clothes are so perfect, & as for your hair, it is beautiful

beyond words. I do hope you will let me tell you . . . often in the next few months how deeply I love you, & how tremendously I admire you in every way, for all this intense feeling has been bottled up inside me for so long that if it does not have an outlet in expression now, I think I shall go insane. You cannot imagine what the past four years have been like, but as things have turned out, I rejoice in every moment of the suffering since it makes the realization wholly perfect. But this sudden change in our relationship has been a shock, coming as it did out of the resignation to absolute hopelessness on my part, & it will take me a good while to collect myself & settle down, so you will bear with me, won't you dear, & I shall try not to be too boring.

Mother's letters, always articulate and entertaining, now were ecstatic. Worthy of Elizabeth Barrett Browning, they dealt, of course, with wedding plans, but irrepressible love dominates them. "I miss you so terribly I am almost insane . . . every time I think of our evening in the moonlight my heart stops beating. I miss you beyond words. I do love you so." "I think of . . . your eyes, & voice & the adorable way you laugh, & I don't know how I can stand being away from you." "I do love you with every bit of me & you just remember that I am wholly yours forever." "My love for you has grown so immeasurably that it is just about all I consist of now." "I really can't wait to have you put your arms around me again—I'm sure this is terribly forward of me to say, but it is the truth."

Harry wrote often, too, but his passion may have been still more eloquently expressed in presents: flowers, a beautiful fitted travel case (which included a clinical thermometer!), golf clubs, and a superb diamond engagement ring.[6]

Harry's path to so happy a resolution had been more tortuous than Ruth's, owing not only to his obligation to his father, but also to his timeless devotion to the memory of his mother. Ruth, honored by his having revealed so important a part of himself to her, was helped to understand it by her unusual bond with her own mother. She wrote him that on the Easter Sunday just preceding their engagement, "I could think of nothing but how your mother was looking down from heaven & loving you." She was thrilled to be told "that you think your mother would have liked me. I . . . want to do always as she would approve . . . & I know her memory & influence will surround us always." Ruth was always sensitive to Harry's feelings for his mother—perhaps the most basic love that he would ever expe-

Ruth Wales du Pont, June 1916.

rience—but she reveled in the true love he felt for her and unendingly counted her blessings.

Ruth was apprehensive about her own mother's reaction to the engagement, and she and Harry broke the news in separate letters. Mrs. Wales had evidently chosen not to contemplate such a possibility, for the news came, as she wrote to Harry, "like a bolt from the blue.... I am so completely stunned.... You have always been such good friends I thought you always would be. It is useless for me to try to tell you what it will mean to give her up but there is no one I would rather trust her to than you. . . . But in the moment of writing I don't see *how* I can do it at all—for she is the only one I have." This letter, to which was added the plea "Please destroy this at once, Ruth's Mother," was followed soon after by a still more plaintive one.

> I've tried so hard all these years to keep the child from marrying for I think so many times it leads to nothing but misery & heartbreak, but I can't find any fault here, for out of all the world if I had to choose I'd trust her to *you* before anyone else, feeling sure that everything human power could do to keep & shield her you will do for her. It is quite a "large order" for you but my faith in you is absolute. . . . Her whole being is centred upon you & her respect & admiration are boundless. I beg you don't *ever* let her get away from it. I want her to love you better & respect you more each day you live. That is the only road to absolute trust & happiness. . . . Your ideals of life are the highest of that I'm convinced. Never let her see anything else. She is terribly proud. Guide her & keep her close to you always.
>
> To be happily married is the only thing worth while in this weary old world & life is short at best. I hope you will be spared to each other for many years & that life as you meet it each day will only bring you closer understanding.
>
> People can meet & endure anything with a pal beside them. It is the lonely road that kills. She is my one chicken I never thought I'd live long enough to be without her. I shall be very proud to have *you* for my only *son*.

These words from a "heart broken old party," never reconciled to her husband's behavior, were evidently taken in stride by the young couple. Harry's common sense, abundant when he was not overwhelmed by self-doubt, and Ruth's adoration of her husband-to-be overrode the feelings of guilt that Mrs. Wales evidently intended to arouse, but her genuine approval of Harry was also reassuring.

Expressions of delight poured on Harry and Ruth from all sides when their engagement was formally announced. Letters to Harry echoed the thoughts expressed by his old friend Oglesby: "For what you have done for your own family [i.e., father] no one has earned [happiness] more faithfully than you, & I hope it will come back 100 fold." Harry's devotion to the Colonel was repeatedly applauded. Louise wrote to Ruth's mother: "[Harry] in his entire life has never done anything to cause my father any worry or anxiety. He really is straight all the way through." Praise for Harry was matched by compliments for his bride-to-be, who was beautiful, "wonderfully attractive," and with brains to match. Her not impartial uncle Elihu Root, who had known Ruth from infancy, wrote the Colonel that she was "fine . . . in every sense, with intelligence, self-control and good temper and the courage to be truthful. I hear only the best things about your son . . . and I think both of them are very fortunate."

On June 24, 1916, having just turned thirty-six and twenty-seven years old, respectively, Harry and Ruth were married in the Episcopal church at Hyde Park. It was a nice touch that the Reverend Sherrard Billings, my father's supporter at Groton, participated in the service. Afterward, Mr. and Mrs. Wales, together for this occasion, held a supper reception under a tent on their lawn. A special car attached to a New York Central train transported friends from New York and back again. Newspaper accounts listed the members of the wedding party[7] and noted that the guests included Assistant Secretary of the Navy Franklin D. Roosevelt, who had brought with him on a torpedo boat from New York the two officiating clergymen and a number of other guests. In a custom unheard of today, some of the "more than 500 costly and beautiful" wedding presents were also listed: a diamond tiara from the bridegroom, pearl necklaces from the Colonel and the bride's father, a diamond and sapphire bracelet from Senator and Mrs. Elihu Root, a feathered fan from Mrs. Vincent Astor, and a diamond bowknotted pin, "with pear-shaped ornament," from Mr. and Mrs. Frederick W. Vanderbilt (Ruth's cousin Lulu).[8] Not listed was the watch that Ruth presented to Harry, which, as she wrote her mother, "knocked spots out of my bank account."

The marriage had an auspicious beginning indeed. Ruth was overwhelmingly happy, and Harry du Pont for the first time in the fourteen years since his mother's death was immersed in a loving relationship with a woman. As the perceptive Louise wrote Mrs. Wales:

> I promise you dear Mrs. Wales that I shall always feel toward [Ruth] & treat her just as if she were my own sister. It seems too wonderful that I am really to have one. . . .
>
> Harry has written me how lovely you & Mr. Wales had been to him. . . . He adored Mamma so that his loneliness had been pitiful & now that will be gone.

And Harry himself, soon after the wedding, reached heights of eloquence.

Henry F. and Ruth du Pont and her parents,
Ruth Hawks Wales and Edward H. Wales.

Dear Mrs. Wales,

The chocolates have just arrived and it is too dear of you to have thought of me at all in the midst of the packing of the presents and the general confusion and exhaustion following the wedding. From the very moment Ruth and I were engaged you took me into the family in such an affectionate way that it made my happiness absolutely complete and I can not tell you how greatly I appreciated the way you made me feel the wedding was mine as well as Ruth's. Your unfailing sweetness, tact & thoughtfulness combined with your tireless energy to do everything for both Ruth & me has reminded me so much of my mother & I only wish she could still have been here for Ruth's sake. I will try & do my best to fill her place & make everything as easy for Ruth as possible when she first goes to Winterthur and when you come there to stay with us.

I think the wedding was perfect from every point of view. I am proud to have been one of the participants in such an absolutely complete success.

Thanking you once again for the chocolates & everything else you have done for me too

With much love Affectionately yours,
Henry F. du Pont

Aside from the love he felt for Ruth, Harry du Pont knew a good thing when he saw it—the excellence represented by his bride. But the fourteen-year-old sorrow still reverberated. He only wished his mother "could still have been here." Ruth Wales was exceptionally well equipped to approach Harry's ideal of filling her place.

❧ · CHAPTER 10 · ❧

Early Married Life

I N 1916, events in America were overshadowed by the war in Europe
and by Americans' ambivalence about their country's increasing and
seemingly inexorable involvement in it. For many members of the
du Pont family, 1916 was also a year of momentous import on a personal level. A bitter court battle raged between the first cousins and former
partners Alfred I. and Pierre S. du Pont, and the Colonel was again deep in
politics, with Alfred as his adversary. On a happier note, Harry du Pont married Ruth Wales. On their wedding trip, Harry and Ruth received two letters from Louise Crowninshield highlighting some issues she anticipated
for the coming months. In July she wrote from Winterthur, "Everyone here
is thrilled at the thought of the moment when 'Mr. Harry brings home his
bride'"; in August she reported that Alfred, "the fiend" (Ruth's label) not
only was likely to win the lawsuit but also would probably succeed in block-
ing the Colonel's nomination for a third term in the Senate.

Louise's news, however, did not disrupt what seems to have been an
idyllic three-month honeymoon, the leisurely pace of which would be all
but impossible today. The tone was set the first night at the Yama Farms
Inn in upstate New York, at a pace somewhat *too* leisurely for my mother's
taste, for she told me that her new husband's initial action of arranging
flowers throughout the bridal suite had quite tried her patience. From then
on, however, her daily letters to her mother were lyrical, beginning with a
description of her husband's "nature ... so thoughtful every minute ...
sweeter than any woman ... & is as near perfection as any human could be."
From Lake George she wrote that he was "perfect," from Albany, "*perfect*,"

The Colonel's relationship with Alfred was a difficult one. As the older son of the next to last president of the company, and one of its largest stockholders at the turn of the century, Henry A. had a good deal of clout. In 1902, when the sale of the family company to an outside concern seemed inevitable, Henry A., to the astonishment of the other directors, offered his support of Alfred's unexpected offer to buy it, with the stipulation that his cousins Pierre and Coleman be included as partners. Alfred's biographer, Joseph F. Wall, conjectures that the Colonel's action stemmed from a "complex mixture of sentimental family pride and calculated business acumen."[2] The Colonel's success in persuading Alfred to this course ensured not only that Alfred's power would have limits but also that he himself and other family members would continue to benefit from the anticipated company profits, which turned out to be enormous.[3]

Several years after the formation of this triumvirate, Alfred's personal life became a maelstrom of controversy. His divorce in 1905 from his distant cousin Bessie and his marriage two years later to a second cousin, the unconventional (and herself divorced) Alicia Bradford, resulted in their social ostracism and was a factor in Alfred's ouster from the partnership in 1916. Alicia was the daughter of Judge Edward Green Bradford, a friend of the Colonel's, and the families were very close. The judge, considered by some to be a self-righteous martinet, was married to Eleuthera du Pont, the Colonel's first cousin. As a teenager, Louise Crowninshield had been Alicia's close friend and confidante, and in their youth the Bradford son and younger daughters, judging from their many letters, had been devoted to Harry.

Judge Bradford resented the fact that Alicia, his first child, possessed gifts of intellect and vitality superior to those of his son and was displeased by her wish to marry the ineffectual Amory Maddox. Not only did he forbid his wife and younger children to attend the wedding, but he went further: he fabricated a tale that the marriage was a mere cover for illicit love between Alicia and Alfred du Pont, who had given Maddox a job in the company. The judge's lie is hard to credit, but many members of the family were convinced by it and shunned the young couple. Consequently, when Maddox's infidelities caused the marriage to fail, and Alicia, perhaps on the rebound, eloped with her infatuated cousin Alfred, a major scandal resulted. Alfred's gift of Nemours to his new bride—the vast house with its

Henry F. and Ruth du Pont early in their marriage.

from Montreal, "more perfect than ever." And so it went. On a Canadian Pacific train they "twosed [*sic*] & spooned, did you evah." On a three-day camping trip in British Columbia, "H. [was] never selfish . . . ruffled or grouchy," in Tacoma "so sweet every minute, it is unbelievable," in Santa Barbara "heavenly . . . the very loveliest creature that ever lived." The hotel in Salt Lake City was worthy of comment, with "bedroom & private bath, immense parlor with grand piano, & a dining room. It is only $10 per day, which I do not think excessive."

The accounts of this interlude with glaciers, waterfalls, fancy hotels, beach cottages, and friends here and there are enlivened by mentions of

Harry's struggles with a pen, which "he holds . . . so tight I don't see why he doesn't dislocate his arm," as well as his shaving problems, compounded by the motion of the train, where he gets "all soaped up before we reach the station, then he works like a madman but leaves a small portion like a goatee." Fortunately, Harry's valet appeared from time to time with razor in hand or to help with the packing. At one hotel he produced a horseshoe of flowers marked "Welcome," which, lest his feelings be hurt, could not be left behind. Nevertheless, the honeymoon was evidently too much for the poor man, for in St. Paul, he gave notice.

Harry was able to pursue several of his special interests on the wedding trip. He gathered plants from a rock, sent seeds of pure yellow dogtooth violets to the head gardener at Winterthur, wrote to his mother-in-law about the "loveliest of wildflowers" near an ice cave, and was captivated by a house in Tacoma with splendid gardens, lawns, and trees hundreds of years old. In Portland, my mother wrote of the bridegroom on the golf course: "He has no other idea in his head & it does my heart good. He has kept a score card of every course we have visited, & he thinks of nothing else." This was of course hyperbole, for Winterthur Farms was also very much on the new husband's mind. The previous year he had been elected a life member of the Holstein-Friesian Association of America, and on the way home from the honeymoon he visited what were thought to be the finest herds between Omaha and Chicago, including the Schroeder Farms in Moorhead, Minnesota.[1] He was "keen to have his [own herd become] the best in the country" and to have Delaware "wake up & do better." Marriage had not affected his obsession with Winterthur.

While Harry and Ruth were on their honeymoon, the political scene in Delaware was heating up. The Colonel's second term in the Senate would soon expire and Alfred I. du Pont was leading an uprising in the Republican Party. Unlike my mysterious great-uncle William, Alfred du Pont existed for me in my childhood as a creature of wicked eccentricity. What sort of person would build an enormous house on four hundred acres, surround it with a nine-foot stone wall, and top the wall with thousands of pieces of broken glass? Only years later did I learn more about this creative, complicated, and often erratic cousin, who was despised by so many family members. Not the least of these was Henry Algernon du Pont, who, never slow to find a target for his vitriol, had in this case good reason to express it.

terrible wall—was one of several ill-considered acts that created further hostility. The couple nevertheless stayed together until Alicia's death in 1920.

These years were a time of turbulence for the Du Pont Company and for the du Ponts who were in charge of it. The company was found guilty of violating the Sherman Act; it underwent a reorganization, to Alfred's disadvantage; it profited from World War I and the munitions bonanza; it weathered a lawsuit against Pierre du Pont. In 1916, the "civil war" between Pierre and Alfred began in earnest. When Alfred was ousted from the company he sought success elsewhere and, encouraged by Alicia's interest in politics, cast his lot with an insurgent reform faction of the Republican Party. Here was a chance, he thought, not only to help Delaware but to get back at two of his hostile cousins, Henry A. and his sidekick, Coleman. In helping to form a third party, called the Progressive Republicans, Alfred not only aided the election to state offices of men of his choice but, still more important to him, ensured the defeat of the Colonel by the Democratic candidate for the Senate. Alfred's quasi-victory statement included the sentence, "The Senate is a place for serving the people in which the Colonel signally failed."[4] And it is true that the Colonel, a part of the regular Republican machine, had been ineffective in office. He had the poorest attendance record of any member of the Senate, and, since his interests centered primarily on military and naval affairs—war expenditures, battleships, lighthouses, the U.S. Military Academy—his loss of the election may indeed have benefited the state.

My mother as a new bride was not much concerned with Delaware politics, but she did want success for her father-in-law. She had found him "fine in every way," and on the wedding trip she described to her mother his "wonderful letter for a man of 76." (He was actually 78.) After his defeat, she remarked that it had been made more palatable by the fact that the winner was a Democrat rather than Alfred's Progressive Republican candidate. The Colonel "has taken it so wonderfully, I am keen about him." Keen she may then have been, but after his last day in the Senate in March 1917, she would be seeing more of him than she had bargained for.

My mother had assumed that the Colonel's decision to return to Washington every winter would "keep him occupied," but her letters suggest that it was she who was busy. The staffing of a big house was a formidable job, and it was made no easier by the Colonel's testiness. The butler "en-

tered the room without knocking [and] they had an awful fight"; "the second cook is leaving"; "the kitchenmaid seems nice but cannot speak a word
of English." At this period, when many "gentlewomen" would have
starved rather than learn to cook, domestic concerns loomed as gargantuan.
Furthermore, Mother's much less elaborate upbringing in Hyde Park
helped to increase her annoyance: "The whole house is run for the servants
& their comfort, & it beats the Dutch." But on another subject entirely, and
in vain, she shared her late mother-in-law's early sentiments and hopes that
the Colonel might find diversion in social engagements. These were not
forthcoming.

Harry and Ruth were much sought after, but the old Colonel was not
popular. The social isolation of a military hero and ex-senator — handsome
enough, affluent enough, and above all someone in the then indispensable
category of "extra man" — is puzzling. Since the Colonel did not cheat at
cards and was not subject to porphyria or fits, the dearth of invitations probably has to be explained by the fact that he seems to have been an epic bore.
His writings and my mother's comments over the years (I never heard my
father speak of him) suggest that his personality became more difficult as
he got older. His prickliness was apparent, and his snobbishness as well.
Never lacking for opinions, he had much to say about "vulgarians" and
"people of refinement" and such topics as the social inferiority of dentists.
Mother would mimic with a few harrumphs his standard question, "What
was her—or his—mother's maiden name?" He was proud of his Huguenot lineage and held in exalted esteem some cousins named Wood. My parents exchanged secret smiles at his mention of the "Woods of Woodstown,"
a title that was immortalized in our family collection of jokes about snob-
bery. The word "pear" invariably elicited from Henry A. the phrase, "Nec
pluribus imper." Another of his witticisms involved a wordplay on "horse
chestnut" versus "chestnut horse" and began, "If an eel pie is a fish pie, &
a fish pie is a jack pie, & a..." Well, enough of that.

Early in her marriage, my mother, very much in love, tried hard to get
along with her father-in-law. Before the wedding, she ended a letter of
thanks for the pearl necklace he had given her with: "I do hope that you
will not find it very trying to have me in the house at Winterthur and please
believe, dear Colonel du Pont, that I shall try always to do my best in every
respect." And she did try. She described the Colonel as "really very sweet,"
and "brave and uncomplaining" during an illness. She appreciated his

kindnesses toward her: books from his library, baskets of plums, persimmons on a bed of cotton, and a gift of $500 for Christmas. "Did you evah?" She and Harry invited him to go with them on a trip to Bar Harbor. But after eighteen months of marriage, her feelings were ambivalent. She wrote once to her mother, "I sure am fortunate in my in-laws," and another time wondered if she might not spend Christmas Day with her own family in Washington: "Little H. is willing, but perhaps it is selfish of me. It is so much more fun in our house than up here."

The Colonel and the young couple liked different kinds of people; Harry and Ruth gave parties at home only in the Colonel's absence or at a nearby hunt club, since many of their friends were non grata. (During his lifetime, no divorced person was ever allowed inside the house.) Ruth was drafted to help entertain the Colonel's Washington visitors for a week, and she wrote Harry, "I am so mad I could scratch & bite. Damn hounds." The couple were always delighted when the Colonel was away. "After dinner we came right upstairs & had a lovely evening together."

In the decade during which this trio managed to coexist at Winterthur, my grandfather wrote an impressive genealogical history of his family, as

Henry F. and Ruth du Pont and their daughters, Pauline Louise
and Ruth Ellen, February 1922.

well as his two Civil War books. The two Henrys worked together to expand their Pinetum, the small forest with examples of more than fifty species of evergreens, which continues to be one of Winterthur's glories. By 1918, my father's complex of farm buildings was completed for cows, calves, heifers, and two bulls, and barns for wintering young stock. There were also a test barn, a creamery equipped to make butter and to bottle certified milk, and an eight-ton ice plant.[5] Harry now began, through experiments in inbreeding, to achieve the purest possible strain of Holsteins; as one observer noted, "Holstein breeding is an art, and Mr. du Pont studied his herd like an artist."[6] Harry's scientific efforts were rewarded with even higher acclaim than his grandfather Foster had achieved. In fact, during fifty years

Ruth Wales du Pont, holding baby Pauline Louise, with Ruth's grandmother, "Denver" Holmes Hawks, and her mother, Ruth Hawks Wales.

of active competition, the Winterthur herd won a "bewildering number of honors" for form, breeding, and productivity.[7] However, early in the marriage, my mother—hardly an enthusiast in the field—was to write on various occasions to her mother: "The Percheron stallion dropped dead in the hayfield"; "the best bull has hurt his eye"; "half of the cows are not 'in calf.' Last year they aborted. Deliver me from *farming*."

In 1918, a daughter was born to Ruth and Harry and named Pauline Louise after Harry's mother and sister. (Had she been a boy, the name would have been "'Henry Antoine . . . A' for Uncle Lenty.") I was the second child, born four years later and referred to before my birth as "little Tommy Cat." My gender was perhaps an even greater disappointment to the Colonel than to my parents, for it soon became clear that there would be no more children. Ruth's mother told her daughter that the stress of a third accouchement would be intolerable for *her*. And even though my mother expressed her desire for a third child (to be named perhaps Harriet, if another girl), her feelings were complicated by her belief that children should not be brought into this "vale of tears"[8] at all, and I suspect that by her mid-thirties she was happy to call it a day. Harry would of course have greatly liked to have a son and heir—and he let me know it—but he evidently acquiesced to his wife's wishes, as he did so often.

Henry F. du Pont with prize bull, 1923.

Times of Crisis

S
EVERAL events that jolted my family even more personally
than those involving Alfred and Pierre took place during this
decade. Louise's husband, Frank Crowninshield, was an Anglo-
phobe whose ancestry no doubt bolstered his penchant for Ger-
many. He had joined the U.S. Army in Cuba during the Spanish-American
War, but in 1915, to the horror of fellow Bostonians and his family and in-
laws, he openly applauded the sinking of the *Lusitania*. In 1917, after his
rude refusal to contribute funds to American soldiers overseas, angry participants at a town meeting in Marblehead, Massachusetts, as reported in
the *Boston Herald,* "advocated that he be tarred and feathered." My mother
wrote, "Poor Louise is wretched. . . . [Frank] is now virtually an outcast . . .
& [Louise] says she feels like a hunted animal." Word spread to the New
York newspapers, Frank was expelled from his Boston clubs, and Louise
wondered if they would ever again be welcome at Winterthur. Col. du Pont,
a dedicated Francophile and never entirely devoted to his son-in-law, must
have been deeply affected by these events. To his credit, he made it clear
that as long as Louise stood by Frank, he and his family must also do so, and
reluctantly, in response to Louise's plea, he spent Thanksgiving with them
in Boston.

Another crisis, far from public but even more deeply painful to the
three Winterthur principals, came to a head in the spring of 1921, when
Harry and Ruth considered moving out. My mother's state of mind for several years had contributed to this tentative plan. In 1918 she was taking
"nerve medicine," and Harry implored his mother-in-law to leave her own

mother, Denver, to spend Christmas at Winterthur. "Ruth is so depressed at the thought that perhaps you won't come it distresses me to see her & to know the day will be absolutely ruined if you do not." Although the couple were "divinely happy" on their third wedding anniversary, the following year there were hints of a recurrence of my mother's melancholy moods. Her letters spoke of the "sorrow & sadness in the world"; she worried "so [much] that I fear I will get sick but I cannot seem to control it"; she supposed that her "very apprehensive feeling is all foolishness." She was unable to put into practice the concept of "mental reflexes," perhaps some form of thought control believed to circumvent emotional problems.

After they had spent two summers in a small rented house in Marblehead, in 1920 Southampton, Long Island, became my parents' permanent summer residence. As he was to do each summer for the rest of his life, Harry returned to Winterthur for a week or more, on this occasion to celebrate his father's birthday. Ruth's mother came to Southampton to keep her company. Ruth's dependence on her mother during this period was inordinate, and afterward she wrote, "I have never told you what a help & inspiration your last visit was to me. I know it is silly to feel so & probably my nerves are out of kilter."

That fall at Winterthur, two factors were clearly related to my mother's distress—the Colonel himself, and the fear that her mother would never again come to stay: "Now Puss if you do not wish to finish me entirely you will never say again, far less, *do* what you spoke of yesterday about never coming here again for the night. Don't consider yourself this time but think of me, I have enough to put up with without being denied the one little outside happiness I can avail myself of. . . . All this is *true* & such a prospect makes me feel so despondent that I cannot contemplate." Tensions in the household were increasing, and my mother's ability to cope with them was declining. Aside from the Colonel, there were often difficulties maintaining a large staff, and she worried unduly about the health of her daughters. A long visit from Margaret Fraser, a du Pont cousin whom everyone liked, was a stopgap comfort.

An incident that occurred in the spring of 1921 involved the Robinsons, Harry's mother's sister and her family. After Pauline's death in 1902, the Robinsons had continued their close relationship with the Colonel and Harry, visiting Winterthur as a family or individually several times a year.

Louise and Harry remained close to their first cousins throughout their lives. Anna Robinson had been deeply affected by her sister's death, and the suicide of Herman, her oldest child, was a dreadful blow from which she did not fully recover.

In late March 1921, my mother's fear that her mother would never again visit Winterthur was dispelled by the arrival of both of her parents when she and Harry returned from Florida. Mr. and Mrs. Wales were, in fact, witnesses to a scene in which my grandfather in no uncertain terms blew his stack. The Colonel's outburst was perhaps in some way related to the recent death of his sister-in-law Anna and seemed to involve the younger Anna and her husband, Arthur W. Butler.[1] A family crisis resulted, some of it captured in Ruth's letters to her mother:

March 30 ... Little H. & I had a most satisfactory talk & he has promised to make some other arrangement at once. Poor boy it makes him sad & it is not his fault. I am to go [on] as usual just for the present until we can formulate some other plan. . . .

H. begs that you will neither write the Col. nor say a word of your ideas or observations to anyone for his sake. He is ready & willing to do anything & therefore asks that you will show him equal consideration.

April 2 ... H. had a talk with the Col. last night & of course the latter is much opposed to our leaving him. Says it is extravagant & will make talk. He is very much hurt & pained. He said that he was angry at the Butlers—& not at me—which I supposed he would say. So things are at a deadlock. Suppose we shall thrash things out some more. . . . I don't want to have it come to a real break if I can help it as I do not want to estrange father & son, & also H. is due to inherit quite a bit yet which we could manage to use.

April 3rd ... H. is much upset as the Col. said if we left him he wd. marry at once. H. said he did not mind that so much but that in Del. a widow by law must inherit 1/3 of the estate. This with Louise's share removed wd. not be enough to run the Winterthur place, & H. says after all these years to have the eventual ownership— which it really amounts to—slip through his fingers, seems cruel, as Wint. is his house & it wd. break his heart to have to close it up. I agree with this. The Col. apologized to me last night in H's presence. Said his animosity had been felt towards the Butlers not me, & asked my forgiveness. He broke down & cried & I really believe he is much upset & not angry at me. Said he wd. rather die than hurt me in any way & kissed my hand & said it wd. kill him if I were angry at him. I said I was not, only hurt that he should have spoken so, & especially before you & Weeps. It seems to me that it would be very small & unworthy of me not to accept

Colonel Henry A. du Pont at Winterthur, in about 1920.

such a whole-hearted apology—which after all is the most he can do in that matter but I am none the less determined to withdraw from the scene of activities all I can. H. suggests that we compromise by my spending [less time at Winterthur]. I must, it seems to me, consider H. in the matter as well as myself, as if through my agency the Col. did remarry & H. cd. not live at Wint . . . I think subconsciously he wd. always blame me, & perhaps come to love me less, which I could not bear. Is this not logical?

These paragraphs touch on several issues: the Arthur Butlers, as the obscure, alleged cause of the Colonel's explosive scene; the scene as triggering my parents' threat to move out; my grandfather's reactions to this threat, with a counterthreat of marriage and my father's reactions to that; my mother's by now increased determination to loosen her ties to the Colonel.

This episode says a great deal about the three principal characters, all of whom were chastened by it. My grandfather's short fuse, autocratic tendencies, capacity for deep remorse, and genuine affection for his daughter-in-law are apparent, as are my mother's love of her husband, her fear of losing his love, her gesture of forgiveness, and her concern for her own and her husband's well-being. My father's conflicting feelings in this matter are the most complex, and it was his duty to provide the necessary diplomacy. With the risk of losing Winterthur, the core of his identity, he had to keep peace between the adversaries, the two people most intimately involved in his life. The Colonel comes across as rage-filled but somehow tragic and gallant, sad and appealing. Although he had been a widower for many years (legend had it that he maintained a mistress in a nearby house), surely a wife—any wife—would have been easy for him to find. His threat, therefore, was not an idle one, and he well knew that he touched on his son's key vulnerability. There is no doubt that the Butlers and my parents continued to be friends; perhaps the contretemps further deepened their intimacy, for Cousin Anna Butler ten months later became my godmother.

My parents before long reached a compromise whereby my mother would spend little time at Winterthur, and in the summer of 1921 they bought an apartment in New York at 280 Park Avenue. My mother's second pregnancy proceeded as uneventfully as her first, and I was born there the following January.

Reflecting on my mother's temperament, I have to conclude that, although she was in many ways delighted by her two daughters, their existence also increased her general apprehensiveness. Among other worries, here were two targets for deadly germs. Small events loomed large. A photographer's visit for a family picture caused her milk to "dry up," and I was abruptly weaned at the age of one month. What she later referred to as her "well-known nerve symptoms"—gastritis, insomnia, and tears—were exacerbated by the toll that life at Winterthur (even the anticipation of it) exacted from her. In November 1924 she heeded the advice of a family mentor, Dr. George A. Dixon, and despite fears that "everyone will know," entered Austen Riggs Foundation, a hospital in the Berkshire foothills of Stockbridge, Massachusetts, for a stay of three weeks. My father endorsed this choice over several other possibilities because of the high reputation of Dr. Austen Fox Riggs as well as the convenience of the location.

Although the foundation even then served a different patient population from the psychoanalytically oriented psychiatric hospital of today, it was still far more psychologically enlightened than other treatment centers that offered the "rest cures" so popular at the time. Dr. Riggs was not a psychiatrist, but his keen intelligence and empathy, along with a fine staff, helped many young adults to resolve problems in their lives. An extensive correspondence between my parents and letters from my mother to my grandmother during this interval shed further light on the strange triangle of Henry Algernon, Henry Francis, and Ruth Wales du Pont.

In spite of the fact that my mother had spent only three weeks at Winterthur in 1924 and had not kept house there for three years, even before the traumatic scene she had been so oppressed by its atmosphere that mere contemplation of it made her ill. This, of course, says something about her emotional makeup and vulnerability to stress. The behavior of the Colonel on that stormy occasion may have also heralded a deteriorating condition in his personality; it certainly intensified my mother's antagonism to him.

During her stay at Riggs, then in some ways comparable to a luxurious inn, my mother caught up on sleep, walked in the snowy woods, and gained relief through talks with Dr. Riggs. Although Dr. Riggs was the brother of Harry's best man and therefore "so to speak a social friend," his promise of discretion encouraged her to describe as she saw them the Colonel's "every weak point . . . vanity, sensuality, etc." She reported Dr. Riggs' observation that Winterthur was a "private sanitarium [and that] the children & I must leave there. [He] sketched out a campaign not to have a quick break but to work gradually towards never being there except for little visits. . . . To cover the old man with soft soap of regret, & he won't realize it as his mind continues to go."

My father's letters at this time (which suggest his own view of Riggs as a "rest cure") express complete support for his wife. "I love you more than tongue can tell & . . . you know that—all I want is your happiness I know that the more rest you get the happier you will be. . . . I knew it would do you a world of good if you could stick it out. . . . If Dr. Riggs thinks you should not come back that decides the whole question & we can arrange it perfectly after this Xmas we could stay longer in Florida & go to S[outhampton] June 1st & next fall to N.Y." Harry's only stated concern was that Ruth not gain too much weight! "Dont worry as it will be OK. All I want is a good healthy happy Mamma Mouse with whiskers but not too fat. I love you extreme."

My mother, my sister, and I did return to Winterthur for parts of the spring and fall of the last two years of my grandfather's life. Ruth's frame of mind, perhaps because of insights gained in Stockbridge, seemed improved, although letters to her mother still were peppered with anti-Colonel venom. There was a pleasant tea at Louise's, "But oh! The famille en masse! The Colonel [who had hung a second portrait of himself in the front hall] is preening himself & strutting around feeling so fine." Unsteady on his feet, he seemed about to have another fall, but "of course, he won't have the luck to break his neck." The Colonel's annoyance that his daughter, like everyone else, was observing the recently instituted Daylight Saving Time made Louise "pretty mad. . . . I guess she would be grateful not to see him." My mother's last existing reference to her father-in-law, two months before he died, noted that he had "bounced the nurse & now has [no one]."

Margaret Ann Murphy, a lass two years out of Ireland, was sent to Winterthur as a last-ditch replacement by a New York employment agency, to tend my grandfather. Thanks to her sweet personality, my dutiful morning visits to his bedroom, as he fed chipmunks on the windowsill and tried in vain to teach "Mazy" French, became less intimidating. Upon the Colonel's death, my mother made one of the great maternal decisions of her life: that

Mazy Murphy act as assistant to the ancient, arthritic Margaret Graham as my nurse. A few years later, Mazy became for me the best kind of mother substitute.

Had "Mr. Harry's bride" possessed a calmer temperament, she might have been more understanding or at least more tolerant of her father-in-law. But her hostilities, once aroused, were unyielding, and Dr. Riggs recognized the legitimacy of her instincts, her need for self-preservation, and the risk of her greater emotional distress should she be forced to remain for long in the Colonel's presence. Whether or not the Colonel was aware of the feelings of his daughter-in-law, in a letter to his sister he indicated his own unhappiness, referring to a "very lonely winter in Washington." He also wrote to a friend, "I shall be entirely alone this winter, as in fact I have been of late during the greater part of the time." Although the Colonel's personality was anathema to my mother, from a different perspective I can understand him as a strong, honorable, and scholarly man desperately attempting to deal with old age and solitude.

And what of my father during these trials? His marriage had brought him love and the capacity for closeness with an adoring wife whose laughter, vitality, and intellect had helped him rejoin the human race. Yet, born to a family in which filial loyalty was revered, he inevitably retained a strong attachment to his father and consequently tried to keep some kind of peace between the antagonists.

Aside from the dissension under his roof, Harry du Pont was in an upswing during the early 1920s: he had sired two children, he had put Winterthur Farms on the map, and he had watched his lovely woodlands flourish. But such developments, which were of course also gratifying to his father, could not heal the family rift that threatened to take from Harry a part of himself, the place closest to his heart. One would expect to see in him some signs of resentment, frustration, or at least fatigue as he carried out the stressful role of peacekeeper, but Harry's equanimity—hospitalized wife and intractable parent notwithstanding—seemed unshaken. With a high sense of leadership and a talent for compromise, he steered a course that, although not ideal, averted a tragic outcome.

My father's basic character—"level headed," as Ruth once described him—stood him in good stead, but I believe that he owed his ability to transcend anxiety and distress just as much to the events of a single week in Oc-

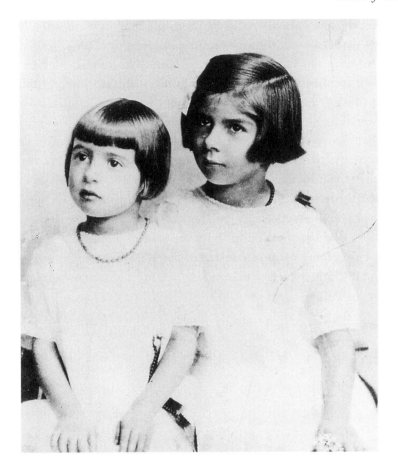

Ruth Ellen and Pauline Louise du Pont, in about 1927.

tober 1923. Even then he recognized it as one that would change the direction of his life. In this week he visited two houses, and what he saw electrified him.

On spectacular land in Shelburne, Vermont, high above Lake Champlain, Harry, as a guest of Dr. and Mrs. William Seward Webb, visited the eighteenth-century brick farmhouse of Watson and Electra Webb, their son and daughter-in-law. At the top of the main staircase to the second floor stood a pine dresser displaying a set of pink Staffordshire plates.[2] The novelty and beauty of pink china against the butternut color of the wood so charged my father that he was never to forget it. The jolt opened his senses to a second experience several days later, this time in Gloucester, Massachusetts, in the house of the architect-decorator Henry Davis Sleeper. Here the intriguing rooms and spaces incorporated to amazing effect early American architectural details of woodwork, furniture, and lighting, unlike anything he had ever seen or imagined. These revelations had almost the power of a conversion. Harry, now forty-three years old, was primed to catch the wave of a rising tide of interest in American decorative arts. Riding swiftly with it, he decided to build an American house of his own. The opening of the American wing of the Metropolitan Museum of Art in 1924 increased the momentum.

My father, whose creativity had flourished outdoors, now turned to this new passion, which carried him above the painful problems of his domestic life. The Colonel's death on the last day of 1926 removed the family conflict, and my father was free to immerse himself in his new calling.

CHAPTER 12

A Child's Perspective

HERE was a man, a country gentleman to be sure, who also delighted in city things: theater, opera, ballet, prizefights, museums, international horse shows, the Ice Capades. My father's ordered life seemed not unlike that of many other well-to-do American men of his time, with lunch and dinner parties, golf and bridge, and Republican politics. He was a dear man, taciturn, wryly humorous, modest, sometimes imperious; my mother wrote that he had "more charm to the square inch than any other human in the world." But when I think about those days, I realize that what I saw in him was a scrim, for behind his conventionality and generally mild manner was the passion that drove him. It was Winterthur.

We lived in four places every year, according to a clockwork schedule. New York was where my sister and I were in school. We spent our summers in Southampton, on the Atlantic shore of Long Island. For one or two winter months, our parents would escape to Florida's west coast, where my sister and I joined them over spring vacation. These moves were automatic, organized in exhaustive detail, and delightful. But the anchor, the basis of everything, was Winterthur—spring and fall weekends, Thanksgiving, Christmas, and New Year's Day, were filled with it.

Of the four places, Winterthur was my favorite, and unquestionably it was home to my father. Here he was born, here he grew up, and here he died. I am certain that he postponed dying until, close to unconscious with cancer, he was flown back from Florida in a cousin's plane. Settled on his and my mother's bed, thin and jaundiced in the extreme, when asked if he knew where he was, he was able to gasp "Winterthur." He died that night, a month before his eighty-ninth birthday.

His father, Col. Henry Algernon du Pont, had died at the same age at Winterthur. On the last day of 1926, two weeks before my fifth birthday, I declined the invitation to gaze on his eminent remains and continued feeding grapes to a Humpty-Dumpty doll behind the curtains in my bedroom. For me, other than no longer having to call on this austere, French-speaking presence every morning with a "Bon jour, Bon Papa," life went on much as before. But my grandfather's death brought great changes for my parents: relief for my mother, who had found ten years of close proximity to her father-in-law increasingly oppressive, and relief as well for my father, both for his wife's sake and for his own. Now the restraints were lifted from his ambitions to create a different house and to have a freer and better life.

The Winterthur landscape must have been very similar in my own and in my father's childhood, and we were both in its thrall. His feelings about the place, as his poignant boarding school letters indicate, were entwined with strong family feelings, and especially with his love for his mother. My own excitement was more directly connected to the land itself, and it recurred every weekend with my return to Winterthur from New York.

Driving from the railroad station we would soon reach real country on the other side of the Gatehouse—owl country, fox country—and would speed down the winding mile-long driveway through the enormous woods and up the hill to the house. My first bedroom looked two stories down on a meadow, Holstein cows, and the Clenny Run stream, whose banks in late spring were crowded with mint, buttercups, and forget-me-nots. Playing outdoors, at first no taller than the turkeys, and before treetops could offer their own hiding places, I was especially aware of the ground and how the trees joined it. The oaks had skirts, and the forked and bulging roots of beech trees, under low-spreading branches, became mossy rooms. In the fall, nuts were everywhere: beech, hickory, walnuts, acorns, and magical horse chestnuts, shiny rounds of mahogany in tight, thorny cases.

There was a good deal of magic at Winterthur, beginning with the excitement of exploring secret places—trees, ponds, hills, bushes near a brook. But some of the magic was man-made. A button was embedded in the trunk of a tulip tree near the house. In an earlier day, when my grandfather touched it, someone in the house would know that he and his horse

were on their way home. This bell seemed to belong to a fairy tale. So did
the Gatehouse, whose scrolled iron doors flew open at the toot of a car's
horn. In the years before I understood that there was a human element in
this process, I both marveled at it and took it for granted.

Magic surrounding my father was also demonstrated in New York on
a smaller scale. Because our lodgings, on the sixth floor of 280 Park Avenue,
were not enormous, although they consisted of three apartments put together, I saw my father here close up more than anywhere else. Unless they
were going to the movies or were about to depart on an ocean voyage or
were anticipating a hurricane, he and my mother always dressed for dinner. My father's valet, a gnome with a Swedish accent and parchment for

Ruth Ellen and Pauline Louise du Pont,
"no taller than turkeys."

The Gate House at Winterthur.

skin, was able to perform astounding tricks. From a flat black disc he could shake out a top hat, gleaming in telescopic height. And when Victor swept my father's long tails or evening coat, he could make the brush play a tune.

My father, tall and handsome, never appeared to be troubled by indecision. He walked briskly and flaunted a series of polished canes. He smoked gold-tipped cigarettes stamped with his initials, also in gold. He passed the plate in our church in Delaware—in retrospect an act far less dazzling than it seemed to a small child, for, with the exception of occasions like Christmas, there was at that time almost no congregation. On trips to Florida, my father seemed to dare the fates when he would alight from the train in Jacksonville for a foray into the station. My heart trembled lest he be left behind, unable to find the track to which our car had been rerouted. When I now read his troubled, timid letters from boarding school, it seems impossible that that boy became the authoritative man I knew in my childhood.

When I was six or seven years old, the much publicized illness of George V of England distressed me, and every morning my anxiety was acute lest I learn that the king had died in the night. My mother found this behavior odd indeed, and the school could not explain it. With the king's recovery, my worries were forgotten. It was not until many years later that I understood that my concern had in fact been for my father's possible death. Although young children often attribute majestic qualities to parents, in the case of Henry Francis du Pont such a comparison was not farfetched, for my father's way of life was indeed regal. Two of his dwellings, Winterthur even then and the house in Southampton, were the size of small palaces. My father's entourage—the butler, footmen in livery, the valet, a large staff for kitchen, house, and laundry, and uniformed chauffeurs who drove black Cadillacs—could also be seen as royal in scope.

One tends not to think of modern monarchs as driving their own cars, taking care of their clothes, or polishing the silver, but that my father did not do such things was attributable only in part to disinclination and the presence of his staff. The truth is that, owing to a remarkable lack of manual dexterity, there were many things that he either did very badly or could not do at all. He had great trouble, for example, tying his shoes. His handwriting was a calamity, a fact that he himself often lamented in letters from Groton. (His grandmother and aunt, writing to his mother, once or twice referred to an improvement in Harry's penmanship, but this change was short-lived.) Harry mentioned in several letters home his uncertainties about shaving, asking his father to buy for him "a razor & the thing you put the soap on with I am not joking so please have them ready for me. . . . P.S. Please do not mention the razor to everyone." Six weeks later, soon before his sixteenth birthday, he wrote, "I shaved this morning without cutting myself, very skill full for the first time." This triumph was not often repeated: until the invention of electric razors, shaving was an art that my father failed to master.

Harry's future mother-in-law noticed his lengthy disappearances into the bathroom, from which he emerged with lacerated cheek and chin, and suggested that he patronize the Hyde Park barbershop. He did so gratefully. Throughout my father's life a valet proficient with razor was nearby; at home, a barber called every morning to shave him or trim his hair. In New York, at least, a special chair, with a sheet to protect the rug, was set up in my father's bedroom for this daily ritual. (It was one that I remember all too well, for to my misery the duties of this same expert included cropping my straight wisps as short as could be. I protested only in secret, twirling with long scarves about my head and dreaming of Rapunzel.)

Another skill my father failed to acquire was that of driving a car. In early days, Dana Taylor, once a young Winterthur farmer, was persuaded to give Harry a summer of driving lessons. Dana said, "He never could remember to shift gears. He had just too much on his mind." Perhaps unaware of Dana's efforts, or in any case undaunted, my mother a year after her marriage wrote to her mother that she had "started to teach little H to run the car & he enjoyed it"—although obviously not enough for this to become a habit. Only once, and perhaps it was in a dream, did I see him behind a wheel, lurching in terrifying curves down Boca Grande's then-empty main avenue.

My mother attributed her husband's ineptness to the fact that when he was in boarding school he had been made to shift from left-to right-hand-edness.[1] Only now do I begin to question this as legendary, for plausible as it sounds, it seems strange that no mention of such a fact appears in the myriad letters exchanged by family members during Harry's boyhood, or in school records. (Of course, it is possible that the practice of hand-changing was at the time so usual as to deserve no mention.) In any case, although it would be satisfying to resolve the question of handedness—perhaps as partial explanation for the man's inability to write without using his entire torso—in a life of singular accomplishment it does not now seem very important.

Along with manual incompetence, there were other activities that my father by inclination or otherwise did not do well. This fact presents itself as somewhat mysterious—for example, in the matter of singing, dancing, and swimming. In many early letters Harry professed that he enjoyed singing, and his voice was praised. But I never knew him to produce a note of song, even in church, or to attempt a dance step (although he attended many a dance), or actually to swim. At every opportunity he went into the water, either in the ocean or in a pool, but only to keep pleasantly afloat. Had he chosen to forget all those singing and dancing and swimming lessons?

Before ending this roster of my father's areas of nontalent, I should mention his blind spot about spelling. Anyone who ever received a letter that he had written—without the help of a secretary—would know that spelling was for him a hopeless cause. His lack of a sense of phonetics, odd in one with a musical ear, led him to sign off in an early letter to my sister with the word "Dady." My mother, highly articulate and a stickler for pronunciation and word usage in general, found this lapse entirely delightful, and "Dady" became one of her many terms of endearment for him. His few but consistent errors of grammar also unfailingly amused her, and she would tease him a bit by repeating after him his often-used phrase, "Why did you do that for?" My own early brush with my father's inability to spell occurred when, unable to find the word "business" in the dictionary (it is not where it should be), I consulted my Pappa, the only person at home at that moment. He had no idea.

Until I was ten or eleven years old, I had met few other fathers; in fact, other than my parents' employees, doctors, and the dentist, I had encountered very few men. My day school, Miss Chapin's School (now called Chapin), was composed entirely of female faculty and students, and heaven forfend that a man or boy should ever sully Miss Robinson's dancing classes at the Plaza Hotel. Consequently, I was acquainted with the other half of the human world mainly through books or hearsay. The sister of a friend was named Marne, after the World War I battle in which her father had fought, and I asked Mother why my own father had not gone to war. "Well, your father would have caught cold right away," was her reply, an explanation I accepted with cheerful matter-of-factness. In actuality, Harry was over age—but it was also clear that he was not cut out for the military.

Although I was aware that my father was not a paternal prototype, I loved him, regretted the fact that I did not see more of him, and at least once experienced dismay that he did not fit a pattern I could recognize. On a bleak day in the schoolyard, with gym teachers displaying a lively dearth of imagination, we children—third-graders, I think—were lined up and one by one as we stepped to a certain spot were invited to tell the teacher "what your father does." At the dreaded moment, unable to come up with the longed for "lawyer" or "doctor," I burst into tears and stammered that I didn't know. At tea that afternoon, in the safety of our New York sitting room, with a fire in the grate and the silver kettle whistling over its flame, I told my mother of this mortification. "Why," said she, "you should have said, 'He's an agriculturist!'"

What my father did was in fact not at all apparent. I was well acquainted, of course, with the farm—the long barn full of Holstein cows, the two bulls, nose-ringed and immense, snorting in their special house, and the calves, some still wet from birth, in yet another building. I would spend hours fascinated by these creatures and watching the pigs thunder through deep mud to fight for the corncobs we threw them. But it was my nurse rather than my father who accompanied me on these outings, and the "agriculturist" did not in the least resemble any of the farmers in overalls.

I knew, of course, that my father was somehow involved with houses, two of which I saw in the making. When I was four, we left the wood-shingled house in Southampton that we had rented for several summers, and, while awaiting completion of Chestertown House, a massive H-shaped structure of whitewashed brick on dunes overlooking the Atlantic Ocean, we lived in its matching eight-bedroom garage, which had already been finished. It was in Southampton that I first became aware of antiques, whose existence soon seemed another commonplace of life.

My father had at this time begun to collect the interiors of old buildings, several from Chestertown, on the eastern shore of Maryland, which provided the Southampton house with much of its woodwork as well as its name. Despite the house's daunting size, its beach location was a delight, as were many of its rooms, especially the pink-paneled nursery and the bedrooms, in pale blues and greens, which looked south to the ocean. However, the canopied beds with their skirts and quilted bedspreads were never to be sat on, nor was the antique cradle to be played with. The living room, which encompassed a grand piano and much-used bridge and backgammon tables, contained among other precious objects two rare and beautiful glass bottles with bubble-like stoppers. These survivors of another era, then as earlier filled with distilled water, had once served to reflect the flames of candles set behind them. When a careless guest broke one of these irreplaceable wonders my father was of course dismayed, but he was also po-

The calf barns and bull barn at Winterthur, 1918.

lite in accepting the man's apology. However, to this day the apocryphal story is told that Harry du Pont, having reassured the culprit that it didn't matter, fainted dead away.

The anecdote, cited as an example of the triumph of human feelings over the manners of a "perfect gentleman," might amuse me if the subject were not my father. In protection of him, I find it demeaning that he could be imagined as having so drastic a reaction to the loss of a mere object, however valuable. Was this not the man reported to have said that were there to be a conflagration at Winterthur, the trees should be saved first; unlike houses, trees cannot be rebuilt. But in the back of my mind is also the awareness that Harry du Pont did indeed cherish this bottle, and that further-

Chestertown House, Southampton, Long Island, built in 1926.

more he was prone to faintness at times, such as at a simple drawing of blood. (He learned to lie down before submitting to such a procedure.)

In the early years of Chestertown House, my father drew up elaborate plans for its conversion after his death to a museum of early Americana, but he came to realize that the house at Winterthur would better lend itself to this end. Increasingly knowledgeable about period furniture, he had become a serious student of American decorative arts. Antiques dealers appeared in abundance. In some instances rather effete or colorless men, they were anathema to my mother, partly because she viewed them, with some justification, as symbols of extravagance, but more I believe because they were competitors for her husband's time. Along with these men was a woman who spent many months hunched on the floor with a tiny paintbrush, numbering in red every single antique object or piece of furniture in the entire house. We were all vastly amused on one occasion when my father noticed that a small Chinese export dish had disappeared from a particular table; he somehow espied it in the handbag of a lady who had been brought to lunch. Her confusion was extreme when a small red number was found painted on the pilfered object.

From 1928 to 1931, while the second major addition to the Winterthur house was more than doubling it in size and reaching out over the meadow, my parents, my sister, our nurse, and I lived in the small farmhouse at the foot of the hill near Clenny Run that had once been home to the Bidermanns.[2] This house was cozy, with chintz, firelight, and tiny bedrooms with slanted ceilings, but, best of all, my parents were more often in evidence. I had misgivings about our future home, too vast in size for comprehension. The maze of roughly plastered corridors and wet cement through which my father often led us was not encouraging. Scaffolding, sandpaper, and the

The 1931 addition to Winterthur.

din of jackhammers were everywhere, and even now when in the vicinity of new construction I am taken back to the sounds and smells of the unfolding museum-to-be.

In 1931, when we finally returned to the remodeled house, my apprehension was allayed. It did indeed seem marvelous. After the badminton court, the bowling alley, and the ping-pong room, perhaps most thrilling to me was the new kitchen wing, which rose nine stories to catch up with the hill. It had its own elevator, red rubbery floors, and, instead of a deep freeze, an entire room behind a glass door in which one could become chilled on even the hottest of days.

Moving into this colossal edifice was an occasion not only of excitement, joy, and confusion but of solemnity. Although at this age I seldom dined with my parents, I did so in what may have been our first official evening in our new home, in the yellow paneled dining room that spanned the entire house. An unfamiliar minister joined us to say grace and to offer a prayer of dedication and blessing for the house. I sometimes would think of this ceremony of awe and reverence before falling asleep, when the lights of cars driving up the hill to the new front door floated through the shutters of my new bedroom and sailed in a pattern across the ceiling.

Just before my fourteenth birthday I was taken out of my first year at boarding school to sail on a Cunard Line cruise ship from New York to San Francisco, by way of Brazil, South Africa, India, and the Orient. I hated the idea of leaving school and friends, but I was soon won over. When the excitement of travel merges with the fast surge of development, the adventure can be an extraordinary one. In this case the additional factor of establishing another home on an ocean liner provided a unique opportunity.

In the rebuilt Winterthur, my sister's bedroom and mine were separated by a bathroom and a small inner hall. Still farther away were our parents' respective quarters, which occupied almost opposite ends of the house. My father, up at sunrise, would leave his sleeping wife and walk down the long hall to his own rooms—bedroom, bathroom, dressing room, and study—where, with hot water and lemon juice, he would start on the business of his day. In this setting, communications often took place via the in-house telephone system.

On shipboard, on the other hand, our cabins—two for our parents, two for their daughters—were a mere ship's width apart, and to have my hal-

Henry F. du Pont, Ruth Ellen (age fourteen), Ruth Wales du Pont,
and Pauline Louise (age eighteen) in Pebble Beach, California,
in May 1936, at the end of their round-the-world cruise.

lowed and entertaining parents as captives for an extended period was in
itself a miracle. During these five months, when at sea we had lunch and
dinner at a table for four on deck or in the ship's dining room. Together on
land as well, we shared unrivaled sights and adventures, sometimes by unusual means of transport: in Rio de Janeiro a cable car to the top of Sugar-
loaf Mountain, and funiculars both there and in Penang; rickshaws in
Madagascar; elephants in India and Ceylon; sedan chairs in Hong Kong and
Shanghai; and a primitive overnight riverboat in Canton. As a rule, however, we journeyed more conventionally by train (sometimes in our own
private car, as to New Delhi or Hua Hin, a town near Angkor Wat) or by au-

The Montmorenci stair being installed at Winterthur in 1936.

tomobile, my father in front with the driver, amused and feigning mild annoyance at his wife and daughters singing rounds in the back seat, but taking in everything. In Bangkok, to our astonishment, he leapt from the car,
having spotted in a crowded bazaar a pink and green Staffordshire tureen
that matched a set already at Winterthur.

It was a glorious time, and when we came home in late May 1936, another miracle awaited us. The marble stairs and hall so prized by my grandfather (into which the original front door had opened) had been replaced
by an early-nineteenth-century spiral staircase of breathtaking beauty,
which rose two floors in lightness and grace to the level of our family bed-

The Montmorenci stair as completed.

rooms. This installation, planned by my father in secret, stood up well as a minor wonder of the world even when compared to the glories we had experienced. Henry Francis du Pont perhaps for a moment believed his life's work to be complete. But now, in his mid-fifties, he was still filled with an energy of which even he may have been unaware at the time and which led him to create the Winterthur that we know today.

· CHAPTER 13 ·

Louise

HARRY DU PONT had luck with the important women in his life, not least his remarkable sister. Mature for her age, and always sympathetic, Louise had stood up for her younger brother since childhood, comforting his tearful sensitivity, defending him against criticism, playing games with him, sharing her friends. During his boarding school misery, her letters were as loving as those of their parents: "I want to write to you just to let you know we think of you all the time." "It must be so awful to be sick without Mamma being there." In 1895 their letters crossed on the subject of their father's bid for the Senate. Harry wrote: "I do not know if Papa is elected or not. . . . It seems so queer to see his name in [all the newspapers]." Louise was more outspoken: "Won't it be awful if Papa is made senator;[1] I should hate to go to Washington. . . . There are the most awful pictures of Papa in all the papers." Characteristically, her letters were frank and colorful:

> Goodbye darling. This is an awfully stupid letter but I have a grouch. Ever yours, Louise.
>
> We have the most awful old cook you ever saw. She is about 7 feet tall & proportionately fat, & never talks but screams. . . Pauline & I were horribly afraid of her. She has a mania for kissing people.

Louise, like many girls of the time, had no formal schooling but had been taught at home by governesses. Nevertheless, she seems to me to have been better educated than many Ph.D. candidates. In the tradition of her mother and her Foster grandfather, she was devoted to the church and to working with children. Before her marriage at age twenty-three she faith-

144

Louise du Pont Crowninshield in about 1894.

fully taught Sunday School, and she had organized a group called Willing Helpers, young girls who visited babies in a day-care nursery and made clothes for them.

A thoroughly natural spirit, Louise had an irresistibly irreverent side. In Washington on one of her fortnightly visits to her father, on returning to his house one night after a late dance she and Harry got stuck in an elevator. With rescue slow in coming, they decided to sit down, but before doing so, to the more conventional Harry's discomfiture, Louise took off her new ballgown to keep it from harm. And it was she who introduced us to the delights of skinnydipping during picnic lunches on deserted Florida islands. At her instigation, women and men would separate for their respective swims—after which it was my challenge, as the youngest, to do battle with her corset. Although because of a glandular condition she had become very stout, Louise possessed such warmth and forthrightness that after a few minutes in her company, one never again thought of her size.

Walter Muir Whitehill, director of the Boston Athenaeum, observed that my aunt's refreshing personality combined qualities not always found together: simplicity, generosity, modesty, high intelligence, perceptiveness, good taste, and administrative ability. In a short biography, Whitehill wrote, "Had she been a man, she might well have run the du Pont works with conspicuous success. As it was, she had a telling hand in an immense number of organizations devoted to the support of the arts, historic museums, houses and sites, and horticulture. Her energy was boundless."[2]

My aunt throughout her life did indeed make her mark in creative and useful ways. From Massachusetts to Florida, she served on numerous cultural boards and on others with primarily humanitarian emphasis. Of the latter, she made a point of acquainting herself not only with the administration of each institution but with the residents themselves. She bought and transformed two islands near the Marblehead mainland, one as a summer camp for deprived Boston children, the other as an endowed bird sanctuary. The "fairy godmother" of Boca Grande, she established a clinic with qualified doctors to run it and built a community house for both cultural events and parties. A Crowninshield niece, Toddy Hammond, said of her, "If anyone on the island needed anything—money, moral support, had a health problem, whatever—they always came to Aunt Louise. She was motivated to do all kinds of things for all kinds of people . . . all over this country."[3]

When Louise married Frank Crowninshield, my father, then at Harvard, was delighted to participate in the furnishing of their Boston apartment. She is said to have discovered American antiques at about this time and, in fact, to have introduced them to her brother. Perhaps it was she who spurred him to buy his first antique objects, a pair of Delft cows, now in the Winterthur Museum, for his Cambridge lodgings. Some two decades later Louise and Harry were both seriously smitten with antiquing, and my aunt became almost as voracious a collector of Americana as her brother. During the Truman administration, at the First Lady's request, Louise Crowninshield joined a committee for the refurnishing of the White House—as her brother did fifteen years later under Mrs. Kennedy. Early in his work on this assignment, Harry du Pont noticed a pair of late-eighteenth-century card tables from Salem, Massachusetts, at one end of the Green Room, the only authentic pieces of furniture in the room. He was startled by the label attached to the underside of one of the tables: "Gift of Mrs. Francis B. Crowninshield."

In 1923, the Colonel bought for his daughter Eleutherean Mills, the former home of his parents, which had unexpectedly come on the market. Having spent so much time there as a child, Louise was overjoyed. She resolved to restore the house (in the interim it had been taken over by the company after an explosion) and to furnish it with authentic American objects. (I well remember the pewter plates at lunch, and the odds against getting food to one's mouth with a two-tined fork.) It was later that year that Louise introduced her brother to Henry Sleeper's American house in Gloucester.

Like her brother, Louise was deeply interested in land, architecture, and artifacts, "the old, the beautiful, the historic,"[4] and was a charter member of the National Trust for Historic Preservation. As a trustee she helped to extend the influence of the organization throughout the country, and turned her energies to the restoration of old houses. Louise also left a permanent legacy to the town of Salem, Massachusetts. In the Peabody Museum there she arranged for the installation of a replica of the cabin of an 1816 schooner that had been owned by George Crowninshield, her husband's ancestor. The ship's namesake, *Cleopatra's Barge II*, was my Uncle Frank's great joy for thirteen summers. The galleries established in his memory display furniture that had belonged to the original Crowninshield skipper, as well as period portraits, silver and glass, and my aunt's fine collection of Chinese export porcelain with a ship design. Louise created in a seafaring setting a counterpart to her brother's land-based accomplishments.

Visits to Marblehead were the high point of my summers, for the Crowninshield brand of hospitality was more relaxed than that of Southampton or Winterthur. My aunt loved fresh air, and the windows and doors at Seaside Farm were always open. The house, surrounded by beech trees and pines, was delightfully situated above the water on high rocks, the

Eutherean Mills. Courtesy Hagley Museum and Library,
Wilmington, Del.

setting for many picnics and clambakes. Inside, the rooms were filled with the antiques and flowers familiar to me, but they always seemed brighter and more cheerful than those at home. Of course the size of the house helped, for although it was big, its scale was a more human one, and the young and pretty staff in flowered uniforms (of whom my uncle definitely approved) added to its charm.

Seaside Farm, like the Crowninshield houses in Delaware and Florida, brimmed with life. There were houseguests, often Robinson cousins, who stayed for weeks at a time, always ready to play cards or Chinese checkers,

Louise du Pont Crowninshield at the wheel, with her husband, Frank, on the roof.

and there were also (and very much a part of the household) dogs and birds. Canaries and parakeets abounded, and a parrot attached to a stand would repeatedly shriek "Keno," my uncle's nickname. Four dogs were the norm, at first hunting dogs for Uncle Frank, joined later by a schnauzer and a poodle, and later still replaced by a gaggle of Pekingese in varying states of decorum. My parents disliked visiting Marblehead, principally, I think, because of the dogs. Mother believed that they gave her hay fever, and my father was happy to back this up, but I suspect that the wagging, barking, and general dogginess intruded too much on the orderliness that was increasingly essential for them as they grew older. It is hard for me to imagine how my father, barely able to conceal his dislike of dogs in my day, had been so committed to the care and breeding of his fox terriers and beagles when he was growing up.

Louise and Harry also had gone separate ways when it came to children. My aunt, sadly without children of her own, lavished presents and parties on nieces, nephews, and the young in general, enjoyed their company, and did not appear alarmed by their potential to destroy. Harry, on the other hand, tended to believe that children, if not quite limbs of Satan, surely represented some forces of evil. He looked forward to the visits of his first grandchild in her infancy, but he anticipated the future uneasily as he thought of her sprung from her crib and rushing freely about. My father's deep distrust of the younger generation was underlined for me after his death when an Oriental rug originally at Winterthur made its way from his Florida house to our Connecticut living room. I thought it lovely, but clearly it must have been an inferior specimen, for on the back, stitched into one corner, was a printed cloth that said: "Albany Room. When Miss R. E. [Ruth Ellen] is in residence"—an eerie message from the grave. I wondered if objects of value were always spirited from my bedroom before I came home to spread the seeds of ruin.

Although my father and aunt had decidedly different personalities, and her serious interests were more wide-ranging than his, they had much in common besides the preservation and restoration of old things. Both were dedicated members of the Garden Club of America and other horticultural institutions. A passion for flowers was as much a part of my aunt's makeup as of my father's, an attribute they shared with many forebears and most directly with their mother. All three would travel great distances for flower shows, would visit gardens whenever they could, and always cared deeply about their own gardens. Their houses were filled with flowers: forsythia and quince and crabapple forced in the winter, azaleas in tubs, bouquets or masses of blooms on the dining room table and almost every other surface. Another bond was their love of drama at Christmas. At Winterthur, "Mr. Harry's party" on Christmas afternoon was legendary. In Boca Grande, my aunt would give a similar kind of party in the Community House, with trunkfuls of presents brought from the north. Shopping sprees were instinctive in the family, and the effort invested in these occasions echoed my grandmother's early generosity and spirit of fun.

As a young girl, Louise had met Bertha King (later, Bertha Benkard) in New York, and she was to become an extraordinary friend to both Louise and Harry; if rivalry existed between brother and sister, it took the form of vying for Bertha Benkard's responsive presence. She shared their keen interest in the decorative arts and in historic preservation; her aesthetic judgment, taste, and perhaps even energy equaled theirs. Her "expert advice & absolutely faultless taste & eye" not only were indispensable to the evolution of Winterthur but also played an important role in my aunt's activities.[5] The restoration of Eleutherean Mills and my father's building of Chestertown House were almost concurrent, and the transformation of Winterthur was soon to follow. These were exciting times, and the several projects that captured the attention of all three created a kind of cross-fertilization. In 1934, Bertha, Louise, and Harry established as a memorial to Bertha's husband, Harry Horton Benkard, an early-nineteenth-century room in the Museum of the City of New York. After Bertha's own death ten years later, brother and sister led a drive to contribute to that museum and to the Metropolitan Museum of Art one room apiece from Bertha's Long Island house, complete with paneling and furnishings, so that "her great knowledge & matchless taste will live for the benefit of all."[6]

Several years later my aunt wrote to her brother,

> I went to see Bertha's room yesterday and I think it is vastly improved and very lovely. I really had a feeling as if she were there. I must have stood in that little doorway a half hour. I also looked around the other rooms of the American Wing. After Winterthur they looked flat, stale and ill done; your arrangements are simply in a different class.
> I never had a chance to tell you how very, very admiring I am of everything

you have done, and am so proud that I am a relation of yours, and even more so,— your sister.

The affectionate bond between sister and brother endured throughout their lives. Harry loved, appreciated, and admired the girl who had cheered on "Dearest Kid" with her appealing letters; the young woman who had all too well understood the depth of her brother's anguish at the loss of their mother, who had helped him as companion to their widowed father, who had applauded his marriage to Ruth Wales, and who had shared his collector's zeal. We were touched by her toast on the occasion of my parents' fortieth wedding anniversary, which ended: "Harry and Ruth made of their life together a fabric woven of creative ability, hard work, public service, kindness to others, and lots of fun; and have kept unscathed through the years the thrill and glamor of their wedding day."

My father acknowledged his gratitude and love in 1968, when in memory of his sister he named the Winterthur library and research facility, the last project of his life, the Louise du Pont Crowninshield Research Building.

৯ · CHAPTER 14 · ৯

Parties and Food

HIS LETTERS from Groton show that Harry's interest in food began early. He complained about a surfeit of apples there, "apple this & apple that every day," but praised the oysters served on the school's birthday and a rich, delicious "black cake full of almonds" consumed on an outing with a friend. When he was older and on a trip, my father sometimes took along food from home: watercress sandwiches and cold chicken for the car, or small steaks for the train, which the valet cooked on a portable stove. He was leery of many restaurants, probably more for reasons of digestion than of palate. My mother had told him that poached eggs were always a safe bet, for "bad eggs can't be poached," so I was not surprised when he asked for them, although they were not on the menu, at a Connecticut inn where I once took him for lunch.

Food and the planning of meals had high priority with my parents, and my father, an old hand after his years of running Winterthur for the Colonel, was primarily in charge. He had enlarged the farm operation into widely separated units for the raising of poultry, pigs, sheep, dairy cows, and beef cattle, and he had built a greenhouse to ensure a supply of fresh vegetables in the winter.[1] My parents entertained a great deal both at Winterthur and elsewhere, and when they were at one of their other homes, large quantities of produce were shipped to them from Winterthur by truck or train.[2]

I was aware of my father's meticulous habits, but I was not prepared to discover in the Winterthur archives the menus for every lunch and dinner served there for at least fifty-seven years, along with the number of guests.

Here is a sample:

> *Saturday Luncheon May 9th, 1931* (about 16)
> Hors d'oeuvres   Eggs   Ducklings   Apple sauce   String beans   Beets   Asparagus
> 2 sauces (Hollandaise, Butter)   Strawberry Meringue Pie (Shell of pastry filled with uncooked strawberries, meringue on top)
> *Saturday Dinner May 9th* (18)
> Cream of chicken [soup]   Soft shell crabs   Saddle of Lamb   Peas   Carrots
> Pate de foie gras in aspic and salad   Nestle Rod Pudding Cake
> *Thursday, December 1st, 1955*
> *Lunch for 2*
> Eggs   Pigs feet   Beets   Spinach   Pumpkin pie
> *Friday, December 2nd*
> *Dinner for 12*
> Terrapin   Mushrooms on toast   Squab broilers   Salad
> Strawberry ice cream   Strawberries

Our food for the most part came straight from the farm and was cooked simply, without rich sauces. Of course the invention of the deep freeze considerably prolonged its freshness. An egg dish was always a part of lunch, as was fruit—mangoes, papayas, melons, persimmons, or homegrown figs and small, sweet red Delaware grapes. Like James Joyce's Leopold Bloom, our family "ate with relish the inner organs of beasts and fowls," and when we were alone—not often—we fell upon sweetbreads, kidneys, tripe, and brains.[3] Pigs' feet were another specialty, as were game birds presented by hunter friends, routinely accompanied by my mother's warnings to watch out for the buckshot. Two prized delicacies came from birds: the carcass of the barely cooked wild duck, and my father's favorite, the pope's nose of the turkey, whose mystique was enhanced by unasked questions about its anatomical origins. During those long-ago holidays the now-endangered diamond-back terrapin crawled about in our cellar awaiting its destiny as the first course on Christmas eve, served as a stew in silver soup dishes. Along with water and two kinds of wine, sherry was also offered for those who considered it a must for a turtle dish.

Although my mother—and of course the head cook—also participated in the planning of meals, my father alone was in charge of the dining room, and he approached it as if he were designing a stage set. His materials—flowers, china, linen—were assembled days in advance, the availability of flowers determining the other choices. Three or four days before a house party a gardener would bring him samples of outdoor or greenhouse flowers that could be counted on to be blooming that weekend. (A flower to be used on the table was not to be seen "anywhere else in the house that day.") In the huge china closet, whose shelves were loaded with stacks of dishes, a footman would climb a ladder and perilously hand down several centerpieces and matching plates. My father and the butler would then decide on the combination of china, glass, and linen that would best complement the flowers. My down-to-earth mother teased her husband a bit about his painstaking methods, but she was proud of him and happy to be relieved of many duties generally assumed by the lady of the house.

I have before me fourteen typed pages from my father's records which list fifty-eight sets of china, along with the number of people each could accommodate. For example: "No. 25 for 16 people—Dinner Spode all over design, pink red and brown flower 16 soup plates, 31 dinner plates, 38 dessert plates, 3 covered vegetable dishes, each three pieces, 4 complete sauce boats, 2 candy dishes, with saucers, one has no cover, 4 vegetable dishes, no covers, 1 big square dish with handles, 1 big square dish with legs, 1 fruit dish with handles, 3 oval cake dishes, 1 salad bowl." Included in the list are eighteen sets of Staffordshire in such colors as pale lavender, mulberry, yellow-green with Canova pink border, and other types of china as well: Napoleon white, Minton, Worcester green, Sèvres, Crown Derby. Weekend house parties, often with twelve or fourteen overnight guests, demanded four or five different lunch and dinner table settings, for they were not repeated from one meal to the next. Breakfast never took place downstairs but was brought to the bedrooms on trays or wheeled tables according to menus checked off by the guests the night before. The tables, if no one was around, were great for coasting the entire length of the dining room.

Like the menus, lists of flowers and their containers for the dining room were recorded for sixty years (from 1908 to 1968). For example, in 1928: "Sunday, December 30th. 6 for lunch Ageratum in white wicker china. Sunday, December 30. 22 for dinner. Gloire de Lorraine [begonias] in Norwegian silver. Monday, December 31. 6 for lunch. Paperwhites in Copenhagen china." Also recorded for a period of fifty-eight years, beginning in 1910, are the day-by-day combinations of flowers, china, and linen which appeared on the Winterthur table:

Lunch, Sunday May 18th, 1930   for 10

Flowers	*China*	*Linen*
Iceland poppy	Green leaf Wedgwood	Yellow mats
	Dark green glass	

Dinner, Saturday, October 23rd, 1931   for 12

Flowers	*China*	*Linen*
White dbl. mums	Pink Rose Lowestoft	Doilies
"Earliest of All"	Battersea [candle] sticks	

Lunch, May 4th, 1937   for 12

Flowers	*China*	*Linen*
Yellow Rose	Silver lustre	Robin's egg blue doilies
	Robin's egg Lowestoft	
	salt glazed plates	

The "doilies" which accompanied the flowers and china were by no means a random selection but were the result of the infinite pains taken by one Marshal Fry of Brooklyn, a purveyor of custom linens, who was as driven as my father by the need to match cloth to china. In their forty-six-year correspondence of 237 letters they discussed quilted linens, experimental stitching, and every conceivable color scheme; octagonal versus square "blue-grey-green" place mats, "violet-initialed napkins," ecru versus gray thread to replace the clear shades of chartreuse no longer available from France. Given Mr. Fry's "interest and enchantment" in working with linens, my father had found an exceptional ally.

The exhaustive detail invested in the setting of a table indicates my father's determination not to leave the smallest matter to chance. He understood very well his need to anticipate contingencies, and he acted accordingly. Since he often remarked that the "average person" noticed very little of his surroundings, the energy with which he repeatedly created as transient a piece of art as a table setting must have fulfilled a deep aesthetic need of his own. If his efforts were appreciated, so much the better, but basically, I suspect that his motivation was highly subjective.

Our dining room of pale yellow eighteenth-century paneling spanned the width of the museum-to-be, and I thought the dining room in the new house on the bridge every bit as beautiful. In that room, eighteenth-century French tapestries covered two of the walls, creating an illusion of the forest. Except for tiny bulbs in sconces which convincingly simulated candle flame, both dining rooms were lighted entirely by candles—in standing torchères in the corners and, on the table, in candelabra or candlesticks of silver, pewter, glass, or china that matched or complemented the dinner service.[4] The dining room at night was always dramatic, the table shining with glasses and silver, the centerpieces filled with flowers or fruit. My father's fondness for the theater tended to increase with the number of scenery changes per play; these exhilarated him in the same way as did the challenges posed by the changing decor of his own table. Guests were not permitted to see the room before 8:30, when—with the butler's announcement of dinner—the curtain went up. My father's pleasure in parties derived from the cast of characters and the food, but probably most of all from the elements of the setting.

My parents were in full agreement on the subject of entertaining, and their lunch and dinner parties were high-spirited and merry. They always sat across the table from each other rather than at its distant ends, and together they arranged (and sometimes rearranged) the seating. For eight or more people there were reusable place cards of the same white porcelain as my father's idiosyncratic menu plaque, always at his place to remind him of the courses to come. My parents believed that an even number of men and women made for livelier conversation, and my mother would struggle to replace a last minute dropout, telephoning one after another candidate from her lists of "local" or "out-of-town" "Extra Men" and "Extra Women" until symmetry had been restored.

The earliest of these parties that I can remember was a fancy-dress "nose" party in 1925. The concept now seems so bizarre that without a photograph I would suppose it to be a dream—and a bad one at that, for I suspect that anti-Semitism was an implicit element in this evening. I crept from my bed and hid on the old marble stairs so that I could see what was happening in the Red Room. There were my parents and their friends, all wearing false noses!

The first official Winterthur event that I attended was my sister's coming-out party, and of course my father welcomed the opportunity to create a stage set. In that June of 1935, dinner was served around the swimming pool, with dancing on a lower level, near the rose garden. To me, age thirteen, the most exciting feature of the evening, other than one or two dinner-jacketed youths falling into the pool, was the big tent with folding chairs in the nearby Clenny Run meadow, put up in the event of rain. Since it was a lovely night, the tent and one hundred rented umbrellas were never used.

Six years later, at a horseshoe-shaped dinner table around three sides of the swimming pool, my parents celebrated their twenty-fifth wedding anniversary. There was no need to rent a tent this time, since the dining room in a pinch could have accommodated the seventy guests, but the decorations were memorable indeed. The pool, lighted from below and by lights high in the trees, was entirely surrounded by silver—silver chairs and tablecloths, silver paper molding the lead seahorse and the diving board. An accordionist was rowed around by a sailor-suited boy in a little boat with a silver sail. A Hungarian trio provided after-dinner entertainment, along with two magicians—one a pickpocket who filched watches and wallets from the male guests.

In the 1930s my father masterminded several of his daughters' activities. The occasion of my sister's January wedding in 1938 was to him as the sound of the bugle to the racehorse. A letter to California friends noted that the bride "looked perfectly lovely" and described the bridesmaids' dresses and bouquets, but its author was more carried away by the surroundings. Winterthur plants and flowers filled the church; buddleias and poinsettias of white and pink, pink begonias, smilax around the windows, and pink roses everywhere—in flattened wall baskets, on the altar and columns, and massed in the font. "I had a 10-foot buddleia in the pulpit & raised to the same height the one on the column opposite, & the sunshine hit them just right during the ceremony." In the same letter he described with equal zest temporary changes to the house: parts of the entrance floor were emptied of furniture, as was the Chinese Room, whose baseboard, bordered with pink primroses, "looked lovely with the paper." Yellow jasmine, blue cineraria, and white freesia were banked beside the bar and the tea and buffet tables. The Breakfast Room (never used for breakfast, and never before for any other purpose that I can remember) "was fitted with a chaise longue for anyone who became exhausted & wished to rest. . . . The dining room table had pink galanthus orchids in Norwegian silver beakers, & silver candlesticks."

Preparations for my own coming-out party in September of the following year again entailed stripping part of the house, and my father outdid himself on this occasion with *two* tents. As he wrote to Marian Coffin, the dancing tent was pale pink and the floor was a most beautiful fuchsia red with a painted pink escalloped border. On the tent poles there were streamers of two shades of pink and one of blue, following the line of the roof of the tent. Also the cornice of the tent was made of two shades of pink braided together. The walk from the conservatory to the dancing tent was lined with pale blue silk, and I had about twenty peach trees along the walk, with the most colossal peaches on them you ever saw in your life. It was really quite ravishing.

The dining tent beyond the dancing tent consisted of white and green stripes and we had masses of flowers around the tent poles, on the tables and in every available place. After dinner we rolled up one side of the dining tent and there was a full-fledged bar with a trellis wall at the back with big bunches of grapes on it.

I find myself disconcerted by the description of this extravaganza designed especially for teenagers, on whom such details were doubtless rather lost, but I am impressed by my father's endearing yet childlike delight.

As to my wedding, in March 1947, I can remember neither his sentiments nor the setting—in fact, I can remember very little. Convalescing from a taxi collision, I was more preoccupied with finding makeup heavy enough to conceal my black eyes and scars, and hoping that once I had washed my face the bridegroom would not be arrested for wife-beating. As this was to be the final major event before the house's conversion, it drew a capacity crowd. Cars stretched from the Gatehouse to the front door. Everyone in the world seemed to have been invited, and they all came— many friends and well-wishers, of course, but the vast number, I suspect, in order to have a pre-museum look at an egg-and-dart molding or a ball-and-claw foot. I had vetoed my mother's suggestion that a sign, "Please Do Not Kiss the Bride," be posted at the head of the receiving line, but long before we had finished shaking hands, my numbed husband and I realized our mistake in not having eloped.

During the two decades of my parents' residence in the expanded house at Winterthur, weekend house parties in spring and fall were the custom. Arrangements began at the railroad station. Three or four chauffeurs would meet the guests, some of whom were accompanied by a lady's maid or valet, and tag each suitcase according to its designated room. On one weekend, twenty people arrived with eighty-five pieces of luggage, which a truck duly trundled to the house. On such frivolous occasions, the friends most often invited were those who played the same games as their hosts—

bridge and backgammon, golf and tennis. However, as the carefully kept guest books indicate, visitors to Winterthur came from many different worlds. The diplomatic corps were primarily English, Swedish, Spanish, and Belgian, and there were lesser members of royal families and other foreign as well as American dignitaries.[5] But the guest list also included artists, musicians and actors, gardeners, collectors, and interested citizens in general.[6] Andrew and Betsy Wyeth, neighbors from nearby Chadds Ford, were friends and frequent dinner guests, and in 1952, Wyeth painted a portrait in oil of my father. Aside from the antiques community, so unappealing to my mother, my parents almost always liked the same people; however, by mutual agreement and in a triumph of compromise, early in their marriage each gave up a childhood friend whom the other heartily detested.

After my parents moved to the smaller house on the bridge, the newly arrived professional staff of the museum and the young and lively Winterthur Fellows brought about changes in entertaining that increasingly reflected an interest in museum activities. Museum trustees and other visitors with diverse fields of expertise introduced a more scholarly approach to the lunch and dinner parties.

ଵ · CHAPTER 15 · ଓ

Harry & Ruth

I N January 1935 my mother wrote to Elihu Root:

Dear Uncle Elihu,

Harry is not a man of strong reactions. He seldom laughs heartily; almost never gets angry; is never worried & rarely sad. Things & people do not impress him as a rule, beyond a kindly & passing interest. I was therefore, in a way, not surprised but enchanted & delighted at his reaction after the visit with you the other day. You bowled him over completely, & he could talk of nothing else for hours. It was the first time he had had the pleasure of seeing you by yourself . . . for a quiet chat. May I tell you that his enthusiasm & admiration for you knows no bounds. He was charmed by your sense of humor—his own is quiet, but very keen, & he is a person of wonderful sensitiveness & appreciation. The whole incident has made me very happy, feeling toward you both as I do.

Do let Harry come again soon. It would be a joy to him. He is a heavenly person & has made me happier than any other wife can ever have been. The nineteen years of our married life have flown for me. The thought of Harry always recalls to me the following line, "As charming as if he were a scapegrace, and as fine as if he had no other charm."

I started out to eulogize yourself, & have ended by a eulogy of my husband. Both expressions are true for me. Why not express one's affection & admiration to its objects?

The letter well describes my father—and my mother's feelings for him, which never changed. Five years later, she was misdiagnosed as having cancer. She wrote to me at college that if either of them had to die, she ought to be the one. "I beg that you will be philosophical about this. . . . [Your father has many interests], but without him I would never have the heart to cultivate mine." This chilling statement notwithstanding, a quarter-century later my parents celebrated their fiftieth wedding anniversary. After my mother's death, I mentioned her letter to my father, and we agreed that although many years had passed, it was still preferable for him to be the survivor.

My parents loved and protected each other—at times to the exclusion of other people, their children included. Once, alone in New York after the death of my third child (my husband having rejoined our older children in London, where we were spending the winter), I tried to seize for myself an evening in their busy lives, with a date set well ahead. I had, in fact, a "collection" of my own—years of events, thoughts, and feelings to share with

Henry F. and Ruth du Pont with Elihu Root and his wife, Clara Wales Root.

them—and of course I was shattered by my loss. I declined my father's suggestion that morning that we go instead to the horse show at Madison Square Garden, but it should have alerted me to inevitable disappointment. We dined early that night, and my mother soon left with a headache. When my father excused himself a few minutes later "to be with your mother" I was no longer in any doubt of their intentions. At the time I was more hurt and thwarted than angry. Later I realized that I had expected the unthinkable from my parents—that they set aside their lifelong aversion to what at school we called "soul talks." They were people of deep feeling, but showing or sharing emotion, except perhaps to each other or in writing, was not part of their makeup. Their commitment to each other was complete, or, in my father's case, almost so; he was still aware of the memory of the first woman in his life. My mother after some forty years of marriage told her twelve-year-old grandson that her husband had never truly recovered from his own mother's death.

Harry and Ruth were an interesting pair, with a great deal in common, and my parents moved heaven and earth to guard against uncertainty. Order and orderliness were crucial to their lives. Plans had to be made months ahead, and tickets were bought accordingly; at least five copies of schedules were typed and circulated throughout the household. Although they would never have admitted it, the unexpected or the unpredictable, as present in dogs and young children, increasingly disrupted their equanimity as they grew older.[1] But they did not lack spontaneity. Mother, a gifted raconteur and mimic, often was a clown, full of jokes and laughter. Once, on a whim at a dinner party, and in cahoots with the hostess, who lent her a shawl and makeup, she disguised herself as a fortuneteller and bamboozled the other guests. My father, to the outside world more reserved, also had a lively sense of fun. Although he was less verbal than his wife (she said that he had no small talk), he was quick-witted and easily amused. During the seemingly endless delays in the installation of the museum's air conditioning, Harry said to the curator, his young friend John Sweeney, "I bet it won't work, and I'll be sending you messages from the Inferno telling you how much cooler it is down here." On a trip to England with Sweeney the year before he died, when the secretary of a grand establishment telephoned in advance of their visit to determine the "title" of his traveling companion, he shot back, "Equerry to H. F. du Pont."

Henry F. and Ruth du Pont dressed for golf, in about 1916.

Especially when he was away from home, my father was relaxed and easygoing. He needed little sleep, and he could nap anywhere—on a bench at the railroad station or, more unsettling to his family, at the theater or on the sofa after lunch with the clergyman and his wife. My mother, on the other hand, slept poorly and was easily fatigued; she was given to superstition and worries about problems real or imagined. If Harry was thirty minutes late, he must have fallen on his walk or been in a car crash. One afternoon, frantic about my sister's delayed arrival (she was unexpectedly on the second section of a train), my mother rushed to telephone J. Edgar Hoover at the FBI, fearing kidnapping and unable to entertain any other possibility.

My parents' temperamental differences seemed not to have affected their compatibility. My father somehow took for granted his wife's basic pessimism, perhaps realizing its relation to her own father's often outrageous behavior and her beloved mother's eccentricities. He spoke of his good fortune in seeming "to notice everything that is attractive and beautiful," whereas instead of immediately appreciating a lovely face or a superb garden, his wife would first spot the gold filling in a tooth or weeds in the flower beds. Although my mother's appealing merriment and ready laugh were contagious, they concealed a dark outlook on life, which, in an undated essay entitled "Non-Accepto," she defined as a "grievous struggle from the start."[2] A firm agnostic, she believed it an "awful act to bring even one human being into the world," and she advanced as a solution the universal use of birth control! At church every Sunday with her husband, she would stand militantly silent during the recitation of the creed.

My father, on the other hand, was devout but seldom spoke about his feelings, although when at school he often revealed them to his mother. "I forgot to tell you that I [do] not read the bible in the morning as it is too dark to see, but I always try to read a little verse." His confirmation had great significance for him, as did services at both the Groton chapel and in church. From his mid-twenties and for forty-one years, Harry was involved with Christ Church, the family church in Montchanin, and as treasurer, vestryman, and finally senior warden, he never missed a meeting. In 1915, the year before his marriage, he undertook its redecoration, with particular emphasis on the chancel and the installation of a window in memory of his mother. In 1945 he further renovated the church "with perfectionism & discipline" and wished that his mother could see the improvements to it—just as he surely would have wanted her to see the new Winterthur.

When I told my father of seeking psychotherapy at the time of my baby's death, he asked whether I had "thought of religion" instead. The minister who presided during my father's later years recalled his "real devotion, real devoutness in his prayer life . . . that he'd never talk about," and his appreciation for the "dignity & restraint" of the Prayer Book service. But he also had less than reverential moments, such as on one Christmas morning when the hymns were by mistake all set to unfamiliar tunes. He paused on the way out to protest to the unfortunate rector—the one who habitually put him to sleep—and announced with some satisfaction to his wife and daughters, waiting for him in the car, "That will teach him not to make a fool of himself next Christmas!" We never let him forget the incident.

Harry and Ruth were in full harmony when it came to matters of health—or, rather, fear of ill health. When they lived at Winterthur, the presence of doctors may have been even more notable than it was in my grandparents' day, and I have already mentioned one instance of the "train-call" phenomenon. My parents' dependence on the medical profession was astonishing, and the response of its members almost equally so, for doctors seemed to appear almost immediately when bidden. A general practitioner from Wilmington called on the Winterthur household every week, whether or not anyone there was sick, and during the flu epidemic of 1918 he took on the daily task of fumigating certain rooms with formaldehyde candles, one to every 500 cubic feet. In 1928, our Delaware pediatrician was prevailed upon to spend a month in England with us, two healthy children, while our parents visited Paris. My sister and I were less than pleased with these medical presences, for they all too often resulted in vile potions or procedures. During one New York winter we consumed daily spoonfuls of what looked like iron filings and, donning huge goggles, tried to lie still under a sun lamp. There is no doubt that thermometers were in our mouths more often than were lollipops.

On one particular morning my father received three doctors—a general practitioner to paint his throat, a surgeon to look at his knee, and an osteopath. On another day, after a heatless train ride, "little H took a slight cold. That night he took 2 A.C. capsules, nitre, ammonia & 2 slugs of hot whiskey & water on retiring, & yesterday took 2 grippe capsules." My father's predilection for nose and throat sprays was such that he had his bathrooms in all four residences equipped with built-in electrical models. He was also acutely sensitive to temperature changes. He wrote to Louise in December 1938 that because of his "every other day colds" he was apprehensive at the prospect of the "long cold drive" to Salem from Boston. He explained rather petulantly that he could not "bring every kind of overcoat" with him. The Winterthur golf pro, Percy Vickers, said, "Mr. du Pont felt a chill in the air more than anyone I ever knew." At the first tee he would begin with two sweaters, long- and short-sleeved, and add to or subtract from them throughout the game. I was intrigued by his beige pullover, thin as a cobweb, which fitted into a small envelope and was carried in his golf bag at all times.

Germs rather than climate were a main source of my mother's anxiety, and fear of them promoted incessant orders for hand washing. Once in Sunday School when I was very young I sought reassurance that the gnat from which I cowered was not a germ on the wing. Water fountains in Central Park teemed with germs and were also banned lest some stranger bash down one's head, resulting in broken teeth. (My mother had heard of such an occurrence, but I managed to accomplish this defacement all on my own when I fell from a scooter.)

These precautions and rituals notwithstanding, our family seemed to be no more and no less healthy than any other. Harry du Pont, in actuality, was blessed with copious energy and could run other people ragged. His scale in the morning and sometimes a tape measure determined the size of the helpings he would take at lunch and dinner, but, after a scant breakfast, he could afford to eat the three or more courses offered at the other meals, as well as some of the "hot dish" that was part of afternoon tea. His restraint, combined with good metabolism and much walking or golfing, protected him from ever gaining too much weight. My mother, less active and perhaps less well-disciplined, was not so lucky and became increasingly rotund over the years. This was especially noticeable since she was small-boned like her spouse (she had weighed only 95 pounds on her wedding day); she said that they had been the "thinnest couple imaginable." My father's interest in the appearance of women in general, evident even in his Groton years, much exceeded his wife's, and my sister and I would often seek his opinion about our clothes. As she grew older my mother was happy to let the rest of us shop for her as well as for ourselves.

As a young married woman, my mother often mentioned books, especially novels, in writing to my grandmother. She had "guffawed" at Booth Tarkington's *The Plutocrat,* was "*enthralled*" by *John Brown's Body* ("a masterpiece" by Stephen Vincent Bénet), and found Hemingway's *The Sun Also Rises* "corrupt, haunting . . . and very remarkable." She wondered whether her mother would be "disgusted or fascinated" by this new work. But over the years, social engagements, letter writing, and, toward the end of her life, an absorption in genealogical research overshadowed her literary interests, as it had her music, and left her little time for reading.[3]

My father could be knee-deep in flower and antiques catalogues or in journals like the *Holstein-Friesian World,* but I never saw him read a book. Serious conversation was scarce at the more frivolous house party weekends although world and local news, as well as politics, were often discussed. With the Franklin Roosevelts in the White House, however, politics was a dangerous topic, and the few guests who favored the New Deal either found themselves invited less often or knew how to keep their views to themselves.

My father, imbued from birth with conservatism and loyalty to the Republican party, never for a moment doubted its superiority. However, except for expressing increasing disapproval of the administration, he was little interested in politics per se. His wife's anti-Roosevelt fury, on the other hand, seems to me to have been pathological. Although most of her acquaintances shared the view that "that man in the White House sold us down the river," I believe that my mother's animosity was unduly intense and that it stemmed from her early years in Hyde Park, where the Waleses and the Roosevelts had been close friends. For instance, when Sara Delano Roosevelt learned of my mother's engagement to Harry, who had been a year ahead of Franklin at Groton and a classmate of James's,[4] she wrote most affectionately to "dear little Ruth" about her "nice, clever" fiancé, "one of very few men who could be worthy of you. . . . I like all his charming tastes and all I hear of him." The Colonel, with Franklin and Eleanor present, spent the weekend of the wedding in Hyde Park with Mrs. Roosevelt.

After Franklin became president, my mother not only held the belief that he was a "traitor to his class" but also, because of several of his public statements—interpreted by some as attacks on the Du Pont Company—felt personally betrayed. In 1936 she made so vitriolic a speech in support of Alfred Landon, the Republican candidate, that one Winterthur resident in the audience said it was sure to gain votes for Roosevelt.

In 1940, my parents, in individual letters to Marian Coffin, registered dismay at her approval of the New Deal. My mother wrote that she was "absolutely horrified by [Marian's] reactions toward Roosevelt." My father, who, like many others, misinterpreted a speech made by the president that seemed disparaging to the du Ponts, expressed his views more moderately.[5] I hardly endeared myself to either parent by voting for Roosevelt in my first ballot ever, but despite the fear of enraging my mother and the wish to avoid arguments, it seemed wrong to hide my decision. After her death we found among her papers letters written in 1954 to the Secretary of the Treasury as well as to the two Delaware senators and its one congressman. These communications made two requests: that the Treasury Department recall all Roosevelt dimes (for which action she was prepared to pay) and that such dimes be no longer minted. The nine years that had passed since the death of her former friend had not lessened her hostility toward him.

Both my parents loved music, my father most of all Wagnerian opera, whereas my mother preferred the march and orchestral pieces in general. Despite arthritis in her fingers, she continued to play the piano well into middle age, mostly for her family's amusement. When I once asked about her failure to pursue her very real musical gifts she replied, I believe without regret, that my "father's genius overshadowed [her] talent." I suspect that her own temperament was the problem and that the demands of daily life had gotten the better of her. Her frequent comparisons of the pre-mu-

Ruth Wales du Pont in the early 1950s.

seum Winterthur to an embassy were valid, but she seemed unable, despite the large staff, to establish priorities that would have freed her from unnecessary chores and worries; she often described herself as "too pleasure loving & too conscientious." Her social life was busy, but her overworked conscience was the real problem, and such things as unanswered letters and day-old bills tormented her. Had she set aside time for music rather than for what Edith Wharton, one of her heroines, called a "mastery over trifles," she might well have made a name for herself in the music world.[6]

Harry and Ruth increasingly saw eye to eye about their way of life, painstaking travel arrangements included. Before the post–World War II proliferation of turnpikes, they generally traveled by train, with an automobile at the ready at each end. When they were en route to Florida from New York, a marvel of logistics would occur during the three-minute stop at the Wilmington station, where a retinue handed over mail, flowers, and, at times, hampers of food. During these lightning exchanges, the first director of Winterthur, Charles Montgomery, could sometimes be found on the station platform himself; once he stood there waving a pair of brass candlesticks for his boss's inspection.[7] My parents' return from England in 1958 was an occasion infamous even in their annals, for the United States Line momentarily objected to the request that three H. F. du Pont automobiles be allowed on the dock at the same time—two to take husband and wife, respectively, to Delaware and Southampton, and the third to transport the bulk of the luggage. (Little did the authorities know that a fourth car, my father's first Rolls-Royce—a startling defection from General Motors—would also be traveling to New York with them on the ship.) On the subject of travel, my father was not without insight and once remarked, "We use the lady at Cook's because she knows how difficult we are."

Harry and Ruth were impatient people. My father's early letters are studded with such comments as "I am in the greatest hurry for," and "with the least possible delay." He must have a suitcase repaired in six days; the chicken house must be finished "immediately as it is quite late enough now"; the duck house is to be built "as soon as possible." This characteristic remained with him forever and was shared by his wife, but since she was less involved with projects, her impatience was most often concerned with the mail and with transportation. Both Harry and Ruth chafed at any kind of delay. Their typical departure from the theater, before or during the first curtain call, was mortifying to me. Crouched and stumbling over pairs of feet as they muttered apologies, they would bolt from the lobby and into the waiting car with the speed of bank robbers. The corollary of this behavior was born of an insistence on punctuality. It guaranteed arrival at the theater with the asbestos curtain still in place, or at the railroad station long before there was even a hint of the train.

My parents' similarity of outlook, which included the honoring of discretion and confidences, an emphasis on loyalty, and a mutual thoughtfulness, kept their relationship in harmony for more than fifty years. They loved and understood each other, thought the same things were funny, and shared many interests, opinions, and prejudices, although my mother's—especially toward Roman Catholicism—were by far the more fanatical. Ruth wrote a letter to Harry every day they were apart, and almost without exception, each letter contained at least one sentence in baby talk proclaiming her love for him and her real anguish at the separation.[8] Harry wrote almost as often and as tenderly. My mother's appreciation of her husband's humor, his accomplishments, his creative energy, and his appetite for action was as striking as my father's delight in his wife's quick wit, her animated personality, and her talents: her music, her flair for both serious and light verse, her abilities as storyteller and mimic, her adeptness at games and puzzles.[9] Harry, sympathetic to Ruth's susceptibility to fatigue, supported her increasing need to rest up, sometimes twice a year, in a small inn in Hot Springs, Virginia, and her faith in the therapeutic powers of the springs themselves.

At first glance, since my mother was the merrier of the two, one would have supposed her to be the more eager to give or attend parties, but in fact my father, nine years her senior, was more enthusiastic about them. In 1928, when she was ill for a month in Paris and unable to leave the hotel, Ruth encouraged Harry to accept all possible invitations to lunch and dinner, and she continued throughout her life to recognize his need for social activity. Whereas she was happy occasionally to dine alone or with a friend, the idea of a quiet meal on a tray (other than breakfast) was anathema to my father, and once the move from the museum had occurred he had more energy to spare than ever. My mother's travel diaries, based on our family's 1936 world journey and her many tours with my father from the 1950s on—weeks in hotels in London, European motor trips, Mediterranean or South

Pacific cruises—faithfully record places and people as well as her husband's greater stamina and appetite for sightseeing. Sightseeing was always for him a source of delight. His journals reflect in particular the joyful observations of a gardener and contain many perceptive comparisons to the Winterthur landscape.[10]

Harry took in stride the fact that Ruth not only did not share his passion for Winterthur but at times really disliked it; she had been known to call the place Frog Hollow. "Imagine, inside your own house, having to reach your husband by telephone!" Of course Ruth admired the museum and its superb surroundings, but they did not charge her emotionally any more than did the Winterthur community itself, to which Harry was so close. Among other things, she had not been able fully to rid herself of memories of the Colonel. My father understood this and realized that his wife, despite her popularity in Wilmington and Philadelphia, could not feel their environs to be her true home. In a limited sense, this was also true of Harry, for he never achieved a deep kinship with more than a handful of the increasingly large and extended du Pont family. I have heard it said of both my parents, with some justification, that "socially, they were New Yorkers." Although Harry had created other places where his wife could be happy, there was no question that Winterthur was where he truly belonged.

Money

THE crucial week in which Henry F. du Pont's aesthetic attention shifted from a European to an American emphasis is well
known, but it is intriguing to wonder when and to what extent
he began to anticipate the changes that he would make at Winterthur when he became its owner. He was able to experiment with some
of these changes in the building of Chestertown House, his "American
house" in Southampton.

Ruth had always loved the Long Island village where her grandfather,
Salem Howe Wales, had been mayor and where she had visited every summer when she was growing up. The prospect of having her own house overlooking the ocean enchanted her. (Although the building was set well back
from the dunes, Ruth's mother, with customary apprehension, this time
about tidal waves, could never bring herself to spend a night there.) My father also of course realized that gaining a piece of her own turf would help
his wife attain further psychological distance from the Colonel.

It is likely that Harry also welcomed this distance for himself. By now
he had started to collect Americana, not only furniture and smaller objects but entire rooms—walls, floors, and plaster ceilings. The architect
John W. Cross drew up the plans; Henry Sleeper assisted with the design,
color, and lighting. My father was closely involved in every step of the undertaking. In the summer of 1926, six months before the Colonel's death,
we moved in. Despite the house's great size, my parents managed to create a feeling of hospitality there in the midst of authentic and beautiful
early American things. Consequently, when Harry du Pont embarked on

his plans for Winterthur, he had the advantage of considerable experience.

The Colonel, through inheritance and a host of business activities, was extremely well off at the end of his life. On his father's death, Harry, at age forty-six, inherited not only a great deal of money but a vast establishment on the 2,400 acres which then constituted the Winterthur land. In addition to the big main house, surrounded by woods, lawns, and flower and cutting gardens, there were working farms that supplied meat, vegetables, and dairy products to our family and to the 250 or so others who lived and for the most part worked on the place. Winterthur was in fact a small town, with its own railroad station and post office, its own water supply, its own butcher, carpentry, and blacksmith shops, and its own laundry. Besides the herd of 450 purebred Holsteins, there were Hereford cattle, sheep and pigs, 45 horses, including some Percherons, and more than 2,000 chickens, turkeys, guinea hens, ducks, and pigeons. The cultivated land produced, in rotation, alfalfa, wheat, corn, beets, and other varieties of fodder.

My father took his new responsibilities in stride. Indeed, he had already mastered and elaborated on the techniques of modern horticulture and farming. Now that he was free to do as he chose, he was ready for the next challenge.

In the years immediately following the Colonel's death there was an explosion of activity. Through careful planning and organization, Harry added to the house on the hill a multi-storied wing more than twice the size of the existing house, remodeled the exterior, and gave as much attention to the grounds that surrounded it. The operation involved five hundred workers, including carpenters, masons, and stonecutters. Most of the stone was quarried on the place. The extensive exterior changes included the addition of dormer windows, a remodeled roof, and a new front door to the west. (A large conservatory on the north side of the house replaced the earlier front door and its porte-cochère.)

The new arrangement ensured more privacy for the rooms that our family continued to use. (At an earlier time, in order to escape from an unwelcome caller, my mother had jumped under a cloth-draped table in the red living room, only to realize that the guest was seated nearby. As the minutes wore on, and as her fear of being caught increased, she wondered how well the pretext of searching for a lost pin would go over. Luckily, there was no need for her to find out.)

When, in April 1931, we returned to our new home from the snug farmhouse where we had lived during the construction, my mother wrote to her mother, "This house is swell but I am not *oriented* as we say among the literati!!" The house represented both my father's aesthetic sense and his undeniable hedonism; its size alone took some getting used to. Winterthur, like Xanadu, had become a pleasure dome, but here antiques existed along with modern features. Not only did we discover twenty-three new period rooms, whose woodwork came from five states and at least twice as many houses, but also a second and third elevator. One of these connected the new service section to the lowest floors, which included the bowling alley and badminton court. (The badminton court was also used for movie showings after dinner parties, and by me for shooting baskets.)

My father, with the help of Marian Coffin, had also superbly integrated the house with its surroundings. To the east, the new entrance hall opened onto a grass and flagstone terrace encompassing six towering tulip poplars; a new stone gazebo anchored its opposite side. Two sets of stairs descended to the gardens far below—a flight of angled, exotic steps that flowed to the rose garden, and a steep Italianate flight that followed in a line from the entrance hall. Interrupted by a landing with sundial and bordered by swooping stone banisters and boxwood, these stairs led to a swimming pool, where water spouted from the mouth of a lead seahorse. Two bath houses reflected the design of the gazebo. To me, reeling from a surfeit of antiques, they were almost as thrilling as the pool itself. Their facilities—washbasin, shower stall, enclosed toilet—were pure art deco and splendidly garish: shiny chrome and magenta porcelain for the women's quarters, chartreuse and black for the men's. With this contrast to the earlier centuries on the hill above, my whimsical father had surprised us again. Signs that read "Bathers are Begged to Take Showers before Entering Pool" were consistently ignored, except when the germ-conscious owners were present.

Henry Francis du Pont had been in a fever of impatience for the completion of his plans, and as he wrote—unrealistically—to his friend Marian Coffin, he "hoped to rush the house through in about 6 months." Thirty extra workers got a taste of his wrath one midnight when, dashing directly from a train, he found some of them quarreling, the others sound asleep. Furthermore, he wanted the gardens finished at the same time as the house, and in the spring of 1929 he chided Marian, "Have you given my iris garden the slightest thought, & if not, how soon [will you] do so?" The nine-hole golf course beyond the Pinetum, built under the supervision of the newly arrived Scottish pro Percy Vickers, who stayed on for my father's lifetime, was completed that year; my mother described it as "too beautiful."

Much later Charles F. Montgomery remembered his boss in this period of frantic activity and, I daresay with some accuracy, called him "profligate." Driven by impatience and accustomed to getting what he wanted, Harry was indeed often careless about money—in fact, until then, he had never in any real sense had to pay much attention to it. "In the building of the great wing," Montgomery said, "money was wasted, and Mr. du Pont was cheated. Cheated out of millions of dollars. The man who supplied the hardware in 1929–30 said, 'Well, hell, it's true.'"

Money, a taboo subject in many families, was also a touchy one for my father. I never heard it discussed at home, and I imagine that this was also the case in Harry's youth. (It could be noted that for the most part only people who have a sufficient amount of money can avoid talking about it.)[1] However, in at least one letter, Harry's father did take up the matter. On his son's arrival at Harvard, the Colonel arranged to send him $100 a month and in Polonius fashion cautioned him to be neither "extravagant or wasteful" nor "mean & ungenerous as nothing is more sure of making you unpopular." Some years later, after a dinner given in his honor by the younger men in the family, the Colonel lectured the assembled company on the "snares & temptations of prosperity" and went on to say that "any allusions ... to the possession or expenditure of money [are] odious & vulgar things."[2]

That Harry, then thirty-five years old, had assimilated at least a part of this philosophy was brought home to me in a startling incident some fifty years later. My husband and I, at Winterthur a year after my mother's death, had dined quietly with my father, together with a much-loved cousin, Carol Irving, and Charles van Ravenswaay, who had come to be the new director of the museum. We had not met before. After dinner, interested by my cousin's earlier account to me of a young family member who had been thrown off balance by an unexpected inheritance, I innocently wondered whether it would not have been better had the young man been prepared in advance for his windfall. My father's reaction stunned us, as he bellowed across the room: "Ruth Ellen, how disgusting! I've never heard anything so disgusting in all my life!" Taken aback, our group at first thought that he must be joking, but the seriousness of his reprimand became all too apparent. One of my concerns was about what on earth the distinguished Charles van Ravenswaay would think he had walked into. He and I became friends, and some time later he sent me the account of the Colonel's speech from which I have quoted above with the comment, "This explains it." Not only had my "odious & vulgar . . . [allusion been] in exceedingly bad taste," but it had certainly touched a nerve.[3]

Although hardly in a usual sense, money did seem to be a problem for my father. Sometimes he carried none at all, and Dana Taylor, his number one chauffeur, often paid for his admission to such events as antiques shows. When he was traveling abroad, he tended to limit the major contents of his wallet to one $1,000 letter of credit, which was in no danger of being used in an Irish village. On his last trip, at age eighty-seven, an Irish bank refused to cash a $10 check on a New York bank until my father explained that he was not only a "farmer" but also a director of the E. I. du Pont Company.

Like some other inheritors of "old money," my father could be very casual about it. Our Delaware pediatrician, along with Graham and an English nanny, spent a month with my sister and me in an inn on the North Sea. Having been given "more money than [she] had ever seen before," the doctor had labored over an accounting of her total expenditures. She was dumbfounded at the end of the visit when my father declined so much as to look at it but was mollified when he told her to keep the balance.

Harry du Pont at one time had accounts in eighteen different American banks. His secretaries claimed that he kept them informed about spending relatively small amounts of cash but was far less open when it came to bigger sums, perhaps fearing that his wife would find out and think his purchases of antiques extravagant. Had she known about it, she might well have thought so when in 1929, as "H. F. Winthrop," her husband outbid William Randolph Hearst for a Van Pelt high chest, obtaining it for $44,000, or the following January at the Flayderman sale at the Anderson Galleries. Major hi-jinks were involved on this occasion. With $130,000 at

Henry F. and Ruth du Pont on board the *Aquitania,* 1927.

their disposal, a Winterthur team consisting of my mother's secretary, Miss McCollum, and my father's two male secretaries proceeded to the gallery in separate taxis and sat far apart from each other. (They managed to spend only $93,660 of the total.)[4] My mother, looking for Miss McCollum that day, was merely told that she was "away." My father's spending habits continued almost unabated throughout his life. In the 1960s, on seeing a 1746 needlework picture priced at $25,000, he was reported to have said, "We better get the darn thing."

Harry's conception of money could be naive in the extreme. A co-trustee of a historical institution exultingly apprised him of a bequest to it from a mutual acquaintance who had recently died. "$350,000," he said. "Imagine!" He was taken aback by Harry's reaction: "Every year?"

My mother was the opposite of her spouse in this respect. She was a bargain hunter, and a compulsive saver of soap remnants, ribbon, string, and paper. To avoid using up stamps, she would often arrange for letters to be delivered by car, even to destinations miles away. And I can see her now in New York, worrying about the time. She did not trust her watch or her table clock, and she was unwilling to make a ten-cent telephone call to determine the correct time. Instead, she would lean from her sixth-floor bedroom window above Park Avenue, a mirror in her outstretched hand, to check the clock on the Grand Central building. She herself was amused by or at least apologetic for these antics, and more than once, when she sent a collection of ten-cent stubs for her mother to redeem at the Hyde Park railroad station, she would add the words, "millionaire's wife at play."

My father seldom fell victim to frugal impulses, but on one subject his behavior never failed to surprise me. Unlike other fathers who cautioned their children about drinking, mine, quite the opposite, became indignant when my friends or I left a glass of anything alcoholic unfinished. I never understood the cause of this peculiarity, which had nothing to do with the wine lover's horror at the waste of a precious drop; he was not much of a drinker himself, and connoisseurs pronounced the contents of his wine cellar far from superior. My father's only other brush with economy that I have uncovered appears in a letter he wrote at the age of thirty-three to Marian Coffin about "an enchanting sun-dial . . . [whose] cost, $750, is quite beyond my means." This restraint seemed unusual, although Harry more than once remarked that among his greatest regrets in a long life were memories of desired objects that he had not bought. Not many, I suspect.

There is no question that my father could be extravagant and headstrong in that he would pay enormous prices for something he really wanted. His philosophy is clearly stated in the eighty-page "letter" he left for future museum administrators.[5] "If an old piece of brocade, damask, etc. [becomes available] it will be expensive, but buy it." Harry remarked to Lloyd Hyde, an antiques dealer whom he met in 1928 and who became a lifelong friend, "There are two ways of going to an auction. Either you buy or you don't." But toward the end of his life he also told Lloyd that the prices he paid had probably evened out over time, since, especially in early days, he had often bought incomparable antiques for very small sums. When it came to the care of plants, no expense was spared. Harry's parents had made special efforts to save an ancient wisteria vine from destruction during the alteration of the house in 1902; during the work of 1929 my father paid $8,000 for a temporary structure that held the vine until it could be reattached to its home on the wall.

Today's taxes would surely have subdued my father, but in 1927 he inherited enough money not only to maintain Winterthur but to transform it inside and out. His good fortune seemed to have been in jeopardy at least twice, however. Had the Colonel carried out his threat to marry again, Harry's diminished income might have forced him to abandon Winterthur, or at least to curtail his activities there. And the stock market crash of late October 1929 certainly affected his circumstances (although two days later, in a letter to a similarly well-to-do friend, the horticulturist Charles O. Dexter, he merely inquired about the blooming season of Mollis hybrid azaleas). The building of the new wing was so advanced that it had to continue. It was the only major construction effort in or near Wilmington during that era.

In December 1931 my father, still paying for the house and for huge amounts of furniture, china, and textiles, was informed by his cousin Beverley Robinson, by then a prominent New York lawyer, of the difficulties of obtaining a mortgage for Winterthur, should one be needed. Quite likely my mother had this time in mind when she alluded to the great generosity of Pierre S. du Pont, for with an extraordinary loan he had apparently once saved her husband from a financial disaster. The lovely personalities of Cousins Pierre and Alice were not the only reasons my parents held them in such high esteem.

Other events added to the concerns of these years. In August 1930 the big cow barn burned down. The cows were saved, but the size of the herd had to be much reduced. A further "death blow" fell when the Treasury Department disallowed any deduction for the loss and instead imposed higher taxes. And another worry appeared: a Washington woman, claiming that Colonel du Pont had been the father of her seventeen-year-old son, sued Harry and his sister for having defaulted on an alleged agreement to help support the boy. To settle the case and to avoid having "Papa's name dragged through the papers, which would be very disagreeable for us as well," Harry and Louise together paid out $25,000, a sum that also included lawyers' fees. The fact that the woman's husband at the time of the alleged seduction was purported to be at the North Pole with Admiral Peary provided a note of levity. Another blow that fell during these years, a sad one for Harry and devastating for Ruth, was her mother's death in 1932.

As the Depression continued, both my father's and my Aunt Louise's letters spoke of financial problems and economies. The Winterthur staff, indoors and out, was decreased, and those who remained took salary cuts. Nevertheless, in both 1932 and 1933 my aunt was able to contribute $50,000 toward the upkeep of the gardens and greenhouses. In 1933, Harry, with perhaps not total ingenuousness, wrote a colleague in the Holstein-Friesian Association, "I am absolutely broke & cannot possibly send you a cent of money." A letter to his sister said, "All of the horrors seem to come at one time." There was thought of "shutting down half of the place" should Beverley lose a particular lawsuit. My father's condition of being "absolutely broke" was of course not absolute but relative; even when describing himself in this way he was known to say, en route to an antiques show, "I hope there isn't anything here we have to buy," as if a purchase were entirely out of his control. Furthermore, in the grip of his "poverty" in early 1933, in order to ensure privacy for his wife after her mother's death, he was able to afford a private railroad car—the equivalent of twenty-seven fares for two nights on the train—to transport themselves and their retinue to Boca Grande. Harry's inheritance of half of the estate of his Aunt Victorine in 1934 brought considerable relief, and by 1936 he must have managed a full financial recovery, for it was then that he took his wife and two daughters on their trip around the world.

From 1951 on, with the opening of the museum, the continuing expansion of Winterthur demanded enormous sums of money. My father needed funds for the additions of the South Wing, the Pavilion, the Library and Research Building, not to mention the installation of air conditioning, the building of storage halls for rugs and textiles, the construction of new roads, and the maintenance of grounds and gardens. He also had to think of his personal requirements and those of his family. Even Harry's formidable income was insufficient to handle all these projects, but luck was with him again. In the late 1940s he had sold for almost $50,000 the whole of his father's small village of Montchanin to one of Winterthur's expert wood-masters.[6] During the 1950s the gradual sale of the Colonel's by then immensely valuable Chicago real estate helped counteract Harry's spending and enabled him to increase his gifts to the museum. For these coups Harry had only his father to thank; he was further rescued by other financial events—for two of which he himself could take credit.

In the 1930s he had established trust funds for his sister and for a secretary, Frank Otwell, which were to revert to the museum after their deaths. Otwell's trust bore fruit over time. When he retired in 1950, his income enabled him to build up a splendid collection of violins, and after his death in 1956, the legacy to the museum was substantial. Evidently my father, in this instance more casual than usual, had forgotten about the trust. According to Charles Montgomery, when it became available, "Mr. du Pont was so surprised and overjoyed. . . . The darn thing had grown to be worth about a million dollars and was soon put to use to build the South Wing." In 1958, the Winterthur Corporation received as the income from Louise Crowninshield's trust the agreeable sum of $147,000, which would repeat itself annually. These windfalls were assisted by the increased value of General Motors, Du Pont, and other stocks over the years.

Another bonanza came about through the passage of a law that seemed to be a gift from the gods. In 1889, Katharine Drexel, a member of a fashionable and well-to-do Philadelphia family, became a nun and founded a Catholic missionary order primarily for the aid of American Indians. Having taken a vow of poverty, she wanted to give away all income that accrued from her trust funds. When federal income taxes became inordinately high during World War I, her financial advisers appealed to Congress. In 1924 a new tax law provided that anyone who for the preceding ten years had given away 90 percent or more of his or her income for charitable purposes could continue to do so and be exempt from paying income taxes.[7]

During the 1950s my father's counselors saw the enormous advantage of this law both for the museum and for my father himself. After proving that he qualified for the deduction because of gifts he had made over the preceding ten years, he was able to contribute annually to the Winterthur Museum objects equal in value to his seven-digit income, and was therefore relieved from paying a huge federal income tax.[8] As an added bonus, the antiques were assessed at their current market value rather than at their purchase prices. The significance of this tax break was staggering for

Harry, the beneficiary, who was able to realize some of his deepest personal ambitions as well as to continue in his hardly spartan lifestyle.

This remarkable arrangement, which prevailed for some forty-five years as tax law, doubtless helped Mother Katharine's causes and perhaps her religious standing (she is now a candidate for sainthood), but it seemed even more specifically designed for the needs of Henry F. du Pont. He already had in storage and would continue to acquire antiques of every description whose ultimate destiny was the museum.

Of course both my father and Winterthur benefited in ways that would otherwise have been unimaginable; the tax exemption made possible during his lifetime many extensive additions, changes, and improvements to the museum and the grounds. As with so many of the details of my father's life, I had heard nothing at all about the tax law until I began the research for these chapters. Although this may not seem surprising, given my father's reticence, it nevertheless strikes me as odd that he did not once mention this extraordinary piece of luck. Was it coincidence or perhaps greater general vigilance by the federal government that in 1969, the year of my father's death, this little known legal oddity began to be phased out by the Tax Reform Act? I am glad that my father did not live to find out about it.

CHAPTER 17

A Passion to Collect

WHEN my father died, the Winterthur Museum and its gardens, his major gifts to this country, were at once recognized as unique treasures. But quite apart from the gardens, farm, and museum, another collection emerged, homely and private: vast numbers of steamer trunks stuffed with tens of thousands of letters, bills, catalogues, lists and records of every description, telegrams, playbills, golf and bridge scores. This array, which now occupies five floors of library stacks, is still daunting to the most dedicated of archivists many years later, but, as its lavish content unfolds, it illuminates various aspects of the collector's life and character and often provides a unique view of social history.

Once when he was questioned about the origins of his acquisitive nature, my laconic father said, "I must have been born with it, for I have always collected. When young I collected birds' eggs, stamps, minerals, etc."[1] It makes me think again of him as a small child and of the deaths of his twin brothers, of his mother's recurring anguish and withdrawal in grief, and of the tragedy repeating itself more intensely with the loss of the family's seventh and last child. Even before Harry was six he surely had experienced powerful feelings of confusion, anxiety, anger, loneliness, jealousy, relief, and, later perhaps, guilt. Much of life at Winterthur during this period was hard for his sister too, but Louise was older, less vulnerable, and I suspect more appreciated by her father; she seemed better equipped to deal with troubled times. But I think that early pain and distress played a part in forming the intense collector's instinct so evident in both brother and sister.

Collecting implies control: it provides an island of orderliness, a bulwark of reassuring, tangible ownership and self-regulated fulfillment in the midst of uncertainty. One theory of collecting holds that "repeated acquisitions serve as a vehicle to cope with . . . problems of need and longing," whose roots most likely are to be found in early childhood.[2] As he grew older Harry survived struggles with academic problems and difficulties with relationships. These had lessened by the end of his college years, but just at that crucial point he had to face the shattering reality of his mother's death. It changed his world, and I think that he turned then even more fervently to the collecting that had comforted him in earlier times.

A certain sense of insecurity stayed with my father forever, as is demonstrated by his remarkable need for contingency plans. Arranging for a stained-glass window for the church, he commissioned two in case an explosion should shatter one of them. At age eighty-seven, en route to Kennedy Airport for the first flight of his life, he arranged for a second Winterthur car to follow the one in which he, John Sweeney, and the valet were riding lest their own vehicle break down. On this trip abroad, my father's last, he ordered twenty more shirts from the London store he had patronized for more than sixty years. (They all arrived with the sleeves set in backward.)

Harry's activities in the years after his mother's death must have helped him deal with his grief. Managing the house at Winterthur made few personal demands, but it required attention to detail, at which he excelled, and left time and energy for experimentation with planting schemes and later with cattle breeding. During summers abroad, his visits to gardens and museums enriched his knowledge of horticulture and indoor design. Not only did he begin to collect plants on a large scale, but he also began to buy French furniture, fabrics, and porcelain for both the Delaware and Washington houses.

When he was away at school Harry had consoled himself primarily through objects—stamps and flowers—rather than people, and this trend was to continue. The sudden realization of his calling when he visited the Webb and Sleeper houses in 1923 opened a world that would absorb him for the rest of his life; it marked the beginning of his serious commitment to collecting early Americana. To the seven hundred objects he bought in 1924 he added twelve hundred more the next year. As had been the case with his first horticultural ventures, the numbers continued to increase exponentially and kept pace with the completion of the Southampton house and the changes and additions at Winterthur.

When Henry F. du Pont thought creatively about houses, he started with the inside, for he believed that one function of a period house was to preserve the integrity of an earlier time. Old rooms installed in new spaces must retain as much as possible of their original identity—proportion, architectural detail, fenestration, woodwork. Chestertown House in Southampton was designed to accommodate the rooms from Maryland and Massachusetts that Harry already owned, stored piece by numbered piece in packing boxes in various barns, and the new wing at Winterthur followed the same principle.

Despite my father's offhand remark that there seemed to be a "lot of woodwork around," the search for valued houses was in itself a thrilling challenge, and his dealer friend Lloyd Hyde was responsive to it. In 1928, Lloyd noticed from the train a derelict Georgian house near Philadelphia; he later located it in a rundown neighborhood, where it had been converted to a Polish athletic club. He assessed it as a supreme example of eighteenth-century architecture and woodwork and bought it for $10,000. Built in 1762 by a prosperous planter and merchant, who had named it Port Royal after his birthplace in Bermuda, this house contained key features that were used or copied in the 1931 addition at Winterthur and provided a challenge to the new architect, Albert Ely Ives. Ives had to provide in his plan for what was to become one of the most beautiful spaces in the addition—the stately Port Royal Hall, which stretched from the new front door straight through the house to the gazebo terrace. The rich interior woodwork for the Port Royal Parlor and several smaller rooms and the model for the new dormer windows came from the same old house. Out of respect for the original owners of the twenty-three period rooms he had salvaged and installed in the addition, my father named them for the most part after their house of origin—Port Royal, Belle Isle, Readbourne. Sometimes he used the name of the city or town where the houses were located—Albany, Oyster Bay, Baltimore.[3]

My father's love of color led to his fondness for wallpaper.[4] In the 1931 wing the most notable example of wallpaper, another discovery of Lloyd Hyde, determined the dimensions of one of our living rooms, which had

The Port Royal entry hall at Winterthur after 1931.

been created by combining the Colonel's dining and sitting rooms and a hall, and which served as a transition between the original house and the new. The wallpaper, painted in China in about 1770, depicted an Oriental village surrounded by high hills and lakes, full of people, houses, shrubbery, boats, and animals, including a large rooster close up. This dramatic paper, in which there were no repetitions, exceeded the height of the room by two feet. As it was too beautiful to be cut away, my father and Albert Ives ingeniously arranged that the ceiling be curved to accommodate every last inch of hills and sky. The paper was of the Chippendale period, and my father was delighted to have a further reason to collect furniture accordingly.

He happily pointed out that Chippendale chairs and tables were sturdy enough to "be used safely without fear of damage"[5]—meaning scourge by the young. The Chinese Room, with its piano and its bridge and backgammon tables, became our favorite place for parties as well as for daily use.

Lloyd Hyde observed that Harry was an "omnivorous collector" but not an "accumulator," as were Henry Ford and William Randolph Hearst. That is, he did not buy things wholesale but more often with a definite plan in mind. Nevertheless, he clearly took comfort and pleasure in the ownership of large numbers of things: cows, antiques, cases of wine, made-to-order shirts, seashells. Shelling on Florida's west coast was fine sport, especially before Gulf of Mexico beaches were overrun by late-twentieth-century tides and tourism. My father, always susceptible to sunburn, wore a wide straw hat, his face shiny with Vaseline, as he wielded an ingenious combination cane and spoon that we had given him one Christmas. He would often proceed, head bent and in single file with the rest of us, along the waterline of Boca Grande's Gasparilla or neighboring islands, hoping to add another rare specimen to our family's shell collection, which was on display in lighted cabinets in the Florida house.[6]

George A. Weymouth, known as Frolic, the grandson of Harry's Harvard roommate and always my father's devoted fan, once invited him to collect bluebells from the woods near his house by the Brandywine. Not one to do things by halves, Harry sent an oversized Winterthur truck and numerous gardeners armed with shovels who dug up hundreds of plants. To Frolic's astonishment, the same crew returned the next day with a note asking for a "few more."[7] Frolic acquiesced, but he sent back a message: "Dear Cousin Harry, Since you have so many antiques, I'm just going to send my truck over for a few." Said Frolic, "H. F. called back and laughed like hell."

My father often seemed insatiable, but he was also discriminating, animated by the intrinsic beauty of a seashell, a plant, a piece of furniture or fabric, or an architectural detail. His zeal for collecting sometimes led him to shameless behavior, however, such as seeking to obtain objects from unsuspecting owners. On one occasion, twenty-six-year-old Frolic was horrified into submission when—en route to an antiques show in Lancaster, Pennsylvania—his elderly cousin commanded him to make an offer on a Windsor bench that he had spotted on the porch of a small house as they drove by. Dana Taylor remembered many such antiquing expeditions of up to a week into nearby states, during which my father called himself "Mr. Francis," oblivious to the fact that outside a farmhouse or country store, a sixteen-cylinder Cadillac with Delaware license plates (the du Pont crest painted on the door was less apt to be recognized) was likely to attract attention and even to suggest the owner's identity. My father's delight in the sport of collecting was reflected in the nonchalance with which he would permit old furniture—often dusty from storage in an attic or a barn—to be piled high inside the car with no concern about possible damage to the upholstery. The booty from these trips would then be stored in a barn or in the creamery at Winterthur until a specific location was ready to receive it.

H. F. du Pont's use of aliases of course stemmed from awareness that

Henry F. du Pont in the mid-1960s. Photo by Robert Hunt Whitten.

the price of antiques would rise steeply if the identity of the buyer were known. On our trip of 1936, his use of a pseudonym in Manila nearly back-fired. Through a tip from Lloyd Hyde, my father located the Portuguese owner of a Chinese export porcelain dinner service with a beautiful grape design traced in blue and gold. Calling himself "Mr. Hyde," he bought it "for practically nothing" and asked that it be delivered to the ship. Only just in time did he remember to inform the purser that packages addressed to the imaginary Mr. Hyde should be brought to Mr. du Pont's cabin.

My father continued to take pains to conceal key purchases from his wife. As late as 1961 he instructed Knoedler's to keep secretly for one year John Trumbull's famous portrait of Washington with his horse at Ver-planck's Point, for which Harry had paid $175,000 on the installment plan. (It now hangs in the Galleries at Winterthur.) During the Depression he bought for $20,000, also on the installment plan, a rare Philadelphia sofa from Joe Kindig, Jr., an antiques dealer with whom he had become friends. In one letter to Kindig he inquired, "Will it be too late for you to wait un-til the week of July 17 to bring these pieces down, as it is hopeless for me to look at antiques when the family is here." To another associate, Charles O. Cornelius, who was asked to prepare room-by-room descriptions of the Winterthur collection, my father wrote, "I know that Ruth will think this a terrible piece of extravagance & I am scared to tell her about it, so please keep the whole matter dark." His guilt about these transactions doubtless added a further fillip of excitement to them.

Perhaps Harry's best-kept secret was that of the spiral staircase whose installation had taken place when we were away. Returning home in May 1936 after our five-month absence, my father of course was not surprised to see it, but I think that he was as overwhelmed by the sight as were his wife and daughters. One year earlier, in a process with clandestine over-tones, the staircase and other architectural elements had been removed from Montmorenci, an abandoned house in Warren County, North Car-olina. My father, who had disliked the rather pretentious and certainly far from American marble stair and hall the Colonel had installed at Win-terthur in 1902, did not want it to remain as his own "memorial" and had instituted a search for a replacement.[8] A dealer from Connecticut, who within a two-year period had looked at staircases in ten different states, at last located a thrilling possibility. My father wrote with some excitement to Thomas Tileston Waterman, his new architect, about plans for seeing it. (Albert Ives had by this time moved to Hawaii.) "There is some woodwork that I might use in the hall. Please keep this strictly under your hat, however, as I don't want it known to anyone in the world. In fact, during the entire trip I am to be known as 'Mr. Francis.' Do you know the best firm that can saw you plaster cornices, etc., move them and copy them? I shall want the head man of the firm to go with us and tell me if they could be moved, give me an estimate, and also tell me whether the old plaster can really be moved or not."

A great deal of correspondence survives concerning the cloak-and-dagger arrangements that preceded the inspection. To avoid any link with Wilmington, my father and the workmen were to board the train for North Carolina at either New York or Washington. Dana was to park the car with its Delaware plates three miles away from the house. He must be by the side of the road at 11 o'clock on a certain morning, bringing a thermos of iced tea (having mixed it, once the tea was cold, with the juice of one lemon). Soon after this rendezvous a troop consisting of "Mr. Francis," Tom Waterman, another architect-curator, the antiques dealer, the contractor, and several workmen, all in North Carolina or Virginia cars, would descend on the house in order to determine the feasibility of salvaging its various parts.

In the second act of the drama a somewhat different crew, this time the Winterthur superintendent and his wife, the foreman and three other carpenters, and the driver of a truck, spent two weeks near Montmorenci in a hotel infested with "bed bugs by the million." During this interval the floors were first removed from the house, then the windows and doors, and finally the stairs. As the dismantling proceeded, truckloads were shipped back to Winterthur. On one trip, the first two steps fell unnoticed from the truck, and, despite a week's search, they were never recovered. This loss turned out not to be disastrous, however, for all the stair treads proved to be too worn to be used and were replaced by new ones cut from Montmorenci's huge columns of the same yellow pine.

Act 3 of the Montmorenci adventure presented still another challenge: adapting the single staircase to its new and much larger location. After months of secret conference and scholarly research, my father, Tom Waterman, several contractors, and the indispensable Bertha Benkard came up with a pragmatic answer: that the stair be reworked from a circular to an elliptical curve, that a duplicate be built of the same material to carry it one flight higher, and that the entire structure be reinforced with steel. Prodigious effort was involved, often until midnight or later, so that the installation would be in place before our return home. Thus the old marble hall, thanks to the reworking of 1822 materials by modern techniques, was transformed into a flying, breathtaking work of art that, perhaps more than any other treasure, has come to symbolize the Winterthur Museum.

In the early days of collecting my father of course made mistakes, beginning with a slant-top desk from his first auction in 1924; in due course its "later embellishments" revealed themselves by completely changing color.[9] But he was aware of his ignorance and turned to architects, curators, art and antiques dealers, and decorators for help. An initial involvement with an unscrupulous dealer from New York was balanced by advice from Edward Crowninshield, Frank's cousin, the first American to deal in Chinese export porcelain. Harry was lucky to find such professionals, and among his most valued associates in later life were those who shared his love and somewhat rarefied knowledge of the field of Americana.

My father entertained members of this group at a house party every summer at Winterthur. He excelled as a host, and the guests, who of course appreciated Harry's collector's drive and his ability to pay for their wares and expertise, also responded to his superlative taste and to his hospitality. As one of their key clients, Harry was both a favorite child and a knowledgeable peer who recognized his need for the best professional help available. He had strong ideas of his own, but he also encouraged those of others he respected. I believe that this summer interlude every year, along with membership in the Walpole Society, provided him with the kind of carefree but intellectually stimulating milieu that he had missed at boarding school and college, an uncritical time of shop talk and bull sessions offering a sense of belonging, a nurturing club whose members all spoke the same language. My mother did not attend these gatherings. The collector's world was not for her.

One of these summer guests, at the opera with my parents, succumbed to an attack of delirium tremens. He mistook a red velvet railing in the box for an ant colony and called out in strident horror, "Red ants! Red ants! Red ants!" Nothing could silence or pacify him. On another occasion, this one my wedding reception, just as my husband and I were descending the stairs crowded by rice-throwing friends, Thomas Waterman, unmoved by the nuptial excitement, could be heard clearly asking, "Harry, what was the name of that house in Virginia with the two identical doors?" My mother was only later amused.

There were members of this group of whom my mother was fond, however, especially Joseph Downs, formerly a curator of the Philadelphia Art Museum and the Metropolitan Museum of Art in New York, and, like my father, a member of the Walpole Society. In 1949 he became Winterthur's first curator. Another favorite was Lloyd Hyde, who years later became my friend as well. Twenty-eight years old when he met my father, he was perhaps unusual in his care not to ask too high a price for any of the objects he found, for he "wanted to have Harry's friendship always, & I admired his collecting so." Lloyd was a great traveler, and many of his discoveries—among them chandeliers from Canton and Barbados, English candelabra from Portugal, a huge set of American china in Paris on loan to the Louvre, a punchbowl from Stockholm, and woodwork from a house in the Battery in New York—were all added to the Winterthur collection.

Bertha Benkard was most influential of all during this phase of my father's life. She was already a distinguished collector of Duncan Phyfe furniture and was at first more knowledgeable in the field than my father was. A vital woman whose hats towered over her frizzy black hair and chalk-white face, Bertha shared Harry's love of horticulture as well. Jay Cantor, in his magnificent book *Winterthur*, observed that she was "so inextricably involved" in the planning and evolution of Winterthur that "she might also be considered as co-author of the project."[10] As my father's beloved ally, she occasionally represented him in his absence and helped him as well with decisions about rugs, paint colors, or the hanging of a curtain. When they were not together on the premises, the two would confer at length by telephone several times a week, usually starting at dawn, to discuss the details of a bed canopy or a tassel or a particular bit of fringe. Bertha Benkard's daughter, Mrs. Reginald Rose, marveled at her mother's ability to be as fascinated with another person's house as with her own, but she believed her mother's enthusiasm to have been entirely genuine. This remarkable woman was selfless to an extraordinary degree; there may have been some truth in Dana Taylor's opinion that "the boss wore the poor woman out, he just figured that he had energy, & everybody else did too." But there is no doubt of the deep devotion between them.

Bertha's existence was likewise a boon to my mother in that she, along with Marian Coffin, supported Harry's interests in ways that my mother could never have managed. And since neither was ever a rival to her, her gratitude was wholehearted.

☙ · CHAPTER 18 · ❧

The Masterpiece Within

W
HEN did Henry Francis du Pont begin to think of turning his Winterthur collection into a museum? Like many subjects, this one was never discussed at home, and with only fragmentary documentation, any answer must be speculative. Perhaps the question could be phrased differently: how do ideas originate, coalesce, and ultimately assert themselves as clear-cut decisions?

There is ample evidence that in the late 1920s, Harry du Pont envisioned making a museum of Chestertown House. In 1927 he had asked Henry Sleeper for information about Mrs. John Lowell Gardner's will—specifically, its provisions for the disposition and maintenance of her Boston house as the Isabella Stewart Gardner Museum. He wanted to know whether it was left in trust or as a company with directors, and he added, "I am thinking of doing something of the kind with my Southampton house."

In 1930, ostensibly for tax purposes, my father established Chestertown House as an educational foundation, to be known as the Henry F. du Pont Chestertown House Museum. He drew up a thirty-page memorandum which is fascinating in that it anticipates much of Harry's thinking about the museum-to-be in Delaware. He wants the Southampton house and its surroundings "kept in perpetuity for the education and enjoyment of the public. . . . Nothing shall be roped off. . . . I shall want the spirit of the house maintained as if someone were living in it." Men and women guards, "suitably dressed . . . must not look at visitors as if they were robbers." The curator should be chosen for, among other attributes, his "ability as a decora-tor . . . [since] a push here and poke there [can] make things look right."[1]

This document contained pages of explicit directions as to which sets of china and glass were to be displayed and where: "If not enough room in the closets . . . I think the little bathroom . . . & my private wine closet had better be gutted. . . . My valet's pressing room is also to be turned into a dis-play room for the rest of my Pennsylvania Dutch China, etc." There were equally explicit provisions for flowers: the locations for twenty-two pots of ferns, ivy, pink begonias, and dark red geraniums, along with at least nine vases for bouquets in specified places and "3 low bowls of flowers always [to be] kept on the gateleg table #1412 in the Living Room [where] prac-tically no yellow flowers should be used . . . ; they should be mauves, pur-ples & blues." My father was not one to leave anything to chance.

The gradual emergence of his motivations is difficult to trace, but it seems that as the creation of a grander museum at Winterthur began to take shape in his mind, his comparable aspirations for Chestertown House faded. Even though the blueprints of the 1928–31 Winterthur wing give no hint of such an intention, the fact that Harry "had occasion to buy an-other Chestertown paneled room . . . much too sophisticated for the Southampton house"[2] points to the direction of his thinking. And there are further signs that well before the completion of the wing he was indeed contemplating it in terms of a museum, for in February 1930, simultane-ous with the incorporation of Chestertown House, the Winterthur Corpo-ration was also established. Among its listed purposes, which satisfied tax demands (such as ministering to "the aged, the sick, the disabled and the poor," and improving the "physical, mental and moral condition of hu-manity"), a more realistic goal was defined: that of furthering the promo-tion of "departments of knowledge . . . to acquire . . . and administer real and personal property as . . . for a museum or museums." This was more like it, and interestingly, in the same week a letter to Beverley Robinson re-quested the deletion of several paragraphs from the Southampton memo-randum. One of them contained the telling phrase: "whether or not my Winterthur house becomes a museum."

"Whether or not"; Henry F. du Pont seems to have been undergoing a rare period of indecision, and, private person that he was, to have chosen to keep his fantasies to himself. The timing could hardly have been worse; the

Southampton house was only four years old, and the huge Winterthur wing, entailing great upheavals for family and staff, was not nearly finished. Not least to be considered was the matter of expense. The Depression was fast becoming a reality, and although my father had not been overwhelmed by it, it had taken its toll, even raising, as noted, the possibility of a mortgage for Winterthur. Would it not be preposterous to contemplate yet another enormously ambitious project just then? How could such a notion be justified to the world, let alone to his wife or even to himself?

Three letters of the time suggest that my father was striving to put to rest any grand schemes that he may have been harboring. A letter of 1931 to Francis P. Garvan, the distinguished collector of silver, attempted to indicate that his collecting days had reached a stopping point. "In the way of furniture, all I need is two small early pine tables . . . a small Chippendale bed, and a very small ball-and-claw-foot table. Of course I might fall for some unusual piece of furniture that might turn up. I am very anxious also to get two eighteenth-century prints or engravings that are wider than they are high." In a similar vein, he wrote to Marian Coffin that "the house here is practically finished, every curtain and chair material is settled upon." And the next year in a letter to Thomas Waterman, soon before their first meeting, he wrote, "My house here is entirely finished." Although in retrospect these words sound ridiculous, there is no reason to believe that my father was disingenuous when he wrote them.

No matter how one interprets these letters—as expressions of "protesting too much" or as ineffectual efforts on Harry's part to talk himself out of further action—it is evident that he was not able for long either to suppress the masterpiece within him or to keep it entirely secret. Early in 1933, his family having been reestablished in the new Winterthur for less than two years, he sent another long memorandum to his Robinson cousin acknowledging his frank intention of creating a museum at Winterthur and of appointing as curator "Mrs. H. H. Benkard . . . should she be available at the time." The memorandum (which he had first drafted in 1930 and probably discussed with Bertha Benkard and no one else) spelled out with the zeal and phenomenal attention to detail of its earlier Southampton model such adaptations and conversions to the existing house as he thought would be necessary to make the museum-dream a reality.[3]

Although Harry's collecting continued apace, no further mention of Winterthur as a museum appeared until September 1938, when he referred to it as such in a letter to William Sumner Appleton, founder of the Society for the Preservation of New England Antiquities. The idea apparently was not again put into writing until 1941, this time in a letter to his sister; the new rooms are "practical for living purposes & from a museum point of view."

Several developments in the preceding years had helped to sharpen my father's focus. The context of one of these—in the unlikely form of a fundraising project for the Girl Scouts of America—was a loan exhibition of American antiques. This major show of furniture and decorative arts, organized in a New York gallery, offered my father a unique opportunity not only to lend objects but also to assume responsibility for the arrangement of displays in the numerous rooms. The Girl Scouts Loan Exhibition of 1929 marked the first public recognition of Harry's expertise in the field (and was to boot of great benefit for scouting.)

Another pivotal influence of the time was that Henry Sleeper, indispensable during the construction of Chestertown House, had been less than helpful when it came to the new wing at Winterthur. Consequently my father "had to spend a great many hours of time in research, looking through the Metropolitan Museum, and public library books, in addition to having the illustrations photostated, etc . . . The whole load of fixing the house has fallen upon me." Although he was angry with Sleeper for his waning interest, what Harry nonetheless learned as a result of his enforced scholarship and "on the job" training certainly contributed to his personal growth. A third factor of importance to Harry's education at the time was his election in 1932 to the Walpole Society. This organization, founded in 1910 for collectors and students of Americana, introduced him to a small and distinguished group of fellow enthusiasts. Requirement for membership included "distinction in the collecting of early American objects of the decorative arts and other arts, attainment through study or experience in the knowledge of these arts; and the social qualifications essential to the well-being of a group of like-minded persons."[4]

As the last clause implies, the society was not a democratic one. Membership at that time was limited to men, evidently white Anglo-Saxon Protestants of a "broad general culture which stamps a gentleman and a

The Beverley Robinsons' house, New York, 1880s, full of the Victorian
woodwork and furnishings that Harry so "heartily disliked" in his youth.

scholar."[5] I daresay that this proviso did not disturb Harry at all, and he was
elated indeed by the encomiums of his fellow members after their first visit
to Winterthur: "[In a short account] it would be quite impossible to do justice to this collection."[6] (As a child, I myself was especially taken by the
"quizing glass" and "gorget" that were part of every Walpolean's quaint
equipment.[7])

The evolution of Winterthur from a country house to a museum between 1931 and 1951 gained momentum from my father's dissatisfaction
with the contrast between his new American wing and the older house. The
look of pink china against pine wood had startled Harry into his first awareness of the appeal of simpler effects; the wood of an eighteenth-century

American dresser differed greatly from the "heartily disliked" Empire mahogany of his youth from which the veneer always "dropped off."[8]

My father wrote that a powerful force driving a collector is a love of his materials. I think that he had a particular reverence for wood, especially pine, maple, walnut, and fruitwoods. From childhood on, he had noticed trees; discovering a bird's nest in the low branches of a magnolia was one of his earliest memories. His building plans always took into account the need to preserve the trees, and he had lightning rods installed on many of them. Late in life, when it seemed clear that he would outlive the tulip poplar that towered by his bedroom, he made sure that its removal would take place when he was far away. I have already mentioned his perhaps apocryphal remark that saving the trees at Winterthur should be the first priority of firemen.

Awareness of wood became a part of my father's makeup, and much of the house-to-museum evolution is based on it. From the beginning, the period and quality of a room's woodwork determined how it would be furnished. The removal of interior woodwork from old houses was already an established art, and, thanks to the gifted Winterthur carpenters, my father early on had collected and put into storage the components of a number of them. The huge museum now enfolds innumerable elements from old houses, incorporating them into its own structure. The facade of one of the four buildings in the courtyard, for example, is the transplanted front wall of Montmorenci, the North Carolina house whose spiral staircase was already a dazzling display at the opposite end of the museum. Other pieces of Montmorenci woodwork contribute to the elegance of two other rooms and a hall. Interior woodwork from Port Royal not only created the 1931 Entrance Hall and Port Royal Parlor but was also put to use in the Port Royal and Maple bedrooms. With woodwork from Belle Isle, a mid-eighteenth-century house in Litwalton, Virginia, two more bedrooms were built, along with an unusually high dado for the Bertrand Room, woodwork for a part of my father's suite, and a small staircase. Thus, elements of wood from individual houses were dispersed and integrated into far-flung parts of the museum, creating in it a kind of organic weave.

In contrast to the 1929–31 addition, completed with lightning speed, the great shift of the next twenty years—entirely halted, of course, dur-

Facade of Montmorenci in North Carolina.

ing World War II—occurred little by little. As worthy interiors became available, the shapes of rooms were modified; the removal of closets and bathrooms permitted the installation of new-found period woodwork and ceilings and the creation of alcoves for folk art and for china, hardware, or glass. This gradual remodeling of the house began to display the shift in American life from the seventeenth century to the federal period two hundred years later.

Jay Cantor remarks of this time that "Winterthur had taken on an identity of its own. It had become a devouring passion consuming [Henry Francis du Pont's] time & resources. It was his creation & he was trying to make it perfect.[9]

The installation of the Montmorenci staircase was an early example of the drive to perfection, as was the dismantling of the adjoining Red Room, as our family continued to call it, even after the red damask wall covering had been made into curtains. My father exulted in the transformation of this space (where my mother had once hidden from the unwelcome caller) into a room rebuilt with woodwork from a 1744 Maryland house; the paneling and windows happened to fit almost exactly.

During these two decades, changes in the house pointed more and more to the museum it would become. My father was exhilarated to learn in 1940 that the dimensions of the billiard room and the squash court directly below it were suitable for conversion to seventeenth- and eighteenth-century interiors, and he arranged for installation of three new rooms in the former squash court on two floors connected by the Belle Isle staircase.[10] In 1940 the eighth floor gained eleven eighteenth-century rooms,[11] small staircases from Connecticut, Pennsylvania, and Virginia,[12] and a 1690 door from central New York, all of which were carried up on a specially built outside elevator. During the following year, six more rooms, two halls, and a china alcove were fitted into former closets and bathrooms. In Morattico, Virginia, Thomas Waterman discovered the woodwork from a 1715 plantation house stored in the attic of a new house on the same property. With this woodwork, the former billiard room was transformed and happily reunited with a wood-paneled landscape of a stag hunt that my father had bought from the original house eleven years earlier.

During World War II, life at Winterthur of course changed radically; many staff members entered active service or went to work in factories; buses and car pools replaced the Cadillacs, and an old horse was harnessed again to his carriage. When the war ended, however, my father's zeal resurfaced at once. Perhaps the most dramatic changes of this era were the dismantling of the badminton court and the bowling alleys, favorite recreation spots for me for almost two decades. Whether or not my father, with his minimal interest in these sports, had imagined other uses for them when they were conceived, his memorandum of 1933 leaves no doubt about his later intentions. The spaces seemed made to order for transformation, respectively, into a cobblestoned courtyard and a collection of shopfronts, with room for the interiors of two actual shops as well.

Du Pont and Waterman were a good team. They trusted and admired each other, and my father's emphasis on aesthetics complemented the architect's demand for authenticity. Waterman's academic background and his belief in the importance of historical accuracy now influenced much of

Harry's thinking; this association, as well as his sister's interests, may also have encouraged his increasing sensitivity to the need for historic preservation. Although he never interfered with organized preservation efforts, in the 1920s Harry had had little compunction about buying woodwork from people willing to sell it. Residents of Maryland's Eastern Shore were later angry at what they sometimes viewed as a plundering of their houses, and the Pennsylvania German owners of a hotel in Berks County refused to serve lunch to Winterthur carpenters whose mission was to tear down one of their beloved landmarks.[13]

With increased sensitivity to the issue, however, my father restricted himself to buying only buildings or architectural details of buildings that were destined to be demolished. He was happy to have saved the 1795 Bulfinch Stairs from destruction, as well as a shop window in downtown New York; and he enjoyed rescuing an 1800 curved settee, which a New Hampshire family had intended to cut up into chairbacks.[14] Harry's satisfaction in saving treasures from oblivion became a vital part of his philosophy of collecting.

Developing gradually throughout the 1930s, my father's wish to create, to preserve, to make a difference had crystallized in the 1940s in his decision to establish the Henry Francis du Pont Winterthur Museum. Now in his sixties, with no son to carry on his name, and with daughters neither equipped nor eager to maintain Winterthur as a family home, it was clear to him that his lifelong work both outdoors and in his collection would best represent the perpetuation of his name and would be the finest of legacies to the country. As early as 1943, when the director of the National Gallery, David E. Finley, explored the possibility that Winterthur might be left to that museum, my father replied that "the collection has already been provided for."

In 1948, when life after World War II had again settled, my father began to plan for the future, with much of the transformation of house to museum already accomplished. Joseph Downs and Charles F. Montgomery had been appointed curator and assistant curator half-time, with the preliminary task of preparing a comprehensive catalogue of the collection. And Thomas Waterman, although he was by then in failing health, drew up plans for a new house beside the Clenny Run bridge where my parents would live after the museum opened.

When my father—perhaps because of his dislike of drawn-out farewells—had set dates rather suddenly for opening the museum and moving to the new house, the efforts of the curators had to be diverted to coping with this revised schedule, and the building crew was instructed to complete the new residence with all possible speed. Shortly after the start of the Korean War, a letter of September 1950 to Eugene Grace, president of the Bethlehem Steel Company, splendidly illustrates the imperiousness and impatience that my father was not always successful in concealing: "I ordered my steel long before Korea . . . and they kept putting it off all the time until I am really quite desperate. . . . If you could do something to expedite this I will be eternally grateful."

My parents left their house—the family homestead for 112 years—in January 1951. There were not many backward glances, for life in the evolving museum had become increasingly complicated. Although during the transition my father sometimes stayed in a newly constructed building on the place, he and my mother spent most of the next months in Florida, Southampton, or in a much smaller apartment in New York, which they shared with my sister and her family. (After World War II, 280 Park Avenue was razed and replaced by an office building.) With the move into their new house on the Winterthur grounds in mid-October 1951, my father's earliest collection of French and English furniture, in storage since its years in the first New York apartment, was returned to use and seemed again very much at home.[15]

⇔ · CHAPTER 19 · ⇔

The Museum Opens

LTHOUGH several of its rooms had been available to the public by special permission for almost ten years, the Henry Francis du Pont Winterthur Museum did not open officially until the last day of October 1951. I can only guess at my father's feelings on this occasion, but pride and happiness laced with nostalgia and perhaps sadness must have been an important part of them. I felt these myself—as well as dismay, when Charles Montgomery's fifteen-year-old son, following orders, first barred me from the elevator and then escorted me to the Albany Room, my own bedroom, to which I had naively hoped to bid a private farewell.

Response to the museum's opening was phenomenal and unexpected. Requests for reservations poured in, tickets were at a premium for two years, and the swamped secretarial staff was unable to keep up. Despite its fine launching, the museum was far from finished. Remaining bathrooms, closets, and service areas had to be removed to make way for many more period installations,[1] a process hastened by my father's foresight, for full-scale mock-ups of these rooms containing their ultimate furnishings were already in place in a storage facility called the Gray Building. Three of the rooms came from mid-eighteenth-century rural Pennsylvania and illustrated arts and architecture brought to this country by early German colonists: the Fraktur Room, which displayed samples of nineteenth-century illuminated manuscripts, and the Kershner Parlor and Kershner Kitchen, which included an enormous fireplace. The installation of the two Kershner rooms in 1958, the last to be completed in the museum proper, also clearly demonstrated my father's receptiveness to new ideas, for, to his satisfaction, they replaced the Pine Kitchen of 1931, whose Windsor chairs and hooked rugs represented "everybody's idea of what 'Early American' should be."[2] This massive undertaking required the jacking up of a chimney six stories high and the removal of twelve inches from a solid stone wall.

By the time the museum entered its eighth year, it was clear that the existing building could not begin to accommodate the growing number of staff and visitors, especially school groups. A major expansion was built onto the south end of the previous addition; it included a small library and lecture hall and a dozen new chronologically arranged period rooms. The installation of a woodworking shop, used between 1757 and 1864 by the Dominy family, Long Island cabinetmakers and clockmakers, gave the museum still another dimension. Not only did the shop exhibit unique craftmanship but, perhaps more important, along with the Kershner Kitchen, it provided an authentic look at a simpler and more representative kind of American life.

My father was in his element. He was especially delighted to promote the developments that involved material changes, and he took pleasure in later ones—the installation of two Shaker rooms, an air-conditioning system for the entire museum, and large spaces for the storage of carpets, bedspreads, and curtains. (In many rooms, fabrics were changed with the seasons.) Two years before he died, he began construction of a superb library with research and conservation facilities, to be named for his sister.

The Henry Francis du Pont Winterthur Museum owed its early development to several people whose thinking extended its creator's outlook: Thomas Waterman in the 1940s emphasized the importance of historical accuracy and architectural conservation, and Joseph Downs and Charles Montgomery buttressed these concepts with academic standards of their own. Downs was appointed first curator of the Winterthur collection in 1949, a position he held until his death five years later. At that time, Charles Montgomery assumed the management of the operation with the title of director. He saw his task as moving the museum beyond the confines of a private collection to a position of national stature. He hoped to counteract my father's tendency to concentrate on the trees rather than on the forest, a tendency exemplified in the previously mentioned memorandum begun in 1930 and expanded over many years.[3] These eighty pages made clear my father's wish for the house to retain a lived-in atmosphere, but they are mainly composed of inventories and gratuitous recommendations, such as ways for disposing of old newspapers or carrying chairs. Other instructions deal with how to acknowledge letters or greet resident professors. Montgomery prayed for tact in his efforts to enlarge his boss's approach "from personal whim to scholarly accuracy," from the concept of a house built "block by block" to the "grand design of a dream." As we shall see, he was notably successful, especially in helping my father to recognize the importance to the museum of developing a strong educational element.

Unlike my mother, who often said that no matter what else happened in life, people should strive for the best possible education, my father for many years had a blind spot on the subject. Although he always valued scholarly advice, perhaps because of his own miseries in academe he seemed never to have given education per se much thought. This had earlier been apparent to me when I approached him about my wish to go to college. His surprised first question was, "How old will you be at the end of it?" I saw his relief when he realized that, after graduation at the age of twenty-one, I would not necessarily be condemned to bluestocking spinsterhood. Perhaps my college experience helped him pay closer attention to the advice of the curators. Whatever his reasons, he responded enthusiastically to an idea of momentous importance to Winterthur.

In the summer before the museum opened, Charles Montgomery suggested to my father with trepidation that the Winterthur Museum and the University of Delaware collaborate to create a graduate program in American arts and cultural history. As it turned out, Montgomery need not have worried; my father "literally clapped his hands and said, 'Obviously we have to do it!'" With the endorsement of the Winterthur board of trustees and a $5,000 gift from Louise Crowninshield for the first two of five fellowships, the program was launched in 1952 and has flourished ever since; Wilmarth S. (Lefty) Lewis, the scholarly editor of the writings of Horace Walpole, some years later remarked that its graduates "have a certain nimbus about them." As of August 1998, 371 individuals had earned master's degrees from the Winterthur Program in Early American Culture, and 209 had graduated from the Winterthur–University of Delaware Program in Art Conservation. Twenty-six of these had gone on to obtain Ph.D. degrees.

Over 75 percent were working in the field, and more than half were at the top of their profession, in such positions as curators, museum directors, professors, art conservationists, or department heads in major institutions throughout the country. My father wrote in his document, "I really believe this phase of the Museum program is quite as important as the Museum itself. Years after all the books on the Museum have been written I feel that the training and education of these young people at Winterthur will make the Museum a living force through the ages."[4]

Charles Hummel and Jonathan Fairbanks, leading figures in the field, respectively referred to the seminal nature and profound influence of the fellowship program.[5] Not only did Charles Montgomery initiate this direction for the museum, but during his stay he instituted many other vital activities.[6] Jay Cantor wrote that he "possessed the vision of a dreamer and the necessary cunning and skill to achieve his goals. . . . If du Pont ever came to regret the hardheadedness he had admired it was only because he found in Montgomery a similarly committed and intractable personality."[7] If they were sometimes at swords' point, the two men nonetheless complemented, admired, and trusted one another. Montgomery extolled my father's visual memory, his sense of proportion and color, his discipline and drive—but perhaps above all he valued his ability to entertain new ideas. Montgomery gave Harry full credit for endorsing the concept of the Winterthur program, a wholehearted affirmation that suggested no uneasiness that it might outshine his own basic creation. And my father entirely reciprocated the appreciation.

❧ · CHAPTER 20 · ❧

Private and Public

W HEN Harry came home to stay in 1903, the big new house must have been lonely indeed without his mother's warmth and vitality. Even then, Winterthur's size, liveried staff, and general formality provoked amused comparisons to Buckingham Palace. Despite the Colonel's deep interest in his ancestry, he seems to have been cut from a cloth different from other members of his family.

Unlike the dedicated Delawareans whose professional lives were invested in the manufacture of explosives, Henry A. worked only half-time at the powder mills. Beyond the confines of Winterthur, he directed his energies to railroad administration, politics, and out-of-state ventures. A continuing contact with French cousins, visits to his mother's summer homes in New Jersey and Massachusetts, and marriage to a New Yorker—whom he had met in Newport—all diverted his attention from Delaware. Furthermore, he increasingly sought satisfaction in public recognition, as through the Medal of Honor, the Senate, and the publication of books and articles. One can imagine that this autocratic, intellectual man, a stickler for manners, who tended toward ceremony and snobbism, was offputting to his more genial and down-to-earth relatives.

I believe it is fair to say that my father himself, although on very close terms with two or three cousins, never became an integral part of the larger Delaware family network. His innate shyness, his absence at school and college over a period of ten years, and his unusual ties to his widowed father were all contributing factors. Certainly throughout his bachelorhood

Harry could be viewed as the quintessence of filial loyalty. He lived in his father's house and moved with him to Washington, managing both households; he went to Europe with him every summer. The Colonel likened Harry's "even temperament" to that of his own father, Henry the Red. Whereas no hint of rebellion or even discontent appears in any record, many years' worth of correspondence reflects Henry's remarkable role as a son. A bread-and-butter letter to Harry, written a year before his marriage, speaks of the "absolute perfection and enchantment" of the garden, and continues, "Will you let me say to you—that I think you are very wonderful in the way you have filled your mother's place making these days of your father's life so happy, so content, in a way I have never seen any other men do. Yet with all this, you have your own strong individuality, are filling so well your own place in this world of ours, that I know your mother would be very proud of you."

I believe that Harry's responsibilities at home, stemming from his mother's death and his father's demands, further set him apart from the camaraderie of his sports-minded cousins. Having never enjoyed riding, hunting, or shooting, my father found little common ground with them, nor did he share their business interests, for many of them worked for the Du Pont Company. It is no wonder that he did not want to broadcast his own "job"—that of house manager for his father! Furthermore, he had little taste for their practical jokes, perhaps because he had been the butt of several of them. Years later cousins remembered an occasion when Harry, about eight years old and dressed in a lace collar and corduroys, "fell" into a pile of manure on an afternoon visit to their house.[1] With the appearance of automobiles, poor Harry was at a further loss, for the others quickly learned to drive. Harry's college roommate, Eugene E. du Pont, was even to build a car of his own from scratch. Perhaps the most flattering description of my father in those days—an observation by Eugene's grandson—was that he was a "separate entity."

What helped to save Harry at this time was his involvement in activities specific to Winterthur—horticulture and cattle breeding—interests shared by his father and more typically pursued by members of an older generation. His concentration in these fields probably distanced him still further from his contemporaries.

I suspect that Harry's shyness was at its worst with his Delaware cousins, for a Boston friend of Louise's, at Winterthur in 1904 for a visit, wrote about her "nice younger brother ... such an easy friendly person [who] has a great sense of humor and is a most thoughtful host."[2] He had driven her all around in the carriage and arranged for numerous boxes of lilies-of-the-valley to be sent to wherever she chose.

My father's reputation among many family members did not much improve until he was older, and his lifestyle to some was forever a source of amusement. In 1924, the Colonel's erstwhile enemy Alfred du Pont joked in a letter to his sister: "I found [my relatives] most entertaining and, in particular, Harry, whom I described as the only decent milkmaid the family had ever produced."[3] Much later still, a teen-aged cousin on a scavenger hunt, charged with collecting the signature of the "crankiest person around," went directly to obtain that of Henry F. du Pont. To most outsiders, Winterthur for many years—even after the museum had opened—remained a mystery, a myth, a forbidding place presided over by an eccentric autocrat who, as one rumor had it, had ripped out the whole first floor of his house to put some old shop fronts into it.

Interviews conducted by John A. H. Sweeney present a very different picture. After my father's death, Sweeney, who had become his devoted friend, especially in Harry's last years, interviewed at length forty-seven people who had been closely connected with him in some way. Since almost half of them had lived and worked on the place, Sweeney hoped to capture the essence of Winterthur during my father's lifetime and of the man himself. These transcribed interviews, like a series of snapshots seen together, provide a rich and intimate background against which Harry's real world and Harry himself come to life in a unique way.

Winterthur was once home to fifty or so families who lived in clusters of houses on the property, some of them before gaslight, privies, and carriages had given way to electricity, plumbing, and cars.[4] The men and women with whom Sweeney talked plunged eagerly into memories of their childhood. For the men, a first job was that of "water boy," bringing jugs to thirsty gardeners, and later they joined a lawn or weed gang. "Oh, those dandelions." Howard Lattomus, born on the place in 1907, remembered Harry's comforting him (with mud as well as words) after a hornet sting. In succession, Howard dug up weeds, milked cows, cultivated corn walking behind a horse, happily graduated to the carpentry shop, where he spent years as a true craftsman, and ultimately became Winterthur's superintendent. Young people growing up at Winterthur had interchangeable tasks; they caddied, drove trucks, and worked on the farm, on construction, in the gardens, or on the tree gang until they found their particular skill, in which they often became expert. "Every man has his skill," my father said.

Their memories go back a long way: to a faded photograph of the coachman, the postmistress' husband, whose uniform with black-banded sleeve suggested widespread mourning for the lovely Pauline; to the fast carriage horses, a dozen or more, and heavier ones for the farm, a Percheron or two with feathery feet, teams for the long-tailed wagons, until the tractors displaced them. There were lambs to be kept warm and taught to nurse, and yearlings whose fleece was sheared and sold. And pigs—iron shots for the newborns, always anemic, whose wolf-needle teeth had to be clipped for the sow's sake. My father loved the pig farm, especially the smallest pigs, and the spectacle of boar mounting sow. These farms, regularly visited by him, made up "Harry's other garden."[5] He loved the poultry farm as well, its Buff Orpingtons and Rhode Island Reds, its doves and wattled turkeys, its guinea hens and their scurrying young.

But most of all Harry prized the cow barn and the magnificent bull he bought in 1917, King of the Ormsbys, the "herd sire & . . . backbone of the Winterthur breeding program" for fifty years.[6] Toward the middle of the century, as the technique was perfected, vials of frozen semen were sold for $1,000 apiece. Winterthur cows annually broke records for milk quantity and butterfat content, won gold medals and national awards, and were shipped all over the world—to Japan, Australia, Puerto Rico, Europe. Pediatricians recommended Winterthur's as the only milk in the area that needed no pasteurization. Harry devised his own system of identification for the seventy-five calves born every year, which included the names of sire and dam's sire and finally the calf's own seven-letter name. Each year the calves' names began with a new letter. The procedure was not helped by my father's inability to spell. By 1932, "Q" had appeared, but neither Groton nor Harvard had taught Harry the Romance language custom of following it with a "U." Consequently, the calf crop of 1932 had an Arabic flavor, with a Qohanna, a Qormsby, and my favorite, Qobsgrl, in which that girl was deprived of two vowels.

The vegetable farmers and their wives were attentive to their boss's preferences, including his wish that a new vegetable be tried every spring. Cardoon, sorrel, celtus—was it that one, I wonder, that tasted faintly of skunk? Harry experimented with types of miniature corn. "The man had something about him you didn't want to disappoint." Strawberries seemed to ripen especially for his birthday and eggplant for his summer visits. He was "crazy about vegetables"—asparagus, tiny peas, okra, and Jerusalem artichokes with blossoms like small sunflowers. Rhubarb and spinach. Plum jam. Refrigeration replaced ice houses, and some freezers were big enough to walk into. "Oh, man, it was nice to see those things all stacked pretty on the shelves."

The flower gardeners remembered their boss with admiration and awe, and they believed that no one else could put together such color combinations. Lavender and scarlet, dark azaleas beneath white and pink dogwood. The bronze of some year-round leaves had to be considered. "He saw the whole picture and made you see it, too." My father's notebooks, in which he recorded the creation of his peony gardens of the 1950s, illustrate an uncanny sensitivity to color. A list of thirty-two colors of peonies covered a spectrum from "milk white, ivory white & wax white" through "palest flesh, pale salmon & deep bright rose pink" to "shining scarlet, dark mahogany & dark red." The gardeners claimed that my father had made horticultural history; plants thrived at his bidding, even though they had been rooted "at the wrong time" or against recommendations, rooted rather than grafted, or transplanted when in bloom. "Because of his insistence, we found that most of the books are wrong."

The people working in the house and museum, like those who worked outdoors, had many skills. They could hang curtains, position rugs and furniture, and construct cardboard mock-ups of furniture, rooms, and even whole buildings. They marveled at Mr. du Pont's grasp of detail, his thoroughness, and his drive. "He didn't postpone things, he did them immediately." And very often he got into the act himself. An observer at the Girl Scouts Loan Exhibition of 1929 told of seeing Harry in shirt sleeves "looking like a hod carrier [and] working much harder than any of the others . . .

The completed Winterthur barn complex, 1920. It burned down in 1930. The house is in the background.

Henry F. du Pont in Azalea Woods at Winterthur, 1958.

hanging pictures and straightening out things. He had a corps of . . . people under him but worked like a slave."[7] This description would not have surprised the museum staff.

The carpenters and painters spoke almost reverentially both of their craft and of the man who inspired it. Carpentry involved doors, window frames and sashes, paneling, and flower tubs. There were miles of lumber for floors and trim from trees felled during the chestnut blight. Wallpapering and painting turned into an art form. Park McCann, a master painter, made and mixed his paint from scratch and, working closely with my father for forty years, shared his acute awareness of subtleties of color and his desire to capture and reproduce original tones. McCann seemed to understand his boss's thinking. "He wanted it to look like blue, but he didn't want it blue." He remembered one particular Saturday when, with guests soon to arrive, McCann gave up his plan of going to the races and instead put fast-drying paint on the walls of a newly installed room. The boss was "tickled pink," he said, using a painter's metaphor. He added, "He treated me like a man all the time."

Besides his valet, the chauffeurs, successors to the coachmen, probably were in closest contact with my father. The job had its drawbacks, given the dress code (leggings and gloves) and the tedious hours of waiting—"You didn't dare leave; the minute you left, he'd pop out"—and the extremes of heat and cold before big Cadillacs had enclosed front seats. But aside from these problems and my father's bouts of impatience, there were compensations. Dana Taylor (who after fifty-two years perhaps knew my father best of all) said, "He was an awful good man. He was a prince. He'd fly off the handle and get mad, and the next five minutes, it's over, forgot. On the whole, he was a wonderful man."

More than one person at Winterthur described the boss as "genuine," and as a man who seemed to make people want to do better. They were warmed by my father's gratitude and his willingness to listen to other people's ideas. He valued honesty and fairness and embodied these virtues himself. They spoke of his caring for the truth and his quickness to forgive. "If you broke something and told him about it, it was all right." He was quoted as saying, "Everybody makes mistakes, and if you do, come and tell me immediately." They admired and envied his energy—"Man, you couldn't keep up with him"—and reminisced about the meetings held in his room at 6:30 in the morning, attended by his valet, Dana (who brought and opened the mail), the butler, a gardener or two, and often a farm representative and the golf pro. They appreciated my father's capacity for work, his directness, and his decisiveness; there was no need to guess how he felt about any subject. They recognized with amusement his annoyance at pretension and obsequiousness; he liked to be leveled with and stood up to. Once, he questioned the odd location of a farmhouse bathroom and was told by Howard Lattomus, "It was put in by someone as contrary as you—your father." Harry laughed.

These men and women often thought of my father as an associate, a mentor, or, in some cases, a parent. They valued his interest in them and their families, and they cited numerous instances of his quiet help—with telephone calls to doctors, loans of a car and driver, funds for nursing homes or college tuition. The high morale at Winterthur stemmed from my father's presence and his policies. Winterthur was a good place to live. Residents bought most of their food there, at wholesale prices; milk was seven cents a quart and beef "pretty near free." In the 1920s, when the 450 cows were still being milked by hand four times a day, my father put in a baseball field, organized teams, provided uniforms, and built a clubhouse. He encouraged dances as well as the formation of an orchestra from local talent.

The Colonel and Harry instituted a Christmas event that soon became known as "Mr. Harry's party." First held in the squash court decorated with a beautiful tree, the parties were subsequently moved to the bigger clubhouse and later still to the Visitors Pavilion. These affairs featured entertainment by a magician, a ventriloquist, marionettes, or trained animals. Afterward came ice cream and cake and presents for all ages—sleds and bicycles and big dolls for the little ones, handbags and wallets for teenagers, and money or food for adults (turkeys, fruit, nuts, and candy). During the Depression, two chickens were substituted for the turkey. My father invested much energy in these parties, chose the entertainment, and bought the presents himself—first at Bloomingdale's, and in later years at Wanamaker's in Philadelphia, where the manager allowed him to shop after hours. The year before he died, he had 219 presents ready for distribution.

The Christmas parties symbolized the spirit of Winterthur and were mentioned by almost everyone interviewed. One man seemed to speak for the others as he described Winterthur not only as a "wonderful place to bring up children" but as a "surprising place, with so much loyalty to it." At my father's funeral, just as the service ended, his elderly valet rose to straighten the spray of white orchids and baby's breath on the evergreens that blanketed his coffin. For several years after his death gardeners first swept leaves or snow from paths my father would have taken on his early-morning walks.

With the opening of the Winterthur Museum to the public in 1951, Henry F. du Pont and his accomplishments began to gain national recognition. As a result, the opinion of cousins and other acquaintances, who had once derided him and his way of life, also began to change. The minister observed, "It was wonderful to watch when Harry was definitely in the saddle," and commented on the disappointment of those who were not invited to parties or museum events. Vindictiveness was never a part of my father's makeup, but remembering his own earlier rebuffs, he must have permitted himself some pleasure in giving preference on the guest list to the people who had shown interest and confidence in his aspirations and successes from the start. The harshest criticism I ever heard him make about another person was, "He never grew up." Several friends and relatives interviewed by Sweeney noted their belief that Harry du Pont, and Winterthur, had in fact helped this part of Delaware to emerge from an earlier day—to "grow up." "He held onto something here which you might call 'civilization' in a way that the others weren't able to do, and it enriched this community culturally."

Passionately immersed as he was in activities at home—gardens, farm, museum—Harry gave much of himself elsewhere as well, as attested by numerous tributes he received in the last twenty years of his life. These ranged from a low-key commendation from the Southampton Historical Society for help with an old house to honorary degrees from seven colleges and universities for his "taste, scholarship and patriotism" (Yale); "exquisite taste and great respect for historic accuracy" (Williams); his creation of a "living museum of our country's civilization and heritage" and his "knowledge and extensive interest in horticulture and botany" (University of Pennsylvania). The University of Delaware, on whose board my father had served as a life trustee since 1917, in citing his "discerning taste and farsighted design" recognized his contributions to agriculture, horticulture, education, and the arts. Doubtless because of its location in du Pont-land, it somewhat misguidedly saluted as well his "notable career in industry." So in part did Pratt Institute, which hailed his "unequalled leadership in such varied fields as finance, horticulture, and decorative arts."

But the museum was at the heart of every academic citation with the exception of the one from Sunshine University in Pinellas County, Florida. Sunshine University gave my father his only degree as doctor of philosophy "in the Field of modern industry." Although my father had faithfully attended more than twenty-five years of monthly meetings of the finance committees of both the Du Pont Company and General Motors, his strengths did not lie there. I believe that Sunshine University had the wrong man. In 1957 a medal bestowed on him by the Preservation Society of Newport Colony had ironic overtones, for one Newport acquaintance was more than once heard to remark that Henry F. du Pont had "stolen" some eighteenth-century woodwork from a local landmark. He had, in fact, saved the woodwork from certain destruction.

The honors that my father received suggest the extent of his involvement in activities away from Winterthur, several of which were specifically horticultural. In 1947 the Horticultural Society of New York cited him, its president of eleven years, for a "task well done" and for his "guidance through the most trying years of the Society's life." The Pennsylvania Horticultural Society awarded him its Certificate of Merit; the New York Botanical Garden, on whose board he had served for seventeen years, gave him the Distinguished Service Award, especially mentioning his "incalculable aid with the general landscaping of [its] grounds"; and the Garden Club of America in 1956, calling him "one of the best, even the best gardener this country has produced," commended his services and gave him its Medal of Honor. My father, in response, reported that his current crop of eighteen thousand narcissus bulbs "of my own division" had been planted exactly according to the method he had devised forty years earlier, in which dry tree branches of different sizes, tossed on the ground, determined the shapes of the beds.

Capping the championships won for decades by Winterthur Farms cows, my father in his early eighties was gratified to be recognized as an expert in farming. For two consecutive years he received the Holstein-Friesian Association of America's top honor, the Progressive Breeder's Registry Award, "in recognition of achievement through an improved breeding program based on production testing, type classification, and herd health for the advancement of Holstein-Friesian cattle."[8]

These tributes of course meant a great deal to Henry F. du Pont, as did two that brought him especially close to his sister. The George McAneny Historic Preservation Medal of the American Scenic and Historic Preservation Society, given to Harry in 1956 and mentioning the American ideals that inspired the creation of Winterthur, had been awarded to Louise ten years earlier.[9] And in 1961, the National Trust for Historic Preservation gave my father the Louise du Pont Crowninshield Award established in her memory, which read in part, for "a Museum . . . which provides a commentary on tides of taste . . . a result of more than 40 years of dedication [whose] naturalized setting is another testament to Mr. du Pont's versatility." My father, deeply moved, told a friend that he had thought of Louise every minute throughout the ceremony. An interesting footnote to this occasion was that the award was presented by David E. Finley, who as the director of the National Gallery had delivered the speech at the opening of the Winterthur Museum ten years earlier.

The Ninth Decade

M Y MOTHER, speaking of her eighty-year-old husband, said that she felt like a dachshund running after a greyhound, and indeed, Henry Francis du Pont entered his ninth decade with unabated energy. His letters so attest.

May 14, 1961

I arose [in Providence] at 5:30 on Saturday, and accomplished my visit to the dentist in New York. Ruth and I lunched with the Charles Wrightsmans. She is a member of the Fine Arts Committee for the White House. We got back in time for the wedding, and I still had enough pep left to walk around the Azalea gardens for an hour before dinner.[1]

April 27, 1967 (En route to Winterthur)

The lunch after [the Pacific Tropical Botanical Garden meeting with Brooke Astor, who is on the Board] . . . was very pleasant. After that I went to the Daffodil Show, saw the exhibit "In the Presence of Kings," which is a must, then I went to a party to meet the new Directors, dined with Melissa Bingham and then went to the "Art and Decorator" Show at Wildenstein.

Harry thought nothing of going by car from Washington to New York, keeping engagements in both cities at each end of the five-hour trip. (He did not fly until after his wife's death, knowing how she would worry.) Of course, having a car and chauffeur and all arrangements made in advance by secretaries and others on his staff facilitated his daily life; without them he would have been quite helpless. He was the first to acknowledge that he owed his ability to accomplish a great deal in his long life to the fact that he had "never had to do anything for myself." He told Lloyd Hyde that he had never set foot inside a post office. He told me that had he ever been obliged to pack a suitcase, he would never have left home.

Harry's seemingly endless supply of energy continued until his final illness. In the 1960s, with many projects completed, he turned his attention to the visitors to the museum and gardens, who appeared in increasing numbers. The Pavilion, with a large cafeteria and dining area, a museum shop, and parking spaces, was built amid tall trees in a valley to the west, close by but out of sight of my parents' new house on the bridge. Its location necessitated a new driveway. Having rejected the suggestions of Umberto Innocenti, the landscape architect he originally consulted, Harry spent many hours with men from the farm, driving down grassy hills and through pasturelands to determine how best to connect this new complex with the highway. Sentimental though I was at the eventual closing of the Gatehouse and the long, lovely driveway through the woods, I had to admit that the new entrance to Winterthur was also a romantic one.

The road winds down through hills, passing a tributary of Clenny Run on its right—bordered in the spring by long stretches of candelabra primroses. On the opposite hill thousands of daffodils, staggered as to color and timing of bloom, are massed in cloudlike drifts. The new driveway bisects two ponds created at the same time, now home to wild iris and Canada geese, and leads to the partly glass-enclosed Pavilion, whose size is deceptive. The Wilmington architect Samuel E. Homsey, enjoined to "make it look like it isn't here," admirably approached this ideal, and even the large lecture hall, added later, is unobtrusive.[2] My father praised Homsey's ingenuity in saving all but one tree in this wooded area and placing the major parking lot almost out of sight on land above the Pavilion.

After the great burst of bloom in the spring, visitors who came to Winterthur were sometimes disappointed to find quiet woodland gardens rather than flower beds. As a result, my father set about finding plants that would extend the flowering season in both spring and fall. The question of timing had always fascinated him, as indicated by his earliest notebooks, and in his last years the Winterthur landscape became "one of the most highly articulated embodiments of succession of bloom ever created."[3]

With the public in mind, Harry had already transformed the old tennis and croquet courts, surrounded by enormous boxwood, into a voluptuous, April-blooming space called the Sundial Garden, but now he turned

Clenny Run at Winterthur.

his attention to plants that would carry the burst of spring into summer and fall. With many additions—including late-blooming lilacs and dogwoods, roses, summer-flowering magnolias, mimosa, and drifts of pale lavender autumn colchicum—he incorporated pasture land into the garden proper, expanded earlier plantings, and in general enhanced his creations of sixty years. The March Bank, Peony Garden, Azalea Woods, Winterhazel and Quince Walks, along with Oak Hill and their many companion areas, were lovingly—and perhaps with some little sense of time running out—made ready for year-round visitors. He wanted his garden-landscape to be as satisfying and as near to perfect as his museum.

Harry's last major outdoor effort was the conversion of the old quarry, whose depths and wall caves were my favorite childhood haunt. In this deep, dank, and lonely hollow in the woods, where delicious water spouted from a pipe, where orange and brown speckled newts crept beneath wet leaves, and where frozen leafmold and paper-thin ice laced trickling streams, my father created another bit of magic. Stairs of flat rock, like irregular stepping-stones, descend among cascading rhododendrons and leucothoë to ferns, iris, marsh marigolds, and primulas of myriad types and colors, now interspersed with molded rivulets in the basin of the quarry. At its far tip these gather into a pool, which in turn, as the land continues to fall, becomes a modest waterfall under an arched stone bridge and, in a series of tumbles through the descending meadow, adds to the flow in Clenny Run.

My father's transformation of the quarry into the last important garden of his life is to me as lovely a creation as one could imagine. His sense of design never failed him and appeared to be chiefly intuitive. In a rare statement at age eighty-two, replying to a question about his "collecting instinct," he wrote, "Somehow or other I seem to feel where each piece [of furniture] should go," but this could apply equally to his sense of landscape design. In the same letter, Harry continued, "I have always loved flowers and had a garden as a child, and in almost every flowering plant there is order, proportion, color, detail and material, and if you have grown up with flowers and really seen them, you can't help to have unconsciously absorbed an appreciation of [these things]."

My father's modesty and essential shyness were lifelong characteristics, and the most diligent interviewers failed to elicit statements more enlightening than those I have quoted. In declining a 1960 invitation to be a panelist at a meeting of the Philadelphia Art Alliance on the Philosophy of Collecting, his terse reply ended, "I speak very badly and indistinctly and have no definite ideas on my philosophy of collecting."

Henry F. du Pont's effectiveness in his last years, however, was not confined to Winterthur. In February 1961 he accepted an invitation from Jacqueline Kennedy to head a twelve-member Fine Arts Committee for the White House. Its function was to restore to the building historically authentic furniture and decorative accessories from the time of its completion and occupancy in 1802. My father wrote that this period was of particular historical significance because the "decorative arts . . . of that time reflect so eloquently the social, political, and economic aspirations of the new, free country."

The White House appointment had come about through the recommendation of Lefty Lewis, who in 1957 had become a trustee of the Winterthur board of directors. Lewis was a brother-in-law of Hugh Auchincloss, whose wife, Janet, was Mrs. Kennedy's mother, and who was an old Newport and New York friend of my father's. According to Lewis, when he suggested that the First Lady write to Harry du Pont herself, Jackie regressed to earlier times and protested, "How could I? Mr. du Pont wouldn't know who I was."

This hurdle was surmounted. My father was unable to attend the initial committee meeting, but in March he met privately with Mrs. Kennedy in Boca Grande. She wanted a graduate of the Winterthur program to fill the newly created post of White House curator, and Charles Montgomery, the museum director, was glad to suggest the able Lorraine Pearce for the position.

Jacqueline Kennedy and my father lost no time in the spring of 1961. Mrs. Kennedy quickly approved his choice of seventeen "young and knowledgeable" candidates for appointment to an advisory committee. He said that he had chosen them with "three thoughts in mind. First, to find those whose training and present positions equip them to supplement the knowledge and experience of the members of our committee; second, to assure nationwide representation; and third, to include those working in the following major area of research into our country's past—the fine arts, the decorative arts, and cultural history." Mrs. Kennedy wrote, "I cannot wait to hear whether or not they have accepted [they all did]—once they have, I shall print our letterhead immediately." My father was charmed by such an enthusiastic and businesslike reply.

At my father's suggestion, two distinguished historians, Julian Boyd and Lyman Butterfield, prepared an essay, "The White House as Symbol."[4] The essay outlined guiding principles for the restoration program, including the need for awareness that the White House had been an evolving institution and that in planning for an appropriate restoration, choices of furnishings should represent a number of administrations. Mrs. Kennedy endorsed the principles outlined, and the essay became a blueprint for the work of the committee.

The nature of the relationship between Jacqueline Kennedy and Henry F. du Pont was established in my father's early visits to the White House and was captured in the more than one hundred letters they exchanged in the next two and a half years. My father was in his element from the beginning. His first letter enclosed photographs of furniture and a fire screen for possible use in the White House "if you like them," and a second, much longer, letter, which he hoped had not "exhausted" its recipient, jumped straight to the point. He and John Sweeney, who had accompanied him as an advisory committee member, would soon send a list of "all the furniture in the different rooms & what we think is needed there," but in the meantime, Harry had gone to work. He "took the liberty" of moving a table from one room to another, "showed the obliging Usher a table downstairs which will go perfectly well in the Red Room," moved chairs near windows, fluffed out some curtains, debated the date of the library woodwork, and commented on the State Dining Room. "Though not exactly to your taste, [it] is an honest statement of a particular period in our history. . . . I think it should be retained as is, possibly scraping the paint off the woodwork to get back to the natural color. . . . We ought to get back the original mantelpiece which I'm sure was smaller. (With various changes), I feel sure . . . this . . . would be a really very handsome room."

Mrs. Kennedy took all this in stride. She thanked her Fine Arts Committee chairman after his first visit for giving up the whole day "to tramping around the White House with us," and immediately answered his second letter. (In the 1960s, overnight mail delivery could still be counted on.)

Although she disagreed with his idea that the paneled woodwork in the Library should be taken out, she approved of his other suggestions and planned to move the candelabra and tureens accordingly. She wrote, "You are so efficient & work so quickly it is too good to be true."

Although she had been delayed by a White House reception for the astronaut Alan Shepard, Mrs. Kennedy and two members of the Fine Arts Committee flew on a lovely spring day in the Kennedys' private plane, the *Caroline*, to Winterthur for lunch, a visit to the museum, an azalea walk, and an early dinner. The First Lady was a highly cultivated person but, having devoted much of her life to the study of French literature, art, and architecture, she may have found this visit her first real introduction to elegant and authentic early American furniture and objects. She wrote, on her return to Washington:

> May 9, 1961
> Dear Mr. and Mrs. du Pont
> I simply cannot find the words to thank you for our day at Winterthur.
> I am sure that people much more eloquent than I could ever hope to be—have tried to tell you what it means to see that incredible museum and gardens, but how could anyone ever express the impression it leaves. All I can say is I will never recover from it—or forget one tiny detail. I just can't believe that it was possible for anyone to ever do such a thing. Mr. du Pont you now have me in such a state of awe and reverence I may never be able to write you a letter again! And all your hospitality and the delicious food and flowers and comfortable guest rooms— everything at your own house. It was a day *never* to be forgotten.
> I now have an ambition for our old age—for us to be gatekeepers at Winterthur!
> Thank you so many many times for that unforgettable day—and for all you have done, Mr. du Pont, to help us so much.
> It is marvelous that this country can produce someone like the Astronaut but I think it is much more awesome to have someone like you.
> Gratefully,
> Jacqueline Kennedy

After this visit, the Kennedy–du Pont correspondence resumed, and in every letter my father's keen interest, scholarship, and attention to detail were equaled by those of the First Lady.

Matters of policy—methods of polite refusal of donations, appraisals of authenticity, tax exemptions, packing and transportation, insurance, the fate of the furniture during future administrations—were problems for

Jacqueline Kennedy, Henry F. du Pont, and Dana Taylor, 1961.

my father and his committee to deal with, but the Kennedy–du Pont correspondence focused more on the rooms themselves. My father's letters reveal his sense of organization, his aesthetic sense, and his concern with historical accuracy. Should the Green Room be Sheraton Hepplewhite and the Red Room Duncan Phyfe? The Bellangé table found in the storeroom is just right for the Blue Room. "In the East Room we might remove those peculiar consoles . . . and in their place put the handsome torchères which are now stuck in the corners. I see no reason why those dreadful busts cannot be removed when you give a party, & have flowers on the mantelpiece. . . . I do not mean that you would take out all the woodwork, but possibly you might modify the cornice & some little details not to make it so aggressively Chippendale." His advice was never patronizing, and despite his age and far greater experience he was consistently low-key and tactful.

> I hope you will not wear yourself out [with traveling] on this wonderful project of yours, [which should] be fun as much as hard work. I did not do Winterthur in a day, & you cannot hurry too much to get the perfect result.
>
> I don't quite understand why you want a pair of Lannuier tables for the Red Room.
>
> I wish you would give [the table] one more look before turning it down.
>
> I hope you will bear with me if I repeat it once more. . . . You will be glad to know that I will not be back until April.

Mrs. Kennedy by no means always agreed with her chairman's views, any more than he did with hers, but her letters, equally thoughtful and sensitive, were more outspoken. She thinks that the big square mirror "is better. I know you would agree with me if you were here on a State evening [to see the reflection of the Color Guard in it]." "Nothing is more elegant than [your stripe], but with everyone peeping over our shoulder ready to criticize, I really don't think we should have 2 rooms the same material, do you?"

Jacqueline Kennedy's intelligence, charm, and beauty were matched by the quality of her letters, and given the tempo of her life as the president's wife, I find it remarkable that she could find such time as she did to write to my father—sometimes in pencil from under the dryer, or "on the bumpiest plane," or in Newport on a boat before the America's Cup race. "That room needs all the welcoming we can cram into it . . . as it is approximately the size of a field in which one would turn Man o' War out to pasture." A hall should have "the feel of a historic house instead of a dentist office bomb shelter."

Such disagreements as occurred between Mrs. Kennedy and Harry du Pont seemed to stem primarily from failures in communication, and given the nature of their respective schedules, these were surprisingly few. My father exultantly wrote in December 1962 that "in the last half hour" he had accepted the gift of some sets of 1824 du Four wallpaper, "just the right paper for the Queen's Room" and incidentally worth $10,000. He was dashed by her "quite distressed" reply, that wallpaper of rose watered silk had already been slated for the room. Mrs. Kennedy ended her ten-page letter: "Don't you think you can explain to [the owner] that there was a misunderstanding. I will write her myself if you think I should. I eavesdropped on your conference . . . & as I heard you take on that den of lions (which I wouldn't have walked into for all the original Bellangé chairs for the Blue Room!)—I have the greatest confidence that you can satisfactorily resolve this misunderstanding!" And she observed, "This is the only time our wires have ever crossed—which I think is a most wonderful thing." Whatever the resolution of this difficulty may have entailed, my father wrote to the new White House curator that he understood the matter perfectly. "It could not be helped. All's well that ends well."

A matter that ended less well and that because of its publicity was of far greater concern to the President and Mrs. Kennedy and to my father was based on a series of articles published in September 1962 in the *Washington Post* by a reporter who gained entrance to the White House and seized the opportunity to gossip about personalities and the prices and authenticity of the furniture. One subject was a Baltimore desk, an unsolicited gift accepted by the Fine Arts Committee the year before, which was given a place of honor in the Green Room and was singled out by Jacqueline Kennedy in her television tour of the White House as a "treasure."

Although the desk had been examined when it arrived and was believed to be of the early nineteenth century, a more skeptical new curator and another expert took it apart and found that in places it had been reworked with new wood. Had this information not been ferreted out by the *Post* reporter, the desk would have been quietly returned to its owner, who, as the president said, was the real loser because of the embarrassment she had suffered. The publicity resulting from these unauthorized articles, in which the authenticity of other donated articles was also questioned, caused much uneasiness, as it had the potential to damage the entire White House restoration project.

As Jacqueline Kennedy wrote my father,

If you were appalled—multiply your reaction by 1,000,000 & you will have mine. . . .

I believe this will all blow over—as *your* support & work are what kept our project free from sensationalism. It is why the country is grateful for what is being done at the W. House—& why they rejoice in the good fortune of having you to direct the committee's work—& why it has remained completely non political.

The work of these exciting and productive years was also ruffled by a confusion about authority. Lorraine Pearce, whose academic approach, similar to my father's, at times differed from Mrs. Kennedy's, wrote to him as early as July 1961 that she felt like "a bewildered captain surrounded by mighty generals." She left her curatorial post a year later. Poor communication between members of the Fine Arts Committee and the White House also disturbed the acquisition process. In London, John Sweeney examined a set of wallpaper depicting scenes of the Revolutionary War and then received conflicting messages about whether to buy it: one from an Arts Committee member then in Paris instructing him to cancel the order, and a contradictory cable from the White House, authorizing the purchase. "There are too many people making decisions," John wrote to my father.

Another source of potential trouble emerged when the French decorator, Stéphane Boudin, engaged by Mrs. Kennedy to help furnish the family's private rooms, gradually began to get involved with the state rooms as well. William Elder, the new curator, wrote to my father, "Mr. Boudin may be all right as a decorator but he has absolutely no knowledge or respect for American furniture or paintings and I have recently learned, no knowledge of French furniture." Elder's conversation with Mrs. Kennedy the next day, however, somewhat allayed his fears—"I do think that she has some doubts now about his capabilities." He was still more reassured after my father's next visit, which, he thought, "did a great deal of good. I got a memorandum from Mrs. Kennedy saying she didn't think you would let her put any French furniture in the Queen's Room."

Harry du Pont, as the elder statesman, was always philosophical and appeared not to be unduly disturbed. He wrote to Elder, "Don't get discouraged, although situations are infuriating," and remarked to John Sweeney that after all, one needed to remember that Mrs. Kennedy—who after many of his visits rearranged the furniture—was still very young. (She was then thirty-one years old.)

My father's relationship with the First Lady remained harmonious until its abrupt ending with the assassination. They were a good team and had much in common: good taste, standards of excellence, a respect for privacy and confidentiality, and a dislike of publicity. Janet Felton,[5] a young secretary to the Fine Arts Committee and much admired by my father, wrote that Jackie always "held him in the highest esteem. She always said how lucky she was that he had consented to be Chairman of the Fine Arts Committee," and further, that Jackie, her former schoolmate, had deeply appreciated the fact that a Republican could put politics aside and so wholeheartedly work for the project of a Democratic administration.

The Kennedy–du Pont letters throughout this association emphasized a spirit of cooperation, mutual appreciation, and affection. My father often commented on his enjoyment of collaborating with his partner in the White House, and on one occasion his disappointment at coming there on a day when she was too busy to see him. And Mrs. Kennedy reciprocated these feelings. She was "so sad to have missed [him]. . . . Last week was a real back-breaker" owing to the unexpected visit of the Shah of Iran, of which she had learned only upon her return from India. As for the White House restoration project, the efficiency of her "most inexhaustible chairman" continued "to amaze and delight" her. "Nothing would have been possible without your tireless and discriminating help"; a year and a half into the project, she wrote, "I am so glad you say there is still lots to do as it will be so sad when it's all over." There may have been exaggeration in this statement, but in a later letter—perhaps the last my father received from this extraordinary woman—there is indeed the ring of truth. In answer to his offer of the "loan" of an architect, Mrs. Kennedy ended on this note of affection: "Dear Mr. du Pont, don't you know that all that is lovely in the White house now . . . is all your contribution. . . . I only wanted your heart and time—and you have given so much more than one could ever have hoped for."

After President Kennedy's death in November 1963 and his family's departure from the White House, President Johnson requested that my father and Mrs. Kennedy join a Committee for the Preservation of the White House, whose purpose was to maintain its "high standards of beauty."[6] The major job of restoration had been accomplished, however, and although letters indicate my father's continued involvement with some aspects of it, the infrequent committee meetings were more concerned with the acquisition of American art. The new First Lady, a Texan like her husband, sought paintings that reflected the "great, lusty part of the expansion westward . . . the human struggle of a period of American history which had great vitality."[7]

Lady Bird Johnson and Harry du Pont hit it off very well, and, as their friendly letters attest, they stayed in touch throughout my father's life, with the additional bond of a shared love of wildflowers and land preservation. My father, in a note to the Johnsons after my mother's death, thanked them for their yellow and white chrysanthemum wreath (which my sister and I had placed on the Christ Church baptismal font) and their "letter of friendship and affection [which] ... will be a great help in going it alone after fifty-three years of happiness."

Harry du Pont's intimate connections with the White House had ended with the Kennedy years, as had so much else. It was as well that his task there had been almost completed, for in June 1963 my father found himself catapulted into a situation that would absorb and challenge him almost to the end of his life. As a member of the Advisory Council of the Cooper Union Museum for the Arts of Decoration since 1947, he had had for at least a year intimations of trouble from Richard P. Wunder, the museum's curator, who had visited Winterthur several times and had become a good friend. Wunder and other staff members had nevertheless been astonished by the dire announcement in June 1963 of its possible closing.

The Cooper Union for the Advancement of Science and Art was founded in 1859 by a "proud New Yorker," Peter Cooper, an industrialist who had realized his dream of bringing a knowledge of art as well as science to the people of his city by the establishment of a tuition-free college in which men and women of any race, creed, or color could receive the technical and artistic training he himself had missed.[8] In 1897, his two granddaughters continued Cooper's plan by founding the museum, the only one in this country devoted exclusively to all forms of artistic design, from 1500 B.C. to the present. A working museum open two evenings a week (unique at the time), it had a collection of one hundred thousand items emphasizing textiles, prints, drawings, and wallpapers, and including medieval fabrics, Persian calligraphy, Rembrandt etchings, tapestries, metal and woodwork, glass and enamels, Picasso ceramics, and more than three hundred oils, watercolors, and drawings by Winslow Homer.

The June 25 announcement of the museum's "proposed discontinuance" by the Cooper Union's president of two years, Dr. Richard F. Humphreys, and its board chairman, Arthur A. Houghton, Jr., was a bombshell not only to the museum's staff and advisory council but also to the art world, to its Greenwich Village neighbors, to its numerous contributors, and to the public in general. Having stated that the use of the museum by the college had become "insignificant," that its location provided insufficient space and was remote from New York's artistic center, and that its dispersal would "free much needed funds" for educational programs of the school, the announcement ended with the ominous information that the staff of the Metropolitan Museum of Art had offered to assist that of the Cooper Union in "studying the possibilities of relocating."[9] The museum was closed to the public one week later. (It reopened that September.)

The announcement created shock and consternation, and by July 9 the Committee to Save the Cooper Union Museum had sprung to life almost spontaneously. Henry F. du Pont and Albert Edelman, from the law firm of Senator Jacob Javits, were both members. In a letter to Arthur Houghton, who was also on the Board of the Metropolitan Museum, the Committee to Save dismissed as "insubstantial" the rationale for dissolution and spoke of the "rising tide of opposition to the proposed action." Further, it announced its intention to go to court if the president and board of trustees continued their stated plan to close the museum and disperse the art objects. "A museum cannot suddenly shed its character . . . and melt its works of art down to money, with which to support a wholly different enterprise."

One week later, a curt response from the trustees' lawyer suggested the surprise if not embarrassment experienced by Houghton and his cohorts to the reaction to their ill-considered plan. "The temporary closing [of the museum] was decided upon to aid the present study requested by the Trustees. No other decisions have been made and no further action has been taken or will be taken until this study is complete. . . . The committee will be notified if, and when, a decision is made."

On the heels of this exchange, membership in the Committee to Save, which by now had its own headquarters in New York, rose from 40 to 128 in four weeks, and further consternation was registered in the press. An editorial in the *New York Times* deplored the "study" of the contents of the Cooper Union Museum by the staff of the Metropolitan, "which could . . . result in choice items . . . filling gaps in the Metropolitan collections . . . [and] the scattering to the 4 winds a host of . . . discriminatingly acquired works of art. . . . The collections . . . are important enough to be kept together . . . as the newly formed Committee to Save the Cooper Union is valiantly trying to do."[10]

On July 22, Albert Edelman, at lunch in Southampton, persuaded my father to assume chairmanship of the Committee to Save, and the next day he wrote him of the enthusiasm with which committee members had received this news. Mrs. Howard J. Sachs, another council member, was appointed vice-chairman. A masterful letter to Arthur Houghton from the Committee to Save was most likely written by Edelman or Mrs. Sachs (who evidently drafted at least several of my father's later letters for him to edit and sign).

July 26, 1963

It would appear from [the] tenor [of your letter of July 16], that it constitutes the totality of the Trustee's response. It is barren of information, or encouragement or disclosure, or of hospitality to consultation, ideas or assistance.

Following the opening acknowledgment there are five sentences, all of them short.

It is said that the closing of the Museum is temporary, but it was not called temporary before.

It is said that the Museum is closed only to the viewing public, as though that should be a consolation.

It is said that the closing was decided upon to aid the present study requested by the trustees. There is not an inkling of the nature or purpose of the "study." . . . Is it a study of whether the Museum should be continued? . . . Or is it rather . . . not . . . a study, but a marketing appraisal?

In the fourth sentence it is said that: "No other decisions have been made and no further action has been taken." The Committee's initiative and resistance were activated by clear evidence of decisions to discontinue the museum and to dispose of its collections by sale. The Metropolitan's present activities in the Cooper Union Museum are understandable only in the light of decisions already made. We have that upon no less an authority than Mr. Roland Redmond, President of the Metropolitan Museum. . . .

In the fifth and last sentence of your counsel's letter, it is said: "The Committee will be notified if, and when a decision is made."

Surely you understand that this is not acceptable to the Committee. Consistent with the Committee's entire stand and purpose it cannot be satisfied with being informed of a decision *after* it has been made. . . .

Despite the first rebuff, the Committee reiterates its offer to consult with the Trustees and to explore together meritorious alternatives to discontinuance, dispersal or sale . . . *before* any decisions are reached.

Houghton, at his Maryland home for the weekend, refused to comment.[11] He later sailed for Europe, and no further interactions of the trustees and Committee to Save are recorded until September. Throughout the summer, however, magazines were exploding with commentaries: *Life* in "A Scheme to Scuttle a Museum," reported on a "furor of opposition"; the *Saturday Review* talked about the "dramatic pitched battle" over the "scholarly New York landmark"; *Cue* wrote of the "shocking event" and "sense of incalculable loss and outrage"; *Antiques* inserted into its issue on painting several paragraphs about the problem "whose complexities have become distressing, not to say unsavory"; "a moral issue . . . [whose] situation is fraught with the gravest implications for every other museum in the country." *Interior Design* devoted a scathing first page to the subject.[12]

> What better time [than before the July 4th weekend] . . . to spring an announcement if you wanted it to be seen by the fewest number of people! . . .

The August 9 issue of *Time*, in an article called "Debate About a Delight," quoted "Longtime Donor Henry F. du Pont, 83 . . . [who was] troubled but positive": "The blow fell without warning. The trustees haven't treated us very well, keeping everything so secretive, but we are still ready to help them find the solution. We must preserve the collection."[13]

After Labor Day, the conflict resumed, and Wunder in a letter to my father questioned Houghton's motives in inviting only my father and no other committee member to a meeting. "Obviously there should be a fuller representation . . . for the gathering is to attempt to whitewash the Committee you head . . . and negate [its] authority."

The Committee to Save, now with almost two hundred members, swinging into action, were delighted by a new development, the offer by the American Association of Museums to conduct an independent study of the problems and future of the Cooper Union Museum.

In February 1964 a special committee of the American Association of Museums, headed by its president, Charles van Ravenswaay, future director of the Winterthur Museum, called a meeting with the Committee to Save the Cooper Union Museum, whose membership by now had increased to 280. At the AAM's behest, my father approached S. Dillon Ripley, the recently appointed secretary of the Smithsonian Institution, in the hope that this organization might consider an alliance with the Cooper Union. Late in the year, my father reported "some blue sky in our battle. . . . It appears that we have found, at last, a responsible executive of an outstanding institution who will champion this cause," and the following spring he wrote to his committee members that the "goal is within our reach."

This relatively calm period, however, was peppered by minor skirmishes with Arthur Houghton, Jr.

A. H., Jr., to S. Dillon Ripley   Jan. 13, 1965:

We understand that [a proposal to the Smithsonian] was initiated by Mr. Henry F. du Pont, as chair of an organization known as the "Committee to Save the Cooper Union Museum." We believe that Mr. van Ravenswaay's committee should be given the opportunity to study and evaluate [it].

A. H., Jr., to S. D. R.   Jan. 22, 1965

The Trustees of Cooper Union were disturbed by the fact that a fully developed plan concerning the Museum appeared to have been formulated without their having been consulted,—when the question of the future of the Museum is one which the Trustees themselves must decide.

A. H., Jr., to H. F. du P.   Apr. 9, 1965

Among [the] recommendations [of the American Association of Museums is] that the Trustees of the Cooper Union enter into negotiations with the Smithsonian Institution. As a separate step, the report recommends that the Smithsonian Institution enter into negotiations with your Committee on the question of financial support. . . .

[After these proceedings], we would be delighted to have representatives of your Committee meet jointly with representatives of the Cooper Union and the Smithsonian Institution.

You can be assured that your continued interest in the Museum is genuinely appreciated.

Whatever may have been my father's private expressions of rage, his dignified reply to this letter is exemplary:

H. F. du P. to A. H., Jr.,   Apr. 12, 1965

I acknowledge receipt of your letter. If you wish to have your meeting with Dillon Ripley . . . without me or any representatives of our Committee being present, you are, of course, free to do so. You are the host.

But I must take issue with the reasons you have given for excluding us. . . .

We are entirely willing to make this a combined effort, but we cannot be expected to carry the large responsibility expected of us without an active part in the consideration . . . of the Museum's future.

In May 1965, Arthur Edelman, in criticizing a press release proposed by the Cooper Union Trustees, was more outspoken.

[Your statements] place the entire emphasis upon the work and proposals of the AAM Committee . . . and all done seemingly at the behest of the trustees of Cooper Union. This is so distorted a story, and so belittling to the vital role and the long arduous efforts of the Committee to Save under the leadership of Mr. du Pont . . . that it would be damaging to the entire morale of the Committee to go along with any such release for publication. . . . As Dr. Ripley well knows, the initiative relating thereto, came from Mr. du Pont on behalf of his Committee.

My father's disposition, put to a test, remained unruffled, as attested by his generous statement in December 1965 to his Committee members: "It is important for you all to realize the extent of the present cooperation of the Trustees of Cooper Union in the consummation of the plan (a 3 year rent-free occupancy is now cited, along with a $300,000 contribution over a 3 year period). This gives you some idea of the new sense of harmony and common purpose that pervades this second chapter in the 'saga' of the Cooper Union Museum."

In October 1967 the long-awaited contract was signed, transferring the Cooper Union Museum to the Smithsonian Institution, an agreement by which the museum was to remain intact in New York but was to assume a national role through its new affiliation. As reported in the *New Yorker,* Albert Edelman, now vice-chairman, remarked, "The battle was raging. [Mr. du Pont] has been absolutely intrepid. He never wearied."[14] Edelman observed that although it was through my father's efforts that the Smithsonian and Dillon Ripley "saved the resource for the country," H. F. du Pont all along believed that the museum should remain in New York. To this, my father said, "My mother was a New Yorker, so I'm not an intruder."

The end of this story included several happy elements. Arthur Houghton resigned from the board, but not before amity had been restored. The museum set about establishing the first center in the country for the study of color, a coincidental development that also seemed appropriate, given the love of color of one of its prime "saviours." In 1968, Richard Wunder, who for a time had been with the Smithsonian in Washington, was appointed head of the newly renamed Cooper-Hewitt Museum of Design, and Henry F. du Pont, then eighty-seven, accepted the chairmanship of its new board of advisers.

Afterthoughts

WHEN I reflect on my father's life, I am always amazed that despite its faltering beginnings it ended so improbably in triumph. I tend to think of those eighty-nine years in segments. Henry F. du Pont was born in what seemed to be charmed country, but Winterthur had more than its share of sorrow, for the deaths of five children cast a shadow over the caring and affluent family who lived there. Harry, at first constitutionally frail and uncoordinated, nevertheless found at Winterthur endless childhood delight. Those halcyon days were interrupted by an often disastrous decade of formal education in Massachusetts, but in his imagination he remained at Winterthur; thinking about it helped to ease his academic and social difficulties. Before he had even begun to enter the "real world" after college, he was stunned by the death of his mother, a loss so shattering that he questioned his ability to survive it.

But aside from his passion for Winterthur, Harry had other things going for him, among them integrity, intuition, and self-awareness. Even in school he had seemed to understand some of his own needs, as in buying himself a lily-of-the-valley boutonniere even though it was "extravacant." Then and later he was often laughed at, but despite his patent vulnerability, he never pretended to be what he was not. His interests were not those of his contemporaries, and he made no attempt to conceal them. In the years alone with his father, it was Harry's good fortune that his chief interests happened to be rooted at Winterthur, and he channeled them with extraordinary dedication into the passions of his life. His early ventures into horticulture had a driven quality. He entered into the Winterthur dairy operation with equal fervor, visiting other herds, studying the complexities of Holstein breeding, always striving to outdo an earlier record.

Adolescence is often thought to usher in adulthood after "carefree" childhood. My father's adolescence was exceptionally prolonged. The years at Winterthur, which included summers abroad, were an unpressured time, and his creativity and administrative ability began to flourish. In Washington, the engaging Ruth Wales responded to Harry's increasing maturity, and with her he at last permitted himself a degree of romantic closeness to another person. Over a four-year period she saw his transformation from a man she initially thought of little consequence to the only one she was ever to love.

The following decade was a crucial one. Harry's marriage was soon complicated by the demanding last years of his father's life, but he managed both to cope with the problems and to nurture a new passion. Seized with the wonder and excitement of aesthetic discovery, he found that, in addition to horticulture and farming, he had yet another calling, this time in the field of Americana, and he applied himself to its study with characteristic intensity. His mission was then clear to him, and the second half of his life, culminating in the emergence of the museum, was devoted to it.

Recognition of the importance of the museum at Winterthur exceeded all expectations. In 1966, Lefty Lewis, remarking on its "extraordinary progress" and its contribution to American studies, said that through its great collections, by then widely used, it had entered the "bloodstream of the museum world."

My father's achievements over his long life were based on an unusual mixture of elements both concrete and intangible. I suppose the obvious should be mentioned first: his inheritance of seemingly unlimited amounts of money, as well as his capacity to use it creatively. But his innate gifts were at the center of his achievement: unparalleled visual memory, an eye for color, a remarkable sense of proportion, an untiring talent for detail. These he intuitively tempered with common sense, self-discipline, and a kind of nonacademic scholarship. And beyond these observable traits there was an almost palpable force, a restless driving need, a touch of genius that impelled him to create his masterworks.

Harry's tastes were varied, but they had developed along traditional lines, and they remained there. Whether or not he was aware of adventurous modern trends—as exemplified by the pioneering enterprise of men like Lincoln Kirstein and Edward Warburg, only twenty-five years his junior at Harvard—they did not enormously excite him, and he held to well-defined conventional limits.[1] Of course he had visited the Museum of Modern Art (to which on its twenty-fifth anniversary in 1955 he increased his contribution to $50), and in his mid-eighties he joined the board of trustees of the Whitney Museum, but abstract painting and sculpture were not for him.[2] In fact, except for portraits or folk art, he was not often moved by paintings at all except as adjuncts to a room. The outdoor world and the decorative arts spoke to him most clearly—wallpaper, fabrics, carved designs, whose subjects were often taken from the world of nature. At Winterthur, there are more than two thousand representations of eagles, either freestanding or two-dimensional, and when I quizzed my father after a children's game of "What animal would you like to be?" his choice of eagle did not surprise me.

It has been said that the Henry Francis du Pont Winterthur Museum, to which my father gave his full name, represented for him a surrogate son. Although I think it unlikely that he would have been aware of such a fantasy, these speculations are probably accurate; the existence of an unspoken legacy seems clear. The fact that he had no son might have merged with the French concept of primogeniture, and he realized that his name would best live on through another kind of creation, one that was perhaps more permanent and trustworthy.[3]

Although he did not enjoy the company of children, Harry had good sense about them. In replying to a friend whose pompous letter defended his decision to send his eleven-year-old son, Harry's godchild, to an English school in order to escape bad American influences and to develop an "earnest . . . purpose in life," my father wrote, "As a matter of fact, I think a child Tommie's age is much too young to be told . . . any of the 'earnest purpose' line of talk. A boy of that age should be taught to tell the truth, to obey, & to play the game square. Otherwise he should be allowed to develop along his own lines."

This vignette calls to mind the Colonel's severe precepts and Harry's slowly realized success at pursuing the "lines" of his own, which included a strong affinity with objects of many kinds. He often attributed human qualities to plants and furniture. He was concerned that plants find a good home after their owners died, and he invited the nurseryman who had sold him his original Kurume azaleas to visit Winterthur to "see them, their children & their grandchildren." He advised a young cousin at an antiques show to look at the individual chairs as if they were people. Like families, Philadelphia furniture could be very different from the Boston version.

I believe that my mother was correct in her sense that her husband had few close friends. My father took a friendly interest in many people: He was observant, thoughtful, sensitive, and often affectionate, but he maintained emotional distance. For the most part, he preferred companionship with those who not only shared his interests but who were also willing to respect his boundaries. The focus of these relationships was on events and tangible objects rather than on an intimate expression of feeling. The fields of Americana and horticulture provided him with a host of like-minded companions, as did the games that he liked—especially golf and bridge, both of which he played rather poorly.[4]

Harry's lifelong attachments to Marian Coffin and Bertha Benkard seemed to be exceptional. Although they were founded on a mutual love of landscape architecture, gardens, and interior design, I am sure that deep feelings were an integral part of these friendships, as was indeed also true in the case of his sister. However, my father's most profound relationship was with his wife, although her death was not as devastating for him as was that of his mother. After fifty-three years of Ruth's loving, entertaining presence, he was bereft, but his interests sustained him, and, at eighty-seven, he knew that his loneliness could not last very long.

I think that my father found great happiness in his life. Who could have guessed at such a future for the fearful, homesick boy at boarding school, or the inept, solitary Harvard student, or the college graduate so affected by his mother's death that he vowed to "give up feeling"? But Harry du Pont surmounted his tragedy and channeled his creative energies so that his crowning achievement became one with the place closest to his heart, where his identity lay.

Postscript: The Golf Cottage

On my way back from the Winterthur archives, as I walked past the Pinetum and through the soon-to-awaken azaleas in the woods, the sun glittered orange-gold as it disappeared behind a network of branches. My favorite

Henry F. du Pont at Winterthur in the mid-1950s.

time of day. As I reached the front porch of the Golf Cottage, geese were honking in broken formation, veering high to the east. The moon rose very pale orange and turned into a shining fullness.

Here in this house on this mysterious evening I suddenly feel my father's presence. I have the sense that I have come at last to know the man whom I loved very much and who so many years ago was always quick to withdraw the rare glimpses of intimacy he allowed me to see. I wonder to what extent I realized at the time that my "love letter to a house" was in essence a plea for a closer relationship with him. In retrospect, I imagine that he must have sensed it as such and consequently have been at a loss for an immediate response. One year later he wrote to me about arrangements for the cottage in a letter that ended (not entirely grammatically): "Knowing how I feel about the hills, streams and woods, I could not be more pleased that you would like to enjoy them long after I'm gone."

When growing up at Winterthur, I sensed a particular bond with my father: he and I seemed more caught up by the land than were others in the family. Certainly we spent more time outdoors. My father walked a great deal, usually by himself, and on my constant excursions—when I was small I escaped whenever possible from my poor nurse—I also liked to be alone. Harry's voluminous notes often tried to capture an impression, a color, a moment in a day, and so did my private scribblings. I like to think that he was aware of how much I identified with him in certain ways—not with any particular eye for antiques or formal gardens but with a reverence for houses and for land and simply for being in the country.

After this dear house at last became mine again, the seed of my wish to communicate with my father, planted long ago in that emotional letter, began to grow, almost as if nurtured within these walls. It was here that my intense wondering about him was renewed, and now, suddenly, I feel that we are on the same wavelength. Attempting to write about Harry du Pont's life and his re-creation of Winterthur has enabled me, I think, to understand what attracted him so fiercely and impelled him to act so decisively. It could even be that a small bit of his elusive force has come my way and that these pages are a gift to him—my thanks for his legacy to me of the Golf Cottage and all it stands for.

Appendix 1

Family of
Mary Pauline Foster du Pont

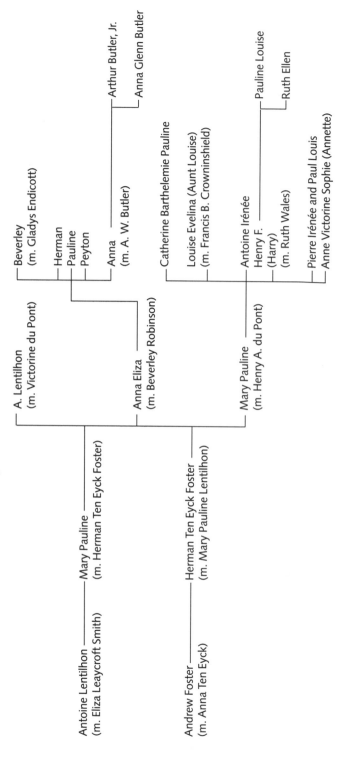

Family of
Henry A. du Pont

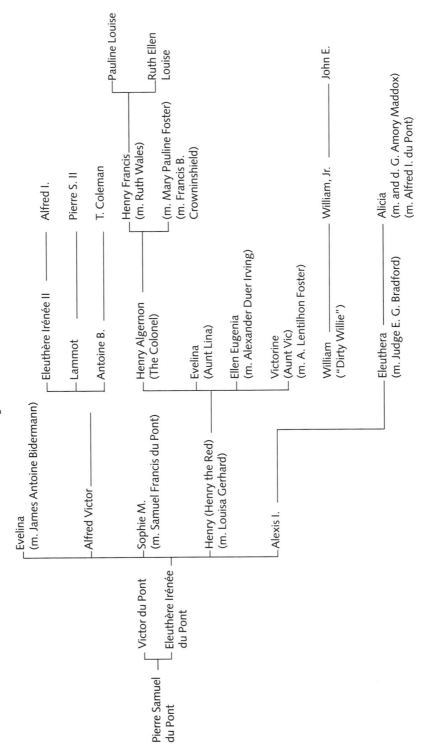

Appendix 2

Fine Arts Committees

Henry F. du Pont served as a member on a number of committees.

The Commission of Fine Arts

David E. Finley, chairman
Linton R. Wilson, secretary
Peter Hurd
Douglas W. Orr

William G. Perry
Michael Rapauno
Felix W. de Weldon

Fine Arts Committee for the White House

Henry Francis du Pont, chairman
Charles Francis Adams
Mrs. C. Douglas Dillon
Mrs. Charles W. Engelhard
David E. Finley
Mrs. Albert D. Lasker
John J. Loeb

Mrs. Paul Mellon
Mrs. Henry Parrish II
Gerald Shea
John Walker III
Mrs. George Henry Warren
Mrs. Charles B. Wrightsman

Advisers to the Fine Arts Committee for the White House

James Biddle, assistant curator in charge of the American Wing, Metropolitan Museum of Art, New York
Julian Boyd, editor of the Jefferson Papers, Princeton, New Jersey
Lyman Butterfield, editor of the Adams Papers, Boston

Richard E. Fuller, president and director, Seattle Art Museum

Gerald G. Gibson, assistant curator of decorative arts, Henry Ford Museum, Dearborn, Michigan

John M. Graham II, director and curator of collections, Colonial Williamsburg, Williamsburg, Virginia

Calvin S. Hathaway, director, Cooper Union Museum, New York

Miss Ima Hogg, founder and curator, Bayou Bend Collections—Museum of Fine Arts of Houston

Thomas C. Howe, director, California Palace of the Legion of Honor, San Francisco; president, Association of Art Museum Directors

Sherman E. Lee, director, Cleveland Museum of Art

Jack R. McGregor, administrative assistant, Metropolitan Museum of Art, New York

Henry P. McIlhenny, curator of decorative arts, Philadelphia Museum of Art

Charles Nagel, director, City Art Museum of St. Louis

Richard H. Randall, Jr., assistant curator, Museum of Fine Arts, Boston

Edgar P. Richardson, director, Detroit Institute of Arts; director, Archives of American Art, Detroit

Marvin D. Schwartz, curator of decorative arts, Brooklyn Museum, Brooklyn, New York

John A. H. Sweeney, curator, Henry Francis du Pont Winterthur Museum, Winterthur, Delaware

C. Malcolm Watkins, curator, Division of Cultural History, Smithsonian Institution, Washington, D.C.

Abbreviations

The following abbreviations appear in the notes and references.

AR	Anna Foster Robinson
HA	Colonel Henry Algernon du Pont
HF	Henry Francis du Pont
HML	Hagley Museum and Library
JAHS	John A. H. Sweeney
LdP	Louise du Pont (later Louise du Pont Crowninshield)
LdPC	Louise du Pont Crowninshield
LGdP	Louisa Gerhard du Pont
PdP	Pauline du Pont (formerly Pauline Foster)
PF	Pauline Foster (later Pauline du Pont)
RdP	Ruth du Pont (formerly Ruth Wales)
RHW	Ruth Hawks Wales
RL	Ruth du Pont Lord
RW	Ruth Wales (later Ruth du Pont)
WA	Winterthur Archives

Notes

Preface

1. Museum directors have been Charles F. Montgomery (1954–62); Edgar P. Richardson (1962–66); Charles van Ravenswaay (1966–76); James Morton Smith (1976–84); Thomas A. Graves, Jr. (1984–92); Dwight P. Lanmon (1992–present.)

2. Although members of the family have written their name in various ways, in the following pages it will appear as "du Pont" (except when referring to the Du Pont Company.)

Chapter 1. The Golf Cottage

1. This 1880 building is still known as the Soda House because of its early use as a storage facility for sodium nitrate.

2. He had opposed an admission fee to Winterthur, a wish of necessity later countermanded by the board of trustees.

3. This was built on the site of the old Bidermann farmhouse, where we had once lived.

4. The construction of the Galleries building was completed in 1992. Parts of it were opened successively then and in 1993 and 1994.

5. J. E. Cantor, *Winterthur* (New York: Harry N. Abrams, 1985), 79.

6. D. R. Belcher and J. H. Willetts, *A Possible Future for the Winterthur Museum*, internal document, 1961, WA.

Chapter 2. Earlier Generations

1. For genealogies of the du Pont and Foster families, see appendix 1.

2. Pierre Samuel, an elected deputy of the Third Estate in 1789, distinguished himself from other du Ponts in the Constituent Assembly by adding "de Nemours" to his name, after the town near which he and his wife had bought a farm.

3. *Rectitudine Sto* (Upright I Stand.)

4. William S. Dutton, *Du Pont: One Hundred and Forty Years* (New York: Charles Scribner's Sons, 1942), 6.

5. P. S. du Pont's "ode in irregular stanzas" begins

> En ce jour au Dieu du Permesse
> Je n'addresserai point mes voeux
> Je vais chanter Choiseul et ses travaux heureux
> C'est au Patriotisme à guider mon ivresse.
> Toi par qui les Romains dompètrent l'Univers
> Divin Amour de la Patrie,
> Viens, porte tous tes feux dans mon ame attendrie,
> Montre moi l'art de vers.

> In this day of the God of the Permesse
> I shall not address my wishes
> I shall sing of Choiseul and his happy works
> It is to Patriotism to guide my rapture.
> Thee, by whom the Romans mastered the Universe,
> Divine love of the Fatherland,
> Come, bear all thy fires in my compassionate soul,
> Show me the art of verses.

—*Autobiography of Du Pont de Nemours,* trans. E. Fox-Genovese Wilmington, Del.: Scholarly Resources, 1984.

6. J. F. Wall, *Alfred I. du Pont: The Man and His Family* (New York: Oxford University Press, 1990), 19.

7. Pierre Samuel was Inspector General of Commerce in 1774; negotiator with Benjamin Franklin of French-American treaties in 1776–78; and Councillor of State in 1784. He was elected Secretary of Assembly of Notables in 1786; elected to Third Estate to represent district of Nemours in 1788; elected president of Constituent Assembly in 1790; elected Secretary General of provisional French government in 1814. His Constitution of 1791 was accepted, and he had a role in the Louisiana Purchase (1802–3).

8. College des Quatres Nations (now the Institut).

9. M. Dorian, *The du Ponts: From Gunpowder to Nylon* (Boston: Little, Brown, 1962), 11.

10. Irénée, in his youth a student of botany as well as of chemistry, was as interested in tree culture and farming as he was in the manufacture of gunpowder. In the early 1800s he ordered from France huge shipments of plants, including fruit and nut trees, grapevines, and collections of seeds. Natural history was said to be his "favorite subject." (The practice of major botanical importing was admirably perpetuated by his great-grandson Harry.) Equally eager to share with France plants native to the New World, Irénée shipped to friends and to public gardens innumerable quantities of small trees, flowers, and seeds, some going to Mme. Josephine Bonaparte for her garden at Malmaison. To a fellow botanist he sent five barrels of white oak acorns from

the Brandywine—"enough to plant a forest." Irénée became active in prominent local and Philadelphia agricultural societies. From N. B. Wilkinson, *E. I. du Pont,
Botaniste: The Beginnings of a Tradition* (Charlottesville: University Press of Virginia,
1972).

11. Ibid., 52.

12. Hagley Farm was the home of James Antoine and Evelina Bidermann for
twenty-one years, before they moved to Winterthur.

Chapter 3. Grandparents and Their Contemporaries

1. As told to Charles W. David (Longwood Library), August 1958.

2. The threat of explosion in the powder mills was always present. A stray spark
could ignite the contents of any one of them—the grinding, the glazing, or the press
mill—and the resulting explosion leap to neighboring buildings. Shocks had been felt
more than forty miles away. At the Brandywine powder mills, explosions occurred in
1817, 1857, 1884, and 1890. The last one so damaged Eleutherean Mills that the family moved out. The building was used by the Du Pont Company until the Colonel
bought it for his daughter, Louise, in 1923.

3. This information is quoted in the *Memorial Booklet of Herman Ten Eyck Foster*, prepared by A. B. Conger for New York State Agricultural Society, Albany, February 9, 1870, HML.

4. To Pauline Foster du Pont, September 23, 1874. Quoted in *The Letters of Edith
Wharton*, ed. R. W. B. Lewis and Nancy Lewis (New York: Charles Scribner's Sons,
1988), 29.

5. Poem by Edith Jones (Wharton), HML.

6. J. F. Wall, *Alfred I. du Pont: The Man and His Family* (New York: Oxford University Press, 1990), (from 1852 correspondence of R. Page Williamson to Mary P.
Williamson), 87.

7. Annual Report (of U.S. Military Academy), June 13, 1927, p. 125.

8. Four buildings were already on the site—two houses, a schoolhouse and a
blacksmith shop—which had been built as early as 1859. In the mid-1890s, Henry A.
built a second railroad station, on Winterthur land, where a post office was also established. This building is now used to house visiting scholars.

Chapter 4. The Colonel

1. My sister and I habitually began Christmas with our own early stocking ceremony in our mother's bedroom.

2. His military uniform, formerly on display in the library, is now the property
of the Historical Society of Delaware.

3. "Thank you for proving yourself to be a monument of endurance and self-
control. . . . I appreciate these qualities having been demonstrated during your many
sittings, all the more as I know you took little or no interest in having the portrait done.

I hope now you will like it." Letter to H. F. du Pont from Ellen Emmet Rand, April 13, 1914.

4. Quoted in minutes of Delaware Society of Colonial Dames of America, November 10, 1902, WA.

5. George A. Custer, another of "Lincoln's lieutenants," graduated in 1861 at the bottom of the class. See Ralph Kirshner, *The Class of 1861* (Carbondale: Southern Illinois University Press, 1996).

6. Quoted in Annual Report of the Association of the Graduates of the USMA, June 13, 1927.

7. That he did not approach his father, a general, on this subject makes one wonder whether he suspected his father of having pulled strings to prevent him from seeing active combat.

8. Major Henry F. Brewerton, quoted in the Annual Report Association of the Graduates of USMA, article by David T. Marvel, June 13, 1927, p. 124.

9. There may be a difference of opinion on whether Henry's heroism was of sufficient magnitude to warrant the bestowal of this highest medal.

10. Henry A. du Pont, *The Campaign of 1864 in the Valley of Virginia and the Expedition to Lynchburg* (New York: National Americana Society, 1925), 89.

11. Varina Davis, *Jefferson Davis: Ex President of the Confederate States of America: A Memoir by His Wife* (Freeport, N.Y.: Books for Libraries Press, 1890; rpt. 1971), 760ff.

12. H. A. du Pont, *The Campaign of 1864 in the Valley of Virginia and the Expedition to Lynchburg* (New York: National Americana Society, 1925). H. A. du Pont, *Rear-Admiral Samuel Francis du Pont, United States Navy, a Biography* (New York: National Americana Society, 1926).

13. C. C. Osborne, *Jubal: The Life and Times of General Jubal A. Early, CSA, Defender of the Lost Cause* (Chapel Hill, N.C.: Algonquin Books of Chapel Hill, 1992), 249.

14. In January 1863, with an excess of confidence in the new ironclad ships, Gideon Welles ordered a naval attack on Charleston with no accompanying support from the Army. Admiral du Pont, knowing that Charleston harbor was heavily defended, had advised against such a plan, but nevertheless followed orders. Taking heavy casualties, he withdrew after one day, reporting, "We have met a sad repulse; I shall not turn it into a great disaster." For this action and for his failure to return a second day, he was roundly criticized by both Welles and Major General David Hunter. Amid the controversy, and after a long and distinguished career, du Pont asked to be relieved of his command. Du Pont Circle in Washington, D.C., is named in his honor.

15. John D. Gates, *The du Pont Family* (Garden City, N.Y.: Doubleday, 1979), 247.

Chapter 5. Early Childhood

1. My father's handwriting was notoriously hard to read, and his sister's not much better, a fact lamented by the Colonel, whose own script was exceptionally fine. My

grandmother's penmanship, most execrable of all, seems to have received less notice, other than from herself. "I am writing on my knee," or, "while everyone is talking," etc. Not only were the loops of her letters identical, but to guarantee illegibility, once all available space had been used, she would proceed—like others of the time—to write whole paragraphs at right angles, across the original words.

Chapter 6. Groton

1. Henry the Red, in 1822 at the age of ten, went off to Mount Airy College, a boarding school in Germantown, Pennsylvania, where he remained until 1828. His son Henry A. spent four years in boarding school from the age of twelve.

2. Cheltensham School; Trinity College, Cambridge. In F. D. Ashburn, *Peabody of Groton* (New York: Coward-McCann, 1944).

3. Ibid., 101, 72.

4. "I am so homesick now I don't know what to do. One mustn't let anyone see. . . . If someone doesn't come to see me soon, I will die of sorrow. Please come to see me. I'm crying so hard I can't write. Aurevoir etc. I kissed the pages." (On the adjoining page, he had drawn a circle and labeled it "baisee," kiss.) The words "Papa" and "Pappa" were spelled interchangeably in family letters, but in both cases were pronounced Pa*pa*.

5. Of the 189 students who graduated from Groton between 1896 and 1905, 57 became bankers, 35 businessmen, 22 educators or publishers, 15 architects, and 10 doctors. (Richard Derby, later Theodore Roosevelt's son-in-law, was among the last group.) Harry was one of eight graduates who, probably as "gentlemen farmers," took up the business of agriculture. Four Grotonians during these years entered diplomatic or government service, including Joseph Grew and Franklin D. Roosevelt.

6. *Catalogue of Groton School* (Ayer, Mass.: Huntley S. Turner, 1896–97).

7. Latin, Latin composition, mathematics (which included geometry, algebra, physics), history, Greek, English composition, and English.

8. *The Grotonian*, February 1899.

Chapter 7. Harvard

1. Robert W. Merry, *Taking on the World* (New York: Viking Penguin, 1996), 35.

2. Undergraduates were permitted at this time to complete the requirements for a bachelor's degree a year in advance, by taking extra courses each semester.

3. "Making Men of the Boys," in *Glimpses of Harvard Past*, ed. B. Baylin, D. Fleming, D. Hardlin, and S. Thernston (Cambridge: Harvard University Press, 1986).

4. In 1899, Louise had married Francis Boardman Crowninshield, whose cousin, Frank Crowninshield, was to become the editor of *Vanity Fair*. Each referred to the other as "bad Frank."

5. Harry's only other long-distance trip had been in 1893 to the World's Columbian Exposition in Chicago, the summer before he went to Groton.

6. In May 1902, in perhaps Harry's last letter to both of his parents, he wrote, "I have discovered a wonderful new way to grow dahlias, so I ordered 12 tubers at the Busy, and before I knew it had sent the bill to Papa it is only for $1.50 but I thought I would explain."

7. The School of Practical Agriculture and Horticulture in Briarcliff Manor, New York, had already accepted him.

Chapter 8. Finding Himself

1. The importing of plants was far simpler before 1913, when restrictions were passed by the Department of Agriculture. In 1948, at my father's request, I abetted his smuggling into this country an English daffodil bulb, Green Island. He fetched it from my stateroom the moment the ship had docked, and it joined its many daffodil cousins at Winterthur.

2. Beginning with the acquisition of two bulls and five cows from Minnesota, the Winterthur herd increased from 75 in 1915 to 450 eight years later.

3. In response to Harry's stated objective, his father reportedly remarked, "It won't cost as much as owning a yacht and it might do a lot for humanity." E. McClung Fleming, "The History of the Winterthur Estate," in *The Winterthur Story* (Winterthur, Del.: Henry Francis du Pont Winterthur Museum, 1965), 40.

Chapter 9. Ruth

1. At this time, Rosa Lewis was landlady of the André Hotel, in Jermyn Street, London, and had also bought the Cavendish Hotel, adjacent to it.

2. Peabody Conservatory of Music, Pupils' Record for Season of 1917, Archives, Peabody Institute of the Johns Hopkins University, Baltimore.

3. Among Ruth Wales du Pont's compositions are a sonata for organ; the introduction and first act of an opera, *A New England Romance,* based on *Ethan Frome;* four dances in the styles of 1750, 1800, 1850, 1900; and at least one waltz, one berceuse (which she had hoped to publish), and many fugues, all but one of which she lost in a railway station. She also wrote original songs and lovely scores for poems she admired, such as Robert Louis Stevenson's "The Night Rider" and "Home from the Hill."

4. In those days, it was not unusual for a Cabinet member, even the secretary of state, subsequently to be elected to the Senate. In 1912, Elihu Root was awarded the Nobel Peace Prize for his efforts toward international peace.

5. Frances Lippitt (later Mrs. Moreton Gage), Butler Ames, and Martha Wadsworth. Four years later, Mrs. Wadsworth wrote Harry, on news of his engagement: "When we were all together on that Panama trip . . . I had a real struggle with myself to keep from trying to bring this about."

6. The jeweler called it a museum piece comparable to the Cullinan diamond, given by the King of England to the Queen.

7. Francis Riggs, best man. Ushers: John de K. Alsop, Butler Ames, Marshall Bul-

litt, Franklin Ellis, R. H. Ives Goddard, Beverley R. Robinson. Ruth Wales had no attendant.

8. *New York Times,* Sunday, June 25, 1916. *Poughkeepsie Eagle* and *Poughkeepsie News-Press,* Saturday morning, June 24, 1916.

Chapter 10. Early Married Life

1. Harry's visit was of great significance, for here he acquired his "foundation herd" of five cows and two bulls. One of the latter, King of the Ormsbys, later at Winterthur sired Bess Johanna Ormsby; these two beasts were probably those most of all prized by Harry.

2. J. F. Wall, *Alfred I. du Pont* (New York: Oxford University Press, 1990), 189.

3. While in the nineteenth century Henry the Red had expanded the company through the purchase of other powder companies, the three cousins who took over its management early in this century saw opportunity in entirely different fields. Cellophane, rayon, fast-drying paints, synthetic rubber, and nylon were early success stories. A further lucrative investment of these years was a 26 percent share of the fledgling General Motors Corporation (since divested). Today Du Pont is a multinational diversified chemical company.

4. A. I. du Pont's statement, quoted in Wall, *Alfred I. du Pont,* 379.

5. Also included were enormous storage capacities for feed, a beet cellar for five thousand bushels, an elaborate forced ventilation system, an electrified cable tramway, and a laboratory for chemical and bacteriological examination of all milk produced.

6. E. McClung Fleming, "History of the Winterthur Estate," in *The Winterthur Story* (Winterthur, Del.: Henry Francis du Pont Winterthur Museum, 1965), 41.

7. Ibid., 43.

8. RdP, Essay, undated, unpublished, WA.

Chapter 11. Times of Crisis

1. Arthur Wellman Butler was an investment banker who later also distinguished himself professionally as an astronomer. He had been previously married to the sister of the sculptor Malvina H. Hoffman.

2. Eliza (Lila) Vanderbilt Webb was the sister of Frederick W. Vanderbilt, a Hyde Park neighbor of the Waleses', whose wife Louise (Lulu) was a distant cousin of my mother. Ruth brought Harry to Shelburne for a visit a year after their marriage and thus he began a friendship with three generations of the Webb family. Electra Havemeyer Webb, my father's junior by nine years, had much in common with him. A lifelong collector whose specialty was early Americana, in 1947 she founded the Shelburne Museum. After her death in 1960, her five children, led by her son J. Watson Webb, Jr., presented the Winterthur Museum with the pine dresser and its pink china, in loving memory of their mother.

Chapter 12. A Child's Perspective

1. Other theories: It is possible that my father suffered from dyslexia, at that time an unrecognized condition. Premature birth (at four and a half pounds) may have also contributed to his poor coordination as well as to academic problems, including those of penmanship and spelling.

2. Twenty years later, an addition to it was deemed impractical, and in 1950 it was torn down. The Regency house into which my parents moved the following year was built on this site.

Chapter 13. Louise

1. She need not have worried, for the Colonel did not gain his senatorship until 1906.

2. W. M. Whitehill, *Louise du Pont Crowninshield—1877–1958* (Winterthur, Del. 1960), 3.

3. Katharine Hammond, quoted in *Boca Beacon,* June 1992, 3.

4. Quote from statement of aims, National Trust for Historic Preservation.

5. J. E. Cantor, *Winterthur* (New York: Harry N. Abrams, 1985), 158.

6. Mrs. Francis B. Crowninshield et al., Letter to potential donors for Memorial to Bertha King Benkard (rooms to be given to Metropolitan Museum and Museum of City of New York). Undated but probably 1945 or '46.

Chapter 14. Parties and Food

1. Harry and his father also built a fig house in 1906, part of a complex of greenhouses that numbered twenty-seven when my father died.

2. The first shipment to Florida every year included one hundred dozen eggs; to Southampton, twelve cases of whole milk and fifty pounds of butter. Twenty to thirty turkeys would be given away every year as Christmas presents.

3. James Joyce, *Ulysses.*

4. "Bougies d'autrefois," discovered at Versailles in 1962 by Jacqueline Kennedy, replaced candelabra on side tables, for it was feared that live flame could damage the tapestries. These were tiny flame-shaped electric bulbs that flickered.

5. The Swedish minister, Axel Wallenberg, and his wife were frequent visitors. Wallenberg was the great-uncle of Raoul, the legendary hero-diplomat stationed in Brussels in World War II who enabled the escape of innumerable individuals from the Nazis.

6. The Duchess of Windsor at a large reception in New York soon after the museum had opened approached my mother:

> Duchess of W.: We have heard marvelous things about Winterthur and how difficult it is to get in.

R. W. du P. (Not a great admirer of the Windsors): Everything you hear is true, and you should apply for tickets about two years in advance.

Chapter 15. Harry & Ruth

1. I am reminded of a remark attributed to W. C. Fields: "People who dislike children and dogs can't be all bad."

2. The essay was introduced by this poem:

"I have finished another year," said God
"In grey, green, white, and brown,
I have strewn the leaf upon the sod,
Sealed up the worm within the clod,
And let the last sun down."
"But what's the use of it?" I said,
"What reason made you call
From formless void this earth I tread?"

3. My mother's wish to join the Society of Colonial Dames may have been influenced in part by the fact that her mother-in-law had become a member of this organization many years earlier. Ruth W. du Pont was also instrumental in the restoration of Tryon Palace in New Bern, North Carolina, the governor's eighteenth-century house designed by her English-born ancestor John Hawks (1731–1790).

4. In actuality, Franklin D. Roosevelt, although younger by a year, was "half uncle" to Harry's Groton classmate James Roosevelt, Jr. James was the grandson of Franklin's father and his first wife, Rebecca Howland, who had died in 1876.

5. "I hope you will forgive me as a very old friend for writing you. . . . Please forget the fact that my name is du Pont or that I have a personal prejudice against the President. This is quite true, but I did not start with one. He was an old friend of mine and an older friend of Ruth's. . . . The violent attack the President made against our family in his inaugural speech in Philadelphia four years ago was not only completely uncalled for but also completely unfair. Why he should have selected us in particular as a target for his attack I cannot imagine.

"You may not know this, but Pierre du Pont had a great part in electing him President the first time. Pierre was then sent for by the President to come to Washington to help out in government matters and went gladly, hoping to be of help in straightening out some of the national confusion; but after a short time working down there, conditions were so unsatisfactory from every point of view that he was obliged to resign from his position, as in fact, have a majority of our reputable citizens who have tried to work for this administration. Since that time, we have been singled out for every type of annoyance that the administration could contrive to visit on us. So I have a very deep personal prejudice, and I think justly so. Apart from that, I feel that the way the President has fostered class prejudice and class hatred should be to his everlasting shame. . . . I fear in four years more you will find yourself without butter for your bread. Esthetic and worthwhile as landscape gardening is, it is, after all, in the luxury class, and this type of profession is in the first group that will have to be abandoned by all our citizens. There will be no more gardens, as no one will be able to employ a gardener. Should we be at war and the 80% tax provision voted by the House of Representatives and the Senate to be imposed on all incomes over $50,000 a year go into effect, nearly everyone who could maintain any kind of an estate would be reduced to penury. . . . To my mind, the most fundamental of the President's failings is the fact that I consider him intellectually dishonest. . . . Ruth came to this regretful conclusion long before the President was even Governor of the State of New York. At the time of his nomination for the presidency, she took it upon herself to approach the Pierre du Ponts and tell them just how serious a thing she felt it would be should Roosevelt be elected. This, of course, carried no weight with them at the time, but they have since lived to regret their decision in the matter of their political stand in 1932."

6. Edith Wharton, *The Age of Innocence*.

7. Charles Montgomery was an antiques dealer and pewter specialist from Wallingford, Connecticut.

8. This sonnet, written in 1962 by Ruth Wales du Pont, is displayed in the Winterthur library.

> I would I knew the words with which to frame
> The all-pervading sense of pure delight
> Attending thee, beloved, in my sight,
> Or roused by vagrant whisper of thy name.
> Rare qualities of grace combine the while
> To give reflections, mirrored, of thy soul
> Honor and godliness, thine aim and goal
> Are radiated by thy very smile.
> Yet of all else, beloved, I hold most dear
> The worship brought by thee to Beauty's shrine;
> Discovering in homely, humble things
> Beauty alone, where e'er she may appear;
> By which same token rapture all is mine;
> I, too, am glorified, and given wings.

9. Ruth's uncle Archie McLean Hawks wrote my mother in 1944 that he and his wife had often discussed "what you *might* have done, if poverty, instead of riches, had been your lot. You could dance, sing, play, act. . . . You could have become a movie star of the Nth magnitude."

10. A journal entry follows:

The wild flowers on the banks each side of the road from Syracuse to Palermo were worthy of Marian Coffin's best planting and colour schemes. Lemon yellow oxalis; pink, blue, yellow, orange, and white wild flowers in profusion. In the gardens of this hotel with eight terraces going down towards the sea but still way above it, the freesias seed themselves like dandelions and have the most heavenly perfume, geraniums (3 kinds) ixias, violets, tulip species, tree peonies, anemones, wallflowers, pansies, cinerarias, callas, stocks (large plants and in all colours), countless annuals, three kinds of jasmine, primula malacoides, white daisies like the ones we have in the greenhouse but huge plants that have been there for years, hyacinths, blue iris, white iris, strelitzia, primroses, clivias, huge beds of white callas, anemones in brilliant reds, blues, etc., sparaxis, daturas, and many of the small flowering trees one sees in the borders of the Longwood greenhouses, heliotrope, forget-me-nots, tiny sweet-scented jonquils, gerberas, ranunculus in all colours, snapdragons, nasturtiums, calendulas, bellis, schizanthus, sweet alyssum which grows wild here. Banksia roses and a few hybrid tea and china roses. The borders of the beds are edged with half a tile.

The wisterias and Judas trees are half out—just like a first Sunday in May in Delaware.

Besides all these flowers there are huge and small palm trees, orange trees, trellis, and many lovely places to sit and see the sea and Etna.

Taormina, Sicily, April, 1954   H. F. du Pont Journal

Chapter 16. Money

1. It is also possible that the reluctance of earlier du Pont generations to talk about their money could have stemmed from sensitivity over war-related profits. Eleuthère Irénée du Pont, so named by his godfather Turgot "in honor of liberty & peace," was of course aware of the ironic implications inherent in the manufacture of gunpowder. Describing himself as a "peaceable friend of liberty," he hoped that the "powder . . . will not be used for war, [but for] exercises against war . . . for the commerce of the Country, for hunting, for the opening of mountains and canals, for public works." From Pierre Jolly, *Du Pont de Nemours: Apostle of Liberty and the Promised Land,* trans. Elise du Pont Elrick (Wilmington, Del.: Brandywine, 1977), 249.

2. Speech given by Henry A. du Pont, November 10, 1915, at a dinner given in his honor "by the Younger Men of his Family," WA.

3. I feel sure that the young man to whom Carol (Mrs. Evelyn du P.) Irving referred was John Eleuthère du Pont, the youngest child of William, her husband's and also my father's first cousin. And I likewise now suspect that the allusion to an unloved branch of his family was in part to blame for my father's uncharacteristically angry outburst.

In January 1996, John du Pont, age fifty-seven, shot to death a wrestling coach who lived on his estate in Newtown Square, Pennsylvania. This event made headlines. The media described du Pont, who in earlier times had studied ornithology and had founded a natural history museum, as a "loner" (later diagnosed as a paranoid schizophrenic) whose thwarted aspirations to a role in the Olympic pentathlon had led him to befriend professional wrestlers and to train local policemen as sharpshooters. This event was of course above all unspeakably tragic for the victim and his family. At the trial, John du Pont was found guilty but insane and was remanded to a mental institution.

4. Fifteen pieces were bought in the Flayderman sale, two of which are still

among the most important of the Winterthur collection: the Newport tea table made by John Goddard for Jabez Bowen of Providence (which sold for $29,000), as well as a drop-leaf table for $8,000 labeled by John Townsend, Goddard's cousin.

5. H. F. du Pont, Unpublished document, 1951–1964. See Chapter 19, n. 3.

6. This complex was bought back by family members four years later, and in 1995 it was turned into an inn with guest suites and a restaurant.

7. By 1954 this law had been amended to specify that anyone who had given away 90 percent of his income in eight out of the previous ten years would qualify for the unlimited charitable deductions.

8. My father's counselors at this time used 80 percent of income as a rule-of-thumb when estimating his federal taxes.

Chapter 17. *A Passion to Collect*

1. HF's interview with Harlan Phillips, 1962, WA.

2. Werner Muensterberger, *Collecting* (Princeton: Princeton University Press, 1994), 11.

3. Albany Room, Baltimore Drawing Room, Belle Isle Room, Cecil Bedroom, Chestertown Room, Chinese Parlor, du Pont Dining Room, Empire Parlor, Essex Room, Hampton Room, Imlay Room, Lake Erie Hall, Lancaster Room, McIntire Bedroom, New York Bedroom, Oyster Bay Room, Pine Kitchen, Port Royal Room, Readbourne Parlor, Readbourne Stair Hall, Walton Room, Wentworth Room.

4. He entered in a contest a flower-patterned wallpaper sample I had designed in the fifth grade; not a prize-winner.

5. H. F. du Pont, early draft of Foreword to Joseph Downs, *American Furniture* (dated September 10, 1951), WA.

6. It is now displayed in the Johann Fust Memorial Library in Boca Grande.

7. My father was a founding member of the Brandywine Conservancy and Brandywine River Museum, established by Weymouth in 1969.

8. This was one of only three or four instances at Winterthur in which a search was made for a specific object.

9. H. F. du Pont, Foreword to Joseph Downs, *American Furniture* (New York: Macmillan, 1952), vi.

10. J. E. Cantor, *Winterthur* (New York: Harry N. Abrams, 1985), 156.

Chapter 18. *The Masterpiece Within*

1. My father suggested that Lloyd Hyde be so named. Once the curator had received his annual salary of $5,000 to $10,000, any money left over from the soon-to-be-established endowment was to go to the Southampton Hospital.

2. H. F. du Pont, Foreword, in Joseph Downs, *American Furniture* (New York: Macmillan, 1952), vi.

3. Excerpts from that memorandum:

New wainscots, cornices, mantelpieces, strips of wood, are to be replaced by old ones currently in storage. The West Bedroom is to have the panelling now stored in Montchanin, as well as furniture covers, curtains, rug and accessories now in the attic, along with a small Chippendale straight leg wing chair covered in plum velvet, and a tip-top pedestal. Showcases are to be built in the Bowling Alley for display of Lowestoft china, my pink Palestine Staffordshire set . . . the sets of blue and gold star Lowestoft, the brown, the set with flowers which has the candlesticks, all in the New York apartment. And from Southampton, more Staffordshire, of two different colors purple, of two different greens, two sets of pink and green, the marbelized set of purple slag. These cases are to be wide and deep enough to display masses of china together. . . . I want a lot of color showing. . . . Naturally, the Bowling Alley will be removed. . . . Maids' rooms 1, 2, 3, 4, 5, and 6, staff living quarters, the butler's suite etc., are to become showcases for more china. The blue armorial set of Lowestoft with Fitz Hugh border is to be kept for entertaining American or foreign visitors of distinction. . . . The royal Copenhagen set made for Catherine of Russia should be displayed in the Locker Room or Billiard Room. The best way for visitors to enter the Museum will be by the service court [and] into the Badminton Room, which will make an admirable waiting room and place to check umbrellas, etc., etc.

4. Walpole Society, Abstracts from Minutes of Annual Meeting held at Hartford, Conn., January 19, 1935.

5. Undated letter to Chauncey C. Nash, secretary of the Walpole Society. Quoted by Elizabeth Stillinger in *The Antiquers* (New York: Knopf, 1980), 167.

6. Walpole Society *Note Book*, 1932.

7. A magnifying glass; a Walpolean badge of membership in the form of a piece of silver worn around the neck.

8. H. F. du Pont, early draft of Foreword to Downs, *American Furniture* (draft dated September 10, 1951).

9. J. E. Cantor, *Winterthur* (New York: Harry N. Abrams, 1985), 188.

10. Queen Anne Dining Room, Hart Room, Pennsylvania Folk Art Room.

11. Dresser Room, Hardenbergh Parlor and Bedroom, Lebanon Room and Bedroom, Pennsylvania German Bedroom, Pennsylvania German Child's Bedroom, Scrimshaw Room, Simsbury Room, Spatterware Hall, William & Mary Room.

12. Bulfinch Staircase, Chippendale Staircase, Wright House Staircase.

13. Fraktur Room.

14. The owners of the settee had the Winterthur truck pull up to their back door as close as possible so that no one could see it leaving. But word had gotten out. At the truck's next stop, the homeowner offered the driver his house and its entire contents in exchange for the Winterthur truck and its precious cargo!

15. This collection was sold in an auction at Christie's in October 1994.

Chapter 19. The Museum Opens

1. Banister Stair Hall, Carroll Stair Hall, Chippendale Bedroom, Dominy Clock Shop, Dominy Woodworking Shop, Empire Hall, Federal Parlor, Fraktur Room, Ker-

shner Parlor & Kitchen, McIntire Porch, New England Kitchen, Queen Anne Bedroom, Seventeenth-Century Room, William & Mary Parlor (installed by 1961), China Trade Room, Pottery Alcove, Pottery Room, Readbourne Passage, Shaker Dwelling Room, Shaker Storeroom, Webb Alcove (installed by 1962), Beverly Room, Centreville Room, Shipley Room & Hall, Williams Room, rearrangement of Wynkoop Room (installed in 1964), Newport Room & Gidley Room (installed in 1966).

2. John A. H. Sweeney, Lecture, Winterthur Trustees, September 23, 1991.

3. H. F. du Pont, unpublished document, 1951–64. The document was addressed to "the Executors of my Will, to the Officers of the Winterthur Corporation & to the Director, Officers & Trustees of the Henry Francis du Pont Winterthur Museum Inc." The memorandum written by my father in 1930 to his executors on the subject of Chestertown House in Southampton was a basis for this "letter": "Naturally, the Board of Trustees . . . will have to give their approval, but . . . I want these changes made." . . . A "professor who is vouched for" should be able to visit the museum "without an attendant." . . . Trustees should not "lean or put their hands on any upholstered chair or on the curtains." . . . "Wing chairs must be lifted by their legs only. . . . Fires are not to be lighted in any of the 18 [many more after 1964] fake fireplaces."

4. Ibid., 11.

5. Charles F. Hummel, curator emeritus of Winterthur Museum; Jonathan L. Fairbanks, Katharine Lane Weems Curator of American Decorative Arts and Sculpture, Museum of Fine Arts, Boston.

6. These included lecture programs, annual seminars on museum operation and connoisseurship, and the development of the Winterthur Library.

7. J. E. Cantor, *Winterthur* (New York: Harry N. Abrams, 1985), 206.

Chapter 20. Private and Public

1. New Year's pamphlet: 1988, Happy New Year from A. Ward Burian et al.: "Cousin Harry and the Manure."

2. Marian Lawrence Peabody, *To Be Young Was Very Heaven* (Boston: Houghton Mifflin, 1967), 312.

3. J. F. Wall, *Alfred I. du Pont: The Man and His Family* (New York: Oxford University Press, 1990), 449.

4. These are still occupied for the most part by Winterthur employees.

5. Paul Hensley, "Harry's Other Garden," in Denise Magnani, *The Winterthur Garden* (New York: Harry N. Abrams, 1995).

6. *Holstein-Friesian World* 6 (May 10, 1969): 1046.

7. Elizabeth Stillinger, *The Antiquers* (New York: Knopf, 1980), 270.

8. E. McClung Fleming, "History of the Winterthur Estate," in *The Winterthur Story* (Winterthur, Del.: Henry Francis du Pont Winterthur Museum, 1965), 44.

9. Her citation reads, in part:

Mrs. Crowninshield has devoted herself actively and untiringly to the restoration and furnishing of a lengthening list of ancient houses. . . . I should say, to the restored houses of Virginia and Delaware, and others of her affectionately adopted New England. In these undertakings she has not only been most generous in the number and the character of her gifts, but she has made them peculiarly gifts of her own, by the application . . . of her own exquisite and expert personal taste. She is indeed a master of the art.

By those who have worked with her in bringing wonderful things to pass, she has seemed a Lady Bountiful, whose kindness and patriotic devotion indeed know no end.

Chapter 21. The Ninth Decade

1. The wedding of George A. Weymouth to Ann Brelsford McCoy.

2. A few years earlier, Samuel E. Homsey and his wife, Victorine du Pont (my father's second cousin), had designed the South Wing of the Winterthur Museum.

3. Denise Magnani et al., *The Winterthur Garden: Henry F. du Pont's Romance with the Land* (New York: Harry N. Abrams, 1995), 150.

4. Julian Boyd, editor, Jefferson Papers, Princeton University; Lyman Butterfield, editor-in-chief, Adams Papers, Harvard University.

5. Now Mrs. Richmond J. Cooper.

6. Executive Order of President Lyndon B. Johnson, March 7, 1964.

7. Press release, Office of Mrs. Lyndon B. Johnson, March 7, 1964, WA.

8. Henry Hope Reed, Jr., "Of Two Sisters . . . and a Museum," *New York Herald Tribune,* Sunday Magazine, August 11, 1963.

9. Cooper Union *News,* Cooper Square, New York, June 25, 1963.

10. Editorial, *New York Times,* July 4, 1963.

11. Article, *New York Times,* July 7, 1963.

12. D. Seiberling, "Scheme to Scuttle a Museum," *Life,* July 19, 1963. K. Kuh, "The Case of the Vanishing Museum," *Saturday Review,* October 26, 1963. "About New York," *Cue,* September 7, 1963. A. Winchester, *Antiques,* October 1963. S. R. Emery, "Requiem for a Museum?" *Interior Design,* August 1963.

13. "Debate About a Delight," *Time,* August 9, 1963.

14. "Smithsonian Outpost," in "Talk of the Town," *New Yorker,* October 27, 1967.

Chapter 22. Afterthoughts

1. The third undergraduate who helped Kirstein and Warburg to found the Harvard Society for Contemporary Art in 1928 was John Walker III, later the director of the National Gallery in Washington. My parents met John and his English wife, Lady Margaret Drummond, through her brother's American in-laws. The Walkers were frequent visitors to Winterthur; although my father and Johnnie sometimes corresponded about their respective museums, my parents' devotion to the Walkers was based more on their charm, vivacity, and bridge playing than on views of modern art.

2. Harry du Pont, at the invitation of my friend Flora Miller Irving (now Mrs.

Sidney Biddle), in 1964 became a trustee of the Whitney Museum of American Art and remained so until his death. Mrs. Irving (at the time vice-president but soon to become president of the museum) was then married to Michael H. Irving, the youngest son of Harry's first cousin Evelyn du Pont Irving and his wife, Carol. The Irvings had inherited Virieux from Cousin Evy's and my father's aunt Victorine du Pont Foster and were therefore close neighbors of Winterthur as well. In response to a second plea for funds toward the construction of the new Whitney Museum—Harry had already anonymously contributed an unspecified amount—in November 1966 he wrote, "Alas, I have to disappoint you, for the plan for the Library Conservation building at Winterthur is about finished and the estimates are just about four times what you need for the completion of your Whitney Museum. I am proud and pleased that I am a member of the Board. It is really beautiful both outside as well as in, and the big rooms are what modern art really needs. I would appreciate it if you would keep my figures confidential." In an unmailed draft of his letter, attached to the last sentence was the phrase "as I really do not want my relatives in Delaware to know what I am spending." (Perhaps his wife, among them.) Harry's embarrassment at extravagance and his desire for privacy never left him.

3. This circumstance was probably all to the good; a male child might not have measured up to expectations or have been able to share in and supplement my father's dreams.

4. When my mother gave up golf, Harry's partners were almost always their women friends, who called him "Tiger" and condoned his driving from the ladies' tee.

References

PAGE

xiii   "I shall be happy to know," HF to RL, October 18, 1957.

xiii   "very striking factor," E. P. Richardson, Memorandum to HF, June 27, 1962, WA.

1   "one of the few remaining relics," HA to PdP, August 27, 1902, HML.

4   "I have been away," HF to PdP, June 28, 1898, WA.

19   "a perfect sunbeam," Louisa Gerhard du Pont to Aunt Sophie (Mrs. Samuel Francis du Pont), August 18, 1874, HML.

21   "I will miss her very much," PdP to AR, January 1888, HML.

23   "best example [of holiness]," AR to PdP, September 17, 1894, HML.

23   "with affection & care," Mary Wingate to PdP, March 11, 1883, HML.

25   "Lent and V left for the White Mountains," HAdP to PdP, August 17, 1888, HML.

26   "something dreadful would happen," AR to PdP, October 12, 1891, HML.

26   "it would be the best thing," AR to PdP, May 30, 1892, HML.

26   "sorrows come soon enough," PdP to AR, March 1886, HML.

26   "Does it seem possible," PdP to AR, February 1887, HML.

27   "sad sad visit," PdP to Sophie dP, March 1876, HML.

27   "Everyone said," PdP to "my dear Cousin," June 30, 1876, HML.

27   "The sight of your grief and tears," D. D. Smith, rector of Christ Church to PdP, March 8, 1883, HML.

28   Beverley and Herman "said," AR to PdP, March 8, 1883, HML.

28   "happy & safe in his Father's arms," PdP to Sophie dP, March 29, 1883, HML.

28   "The blow was so terrible," PdP to Sophie dP, March 1886, HML.

28 "Phillippine has been so entirely a part," PdP to AR, December 1884, HML.

28 "that awful nausea," PdP to AR, November 30, 1884, HML.

28 "even if it should all go right," PdP to AR, December 1884, HML.

28 "It has been dreadful to have Henry away," PdP to AR, January 1885, HML.

28 "a great event, a cake with 35 candles," PdP to AR, April 21, 1885, HML.

28 "If only I could be good for something," PdP to AR, April 21, 1885, HML.

28 "We are all flourishing here," PdP to AR, September or October 1885, HML.

29 "the butcher will not fail," PdP to AR, December 1885, HML.

29 "The baby lamb is as saint-like as ever," PdP to AR, September 1885, HML.

29 "What a dear little baby she was," PdP to AR, March 1886, HML.

29 "I cannot bear to go anywhere," PdP to AR, April 1886, HML.

29 "I am sick in bed," PdP to AR, May 1886, HML.

29 "I have a splitting headache," PdP to AR, August 1886, HML.

29 "Do come to New York," AR to PdP, September 1884, HML.

29 "Nothing will cure your cough as well," AR to PdP, March 4, 1883, HML.

29 "I see now that you feel," AR to PdP, January 30, 1885, HML.

29 "You have quite enough seclusion," AR to PdP, July 9, 1886, HML.

30 "a bad thing for people," PdP to AR, June 23, 1890, HML.

30 "only 3 girls had . . . a good time," AR to PdP, August 16, 1890, HML.

30 "not available in our much abused Wilmington," PdP to AR, December 1885, HML.

30 "It was like having a glimpse of New York again," PdP to AR, Thanksgiving 1885, HML.

30 "We went last night to see Mary Andersen," PdP to HA, December 11, 1888, HML.

30 "I envied you the Opera," PdP to AR, January 1885, HML.

30 "How nice it must be," PdP to AR, 1885, HML.

33 "it would be so nice to have you," PdP to AR, April 1886, HML.

33 "I was so delighted to hear," PdP to AR, Apri 1886, HML.

33 "I am so glad you decided to wear your white dress," PdP to AR, June 2, 1890, HML.

33 "Mrs. Cleveland is really very pretty," PdP to AR, September 20, 1887, HML.

33 "Louise was choking with the croup," PdP to AR, March 1886, HML.

34 "should have felt dreadful to think," PF to HA, September 24, 1873, HML.

34 "I am fully conscious," HA to PF, March 5, 1874, HML.

35 "characteristically dated 'on the train,'" HA to PdP, April 11, 1889, HML.

35 "absurd," re ill-mannered cousin, PdP to AR, December 1883, HML.

35 "The results are a signal tribute," HA to PdP, October 23, 1889, HML.

35 "pardon my dereliction," HA to PdP, April 23, 1890, HML.

35 "altogether . . . not in very good shape," HA to PdP, October 23, 1890, HML.

35 "It seems dreadful to leave you," PdP to HA, April 21, 1883, HML.

35 "I wish you knew how to play solitaire," PdP to HA, November 30, 1886, HML.

35 "It is a pleasure to think," HA to PdP, March 23, 1887, HML.

35 "There is no one here [for us] to know," PdP to HA, August 1889, HML.

35 "quietness and repose of our beautiful home," HA to PdP, September 1, 1889, HML.

36 "How did Henry enjoy his stay with you," Eliza Lentilhon (Mrs. Peter V. King) to PdP, August 21, 1886, HML.

36 "Henry I am sure did not speak," PdP to AR, March 1886, HML.

36 "This is a sad anniversary for us," HA to PdP, March 5, 1899, HML.

40 "well advanced in his studies . . . character & conduct," Samuel Francis du Pont to Jefferson Davis, April 10, 1855, HML.

40 "of the right name and nature," Henry A. Wise (friend of HA's uncle) to President Franklin Pierce, February 7, 1856, HML.

40 "the unrivalled" gun powder establishment, Samuel F. du Pont to Jefferson Davis, April 10, 1855, HML.

41 "To see service with troops," HA to his uncle Samuel Francis du Pont, August 27, 1861, HML.

41 "distinguished services," HA to Major Henry F. Brewerton, October 1, 1895, HML.

41 "bad relations," HA to HF, December 4, 1926, HML.

41 "the unforeseen and almost unparalleled," quote of Confederate General Imboden (in reference to a defeat in the Battle of Piedmont), ibid.

42 "who galloped forward to the firing," HA to Major Henry F. Brewerton, October 1, 1895, HML.

42 "most distinguished gallantry," letter of Major John C. White to HA, October 31, 1915, WA.

43 "offensive, ungentlemanly," HA to James W. Piper, May 21, 1866, HML.

43 "a very old . . . friend," HA to his mother, Louisa Gerhard dP, July 5, 1897, WA.

43 "one of the most important," HA to HF, October 19, 1893, WA.

43 "I could not help remembering," HA to Alfred I. du Pont, December 2, 1922, HML.

44 "Some people think," HA to Rodney Sharp, October 25, 1926, WA.

44   "mental & bodily fatigue," HA to PdP, September 14, 1900, HML.

44   "avalanche of cares," HA to PdP, March 5, 1897, HML.

44   "completely used up," HA to PdP, April 26, 1895, HML.

44   "l'un n'empêche," PdP to AR, January 1886, HML.

45   "many cares," HA to HF, March 21, 1894, WA.

45   "pleasure & pride," HA to HF, January 16, 1896, HML.

45   "cannot help thinking," HA to PdP, January 9, 1897, HML.

45   "awfully sorry & distressed," HA to PdP, December 11, 1897, HML.

45   "Your conceit," PF to HA, September 23, 1873, HML.

45   "I have always been," PF to HA, September 29, 1873, HML.

45   "It is your bounden duty," PF to HA, October 2, 1873, HML.

45   "When doing your best," PF to HA, October 21, 1873, HML.

45   "It never seemed," PF to HA, November 10, 1873, HML.

45   "that I would not be good enough," PF to HA, December 2, 1873, HML.

46   "Sometimes when I think," PF to HA, October 21, 1873, HML.

46   "I knew that I was desperately," HA to PF, September 25, 1873, HML.

46   "I suppose you are right," PF to HA, October 29, 1873, HML.

46   "charming and interesting," HA to PF, March 3 or 4, 1874, HML.

46   "If I had read it," PF to HA, December 6, 1873, HML.

46   "I love you with all my heart," HA to PF, January 5, 1874, HML.

46   "I love you very dearly," HA to PF, March 2, 1874, HML.

46   "With fond love," HA to PdP, August 29, 1884, HML.

46   "So goodnight dearie . . . all my love," PF to HA, June 23, 1874.

46   "Love ye dearie," PdP to HA, August 7, 1888, HML.

46   "Always affectionately," PdP to HA, July 18, 1901, HML.

48   "very swell appearance," PdP to HA, January 16, 1899, HML.

48   "the least the President," PdP to HA, March 10, 1899, HML.

48   "The idea of your telegraphing," PdP to HA, December 14, 1896, HML.

48   lack of "prudence," HA to PdP, March 13, 1899, HML.

48   "mania on the subject of coolness," HA to PdP, ibid.

48   "Referring to your letter," HA to Reverend William M. Jefferis, March 24, 1902, HML.

48   "wholly uncalled for and ungentlemanly," Reverend William M. Jefferis, telephone call to HA's secretary, April 9, 1902, HML.

48   "doleful" . . . but "Papa looked much the more," PdP to LdP, August 25, 1897, HML.

49   "Good bye, my Darling," HA to PdP, September 13, 1902, HML.

49   "My sweet loving Pauline's," HA on PdP's envelope, September 1902, HML.

50   "Play anywhere," HF to Harlan B. Phillips, oral interview, April 11, 1962, p. 7, WA.

50   "a huge cake. He cannot speak a word of English," HF to PdP, October 20, 1900, WA. ("Little 4 year old Warrick Poter [*sic*] his father is Mr. Bobb Potter and his mother was Lily Fish?")

50   a fine account of Christmas dictated in French to PdP and mailed to his Robinson cousins, January 18, 1887, HML.

51   "I know how anxious you feel," Dr. Beverley Robinson to PdP, September 17, 1893, HML.

51   "This could send Anna & me on a spree," ibid.

51   this "pays our debt," HA to PdP, March 20, 1890, HML.

51   "The snow is so wet," PdP to AR, December 27, 1883, HML.

51   "I fear [the heat] will make them ill," PdP to HA, September 10, 1884, HML.

51   "We have had a regular hospital here," PdP to AR, October 30, 1884, HML.

51   "We are like nickels," PdP to AR, April 21, 1885, HML.

51   "Last year [the children]," ibid.

52   "so thin & pale & [seeming] so weak," PdP to AR, March 29, 1885, HML.

52   "dear little Harry," Eliza Lentilhon (Aunt Lilie; Mrs. Peter Vandervoort King) to PdP, August 21, 1886, HML.

52   "poor little Harry," PdP to AR, September 1, 1886; March 1887, HML.

52   "strong & well," AR to PdP, August 9, 1886, HML.

52   gain "flesh & strength & appetite," Ida Guepp to PdP, August 17, 1890, HML.

52   "have him where I could get at him," PdP to AR, March 27, 1885, HML.

52   hoped for "strong boy," Aunt Lilie to PdP, August 21, 1886, HML.

52   "delighted by the trained horses," PdP to AR, November 1884, HML.

52   "Said he, 'Ah-ha, by taking'," PdP to AR, January 1886, HML.

52   "After persuadings & tears," PdP to HA, October 21, 1890, HML.

54   "will be induced to play," PdP to HA, August 1889, HML.

54   "I have done my best," PdP to HA, September 1889, HML.

54   "still standing aloof," HA to PdP, September 5, 1889, HML.

54   "It distresses me," HA to PdP, September 3, 1889, HML.

55   "Harry shows no more fondness," PdP to AR, November 1884, HML.

55   "commencing to read," PdP to AR, January 26, 1887, HML.

55   "cunning," PdP to HA, September 6, 1884, HML.

55   "looking like a little man," PdP to HA, September 2, 1884, HML.

55   "a most charming boy," PdP to HA, April 1891, HML.

55   with "beautiful manners," AR to PdP, May 4, 1893, HML.

55   "As I expected," PdP to AR, November 1887, HML.

55   "well & happy," HA to PdP, March 13, 1890, HML.

56   singing "so sweetly," PdP to HA, February 20, 1890, HML.56

56   a wedding . . . "magnifique," AR to PdP, March 9, 1890, HML.

58   "brave & manly front," HA to HF, October 19, 1893, WA.

58   "Je suis si homesick," HF to parents, November 1893, WA.

59   "I am homesick only during the day," HF to parents, October 14, 1893, WA.

59   "I am not at all homesick this morning," HF to parents, October 22, 1893, WA.

59   "I am not homesick all the time," HF to parents, April 12, 1896, WA.

59   "big Egg, a Nooga egg," HF to parents, April 15, 1895, WA.

59   "It is now 20 minutes past 9," ibid.

59   "thoroughly" appreciated his feelings, HA to HF, October 19, 1893, WA.

59   "power to make," ibid.

60   "Je t'embrasse de tout coeur," PdP to HF, October 14, 1893, HML.

60   "pretty anthem," HF to parents, October 22, 1893, WA.

60   "I never knew how much," HF to parents, January 20, 1895, WA.

60   "long sniff at my daffodils," HF to parents, April 15, 1895, WA.

60   "too much trouble & very few," HF to parents, April 26, 1896, WA.

60   "the gardiner's" fine violets, HF to parents, October 17, 1895, WA.

60   "lovely dark claret," HF to PdP, March 6, 1899, HML.

61   "nosegay of sweet peas," HF to parents, October 22, 1894, WA.

61   "I am wearing one now" (water lily), HF to parents, June 9, 1895, WA.

61   "up to the gardiners," HF to parents, January 27, 1895, WA.

61   "Mr Peabody after dinner called me," HF to parents, February 25, 1894, WA.

61   denied . . . family spoke French at home, HF to parents, March 1894, WA.

61   "I am very much pained," HA to HF, March 13, 1894, WA.

62   "I have been thinking," HA to HF, March 21, 1894, WA.

62   "It makes me so mad," HF to parents, May 3, 1896, HML.

62   "Mr. Billings asked me," PdP to HA, March 6, 1895, HML.

63   "I can't describe the feeling," HF to parents, March 27, 1896, WA.

63   "bright yellow cravat," HF to parents, December 1, 1895, HML.

63   "Dan Draper's golf stockings," HF to parents, September 27, 1896, WA.

63   How to decline Joe Grew's Thanksgiving invitation, HF to parents, October 21, 1894, WA.

63   Asks parents not to speak French on next visit, HF to parents, November 25, 1894, WA.

63   "it would not be appreciated," HF to parents, April 14, 1895, WA.

64   exposing Harry "to the night air," PdP to AR, December 22, 1894, HML.

64   "Two more Sundays," HF to parents, May 10, 1896, WA.

64   "rayon de soleil," AR to PdP, October 23, 1893, HML.

64   "silking" teeth . . . filling "from the upper right," HF to parents, May 30, 1897, WA.

64   "About my close," HF to parents, October 31, 1897, WA.

64   "Please have [my white cravat] cleaned," HF to parents, December 2, 1895, HML.

64   buy some "turned down collars," HF to parents, March 1, 1896, WA.

64   "necktie that is not orange," HF to parents, February 25, 1894, WA.

65   Christmas list, HF to parents, December 8, 1894, WA.

65   "Get them right away," HF to parents, January 27, 1895, HML.

65   a "waterbury watch," HF to parents, May 5, 1895, WA.

65   nail scissors, comb, and clothes brush, HF to parents, May 10, 1897, HML.

65   "silver case to carry," ibid.

65   a pocket "Kodak," ibid.

65   not "swell, just plain cushions," HF to parents, May 17, 1896, WA.

65   "some fashionable English," HF to parents, May 10, 1897, HML.

65   "ever ready electric light," HF to PdP, December 5, 1898, WA.

66   "on pins & kneadles," HF to PdP, October 23, 1895, HML.

66   "I have not gone up," HF to parents, January 12, 1896, WA.

66   "mental weakness," HF to parents, June 24, 1898, WA.

66   "much harder," HF to parents, December 1897, HML.

66   golf "morning & afternoon," HF to parents, ibid.

66   "If my average isent better," HF to parents, May 17, 1896, WA.

66   having "past," HF to PdP, December 15, 1897, WA.

66   "lattin," HF to parents, September 29, 1895, WA.

66   it will be "all right," HF to PdP, January 11, 1898, WA.

66   "I dont think I have done any worse," HF to parents, May 3, 1896, WA.

66   "so very interesting," HF to parents, November 1, 1896, HML.

66   "despite studying faithfully," PdP to HA, February 6, 1897, HML.

66   "Harry simply cannot," PdP to HA, February 24, 1898, HML.

66   *"Are you working hard,"* HA to HF, October 30, 1894, WA.

66   "Never forget that the du Ponts," HA to HF, March 19, 1896, WA.

67   "The marks [4th form] came yesterday," PdP to HF, October 27, 1896, WA.

67   "Dear Mama & Papa, Your letter came," HF to parents, October 11, 1896, WA.

67   "genius does not lie," HF to parents, October 3, 1897, WA.

67   "Of course it is hardly nothing at all," HF to parents, June 24, 1898, WA.

67   "If I should go down," HF to parents, February 5, 1898, WA.

68   "behind & undeveloped," PdP to HA, May 27, 1898, WA.

68   "I cannot tell you how relieved I feal," HF to parents, February 14, 1898, WA.

68   "feel so much more responsible," HF to parents, May 27, 1898, WA.

68   "as I would like to have my books," HF to PdP, June 23, 1898, WA.

68   "You are now rewarded," HA to HF, October 2, 1898, WA.

68   "geometery," HF to parents, October 2, 1898, WA.

69   "the boys seemed," PdP to HA, February 22, 1899, HML.

69   "acting is great fun," HF to PdP, January 23, 1899, WA.

69   he was not "small & pretty," HF to PdP, January 27, 1899, WA.

69   performance as "capital," PdP to HA, February 22, 1899, HML.

69   "so glad for him to have done something," ibid.

69   "splendid baritone voice," HF to parents, June 13, 1897, WA.

69   "ouverture to Tanhauser," HF to parents, March 21, 1897, WA.

69   "extremely interested," HF to PdP, January 23, 1899, WA.

69   shining mass, HF to PdP, March 21, 1899, WA.

69   during a "slay" ride, HF to PdP, March 23, 1899, WA.

69   "everything is leaved," HF to parents, May 1897, WA.

69   "The country is beautiful now," HF to parents, October 5, 1897, WA.

69   "when the sun came out," HF to parents, March 8, 1896, WA.

69   "very pretty" curtain, HF to parents, February 17, 1895, HML.

69   "school saloon," HF to parents, September 20, 1896, WA.

69   "a curtain with the most gaudy colors," HF to parents, May 3, 1896, WA.

69   "first was a light yellow," HF to parents, May 24, 1896, WA.

69   his "eagle eye" HF to PdP, January 6, 1897, WA.

69   "the old green dress," HF to PdP, February 12, 1898, WA.

70   the "bleu waist from Aunt Anna," HF to PdP, February 16, 1899, WA.

70   "unable to manage my tails," HF to parents, March 7, 1897, WA.

70   somebody to room with, HF to PdP, October 23, 1898, WA.

70   "I never had such a letter," HF to PdP, March 10, 1899, WA.

70   "I hope he will like my letter," HF to PdP, March 17, 1899, WA.

70   "dreadfully, as he always went out," HF to parents, April 26, 1896, WA.

70   "terrible nightmare," HF to parents, February 21, 1894, WA.

70   "had a fit in church," HF to parents, May 17, 1896, WA.

70   "very homesick, and seems too old," HF to parents, October 11, 1896, WA.

70   "It will be so sad for Hermann," HF to PdP, January 29, 1899, WA.

70   "Does Pappa wear a nightshirt?" HF to PdP, March 6, 1896, HML.

70   Is Pappa elected to the Senate or not?" HF to parents, May 12, 1895, WA.

70   "Was Pappa in the artillery or cavalary," HF to parents, March 1, 1896, WA.

71   doubted that Pappa would enjoy the play, HF to PdP, January 31, 1898, WA.

71   advises mother about golf clubs, HF to parents, March 22, 1896, HML.

71   his "very selfish view," HF to PdP, February 6, 1899, WA.

73   geology would prove "interesting," HF to parents, October 1, 1899, WA.

73   "very entertaining so far," HF to PdP, October 8, 1901, WA.

73   "Philosophy is very hard," HF to PdP, October 14, 1901, WA.

73   "more than glad," ibid.

74   "studying like the mischief," HF to parents, May 23, 1901, HML.

74   "You never mention Hermann," PdP to HF, October 1899, WA.

74   "I suppose all the Groton boys," PdP to HF, January 1900, WA.

74   "Don't you think," PdP to HF, October 8, 1900, WA.

74   "Your letter has just come," HF to PdP, October 9, 1900, WA.

74   "successful" tea parties," HF to PdP, November 2, 1900, WA.

74   "conversed affably," HF to PdP, November 8, 1900, WA.

74   "Lots of fellows came in," HF to PdP, May 1901, HML.

75   "As usual my partner," HF to parents, January 6, 1900, WA.

75   "hopeless as usual," HF to PdP, October 15, 1901, WA.

75   "would have been pleased," PdP to HA, February 9, 1901, WA.

75   "very good fun," HF to parents, February 27, 1900, WA.

75   "*Gotterdammerung* and *Carmen*," HF to PdP, December 7, 1899, WA.

75   *Figaro,* HF to PdP, December 6, 1899, WA.

75   *Cyrano,* "wonderful," HF to PdP, October 11, 1899, WA.

75   *Ben-Hur,* "the staging was wonderful," HF to PdP, January 10, 1901, WA.

75   "I never expect," HF to PdP, April 27, 1901, WA.

77   "The outside curtains," HF to parents, November 12, 1900, WA.

78   "I do not think you understand," HF to PdP, January 22, 1901, WA.

78   "I really think you might have the heat," HF to parents, January 20, 1901, WA.

78   "kennel friend at Wellesley," HF to PdP, March 27, 1902, WA.

78   lilies-of-the-valley "as perfect as ever," HF to PdP, April 1902, WA.

78   "Primula Obconica," HF to PdP, March 27, 1902, WA.

78   "robbing all the gardens," HF to PdP, October 16, 1901, WA.

78   "one of the best surgeons," HF to parents, June 6, 1901, HML.

79   "London is fascinating," HF to parents, June 27, 1901, HML.

79   "The scenery from Viège," PdP to HA, July 18, 1901, HML.

79   "sudden resolution," HF to PdP, October 24, 1901, WA.

79   "much to be admired," HF to PdP, ibid.

79   "We heard all about," HF to PdP, April 27, 1902, WA.

80   "Sunday will be all taken up," HF to PdP, March 27, 1902, WA.

80   "too much bowing," HF to PdP, October 1901, WA.

80   Congregational church "awful," HF to parents, November 12, 1899, WA.

80   "perfectly disgusting," HF to PdP, October 8, 1901, WA.

81   "grow in goodness," LGdP to HF, August 13, 1896, WA.

81   "a good, useful, honorable," HA to HF, May 25, 1897, WA.

81   hoped for nothing more, PdP to HF, May 20, 1901, WA.

81   "You must be worthy," HA to HF, March 21, 1894, WA.

81   "back seats," HA to HF, March 19, 1896, WA.

81   "I thought I would die," HF to PdP, November 2, 1901, WA.

81   "I went all the way down town," IF to PdP, March 27, 1902, WA.

81   "Did I not tell you," HF to PdP, February 4, 1901, WA.

81   "Don't you want to consult," HF to PdP, April 1902, WA.

83   "Don't get too tired," HF to PdP, August 6, 1902, WA.

83   "Do be careful," HF to PdP, August 22, 1902, WA.

83   "The beach is entirely too far," HF to PdP, August 20, 1902, WA.

83   "Your mother suffered," HA to HF, September, 7, 1902, WA.

83   "I had a lovely time," HF to PdP, April 29, 1902, WA.

85   "rather tired," W. Hadden to HF, January 22, 1903, WA.

85   "I am much excited," LdPC to HF, September 16, 1903, WA.

85   "leggings or plain black trousers," HF to Brooks Brothers, November 22, 1907, WA.

85   "do you think I had better have," HF to Brooks Brothers, October 8, 1907, WA.

86   "plenty of extra material," ibid.

86   "Joseph Benoit's coat & vest," HF to Brooks Brothers, November 16, 1909, WA.

86   "It seems to me that," HF to Brooks Brothers, November 14, 1908, WA.

86   "Complete bedroom drinking water sets," HF to Gilman, Collamore & Co., April 18, 1907, WA.

86   "lately have been quite tough," HF to Henry Maillard, May 13, 1913, WA.

86   "but there is no use wasting time," HF to Henry Maillard, January 13, 1913, WA.

87   "cocaine fiend," HF to LdPC, March 3, 1905, WA.

88   "You are so like your mother," Emily Janeway to HF, May 8, 1906, WA.

89   "which we are refurnishing," HF to Little and Brown, Architects, Febuary 28, 1910, WA

89   "I have decided not," HF to Little and Brown, Architects, January 4, 1911, WA.

89   "I think the public," HF to W. W. Rawson & Co., October 3, 1908, WA.

90   "I shudder with horror," HF to Marian Coffin, October 4, 1911, WA.

90   "All you need to do," HF to Anna Robinson, October 6, 1911, WA.

90   "Dearest Harry—I write in triumph," Anna Robinson to HF, fall 1911, WA.

90   "I hope the Colonel," HF to John W. Chapple, October 2, 1911, WA.

91   "deep black red snapdragons," HF travel notebook, September 13, 1909, WA.

91   "distinctly green," HF Garden Diary, April 7, 1910, WA.

91   "brazenly rang the front door bell," HF to Marian Coffin, September 25, 1912, WA.

91   "without a trace of pink," HF to H. W. Pfitzer, July 7, 1913, WA.

92   "having been bandied about," HF to A. J. Woodruff & Co., December 26, 1913, WA.

92   "12 clumps of Viola," Barr & Sons, London, to HF, October 11, 1912, WA.

92   "in my trunk," HF to Barr & Sons, London, August 6, 1914, WA.

92   "whole set of Autumn crocus," HF to Ellen Willmott, August 13, 1914, WA.

92   "patriotic work," Charles Sprague Sargent to HA, November 26, 1918, WA.

92   "I assure you," HF to parents, January 20, 1901.

95   "It is simply *corking*," RW to RHW, undated, 1903, WA.

95   "being able to laugh," from school essay, "Advantages of a Sense of Humor," April 11, 1906, WA.

95   "I hang on the mail," RdP to RHW, March 18, 1921, WA.

97   "Mrs. Cushman . . . remembered," RW to RHW, January 11, 1912.

97   "Ed and Mame were saying," August 26, 1907, WA.

97   "They keep 150 horses," RW to RHW, October 23, 1910, WA.

97   "certainly keeps people," ibid.

97   "writing . . . very hard," RW to RHW, "Mon," 1911, WA.

97   "chorus for a ragtime," ibid.

97   "all the rag I knew," RW to RHW, February 6, 1915, WA.

97   "Had a wonderful lesson," RdP to RHW, January 11, 1917, WA.

97   "I am terribly busy," RdP to RHW, October 22, 1919, WA.

98   "Most terrible day," RW diary, May 10, 1909, WA.

98   "I cannot bear to think," RW to RHW, August 16, 1914, WA.

98   "The imagination cannot picture," RW to RHW, Thanksgiving 1914, WA.

98   "You bet I am glad," RW to RHW, January 22, 1915, WA.

99   "Du Pont called me up," RW to RHW, 1911(?), WA.

99   "No one could be nicer," RW to RHW, March 20, 1912 [on board United Fruit Co.'s SS *Parismina*], WA.

99   "almost engaged," LdPC to HF, July 18, 1913, WA.

99   "Do let us go on," RW to HF, February 4, 1915, WA.

99   "terribly funny," RW to HF, March 8, 1915, WA.

99   "to give the gossips," ibid.

100   "Now I want to talk," RW to HF, March 31, 1915, WA.

100   "your true friend," RW to HF, August 9, 1915, WA.

100   "approximates to the majority," ibid.

100   "beautiful & . . . very high-bred," RW to HF, September 4, 1915, WA.

101   "you [could not] help being 'desirable,'" ibid.

101   "chimerical & far-fetched," RW to HF, March 26, 1916, WA.

101   "impossible," RW to HF, April 7, 1916, WA.

101   "Do let me hear," RW to HF, November 11, 1915, WA.

101   "Do stop buying cows," RW to HF, January 13, 1916, WA.

102   "It changes the whole day," RW to HF, March 28, 1916, WA.

102   "an uncongenial alliance," RW to HF, April 7, 1916, WA.

102   "so happy at home," ibid.

102   "For one second consider marrying," ibid.

102   "a marvelous bunch," RW to RHW, March 1914, WA.

103   "My dearest Harry . . . Yesterday was the," RW to HF, May 9, 1916, WA.

104   "I miss you so terribly," RW to HF, May 14, 1916, WA.

104   "I think of . . . your eyes," RW to HF, May 20, 1916, WA.

104   "I do love you," RW to HF, May 30, 1916, WA.

104   "My love for you has grown," RW to HF, June 1, 1916, WA.

104   "I really can't wait," RW to HR, June 8, 1916, WA.

104   "I could think of nothing," RW to HF, May 7, 1916, WA.

104   "that you think your mother," RW to HF, June 2, 1916, WA.

105   "like a bolt from the blue" RHW to HF, May 7, 1916, WA.

106   "I've tried so hard," RHW to HF, May 1916, WA.

106   "heart broken old party," RHW to HF, ibid.

106   "For what you have done," J. H. Oglesby to HF, May 1916, WA.

106   "[Harry] in his entire life," LdP to RHW, May 30, 1916, WA.

107   "wonderfully attractive," Marshall Bullitt to HF, May 22, 1916, WA.

107   "fine . . . in every sense," Elihu Root to HA, June 8, 1916, HML.

107   "knocked spots out," RdP to RHW, July 6, 1916, WA.

107   "I promise you," LdPC to RHW, May 30, 1916, WA.

108   "Dear Mrs. Wales, The chocolates," HF to RHW, June 29, 1916, WA.

110   "Everyone here is thrilled," LdPC to RdP, July 9, 1916, WA.

110   "the fiend," RdP to RHW, August 14, 1916, WA.

110   "nature . . . so thoughtful," RdP to RHW, June 28, 1916, WA.

110   "perfect," RdP to RHW, July 4, 1916, WA.

110   "*perfect,*" RdP to RHW, July 6, 1916, WA.

111   "more perfect than," RdP to RHW, July 1916, WA.

111   "twosed [*sic*] & spooned," RdP to RHW, July 25, 1916, WA.

111   "H. [was] never selfish," RdP to RHW, August 8, 1916, WA.

111   "so sweet every minute," RdP to RHW, August 22, 1916, WA.

111   "heavenly . . . the very loveliest," RdP to RHW, September 6, 1916, WA.

111   "bedroom & private bath," RdP to RHW, September 16, 1916, WA.

112   "he holds . . . so tight," RdP to RHW, July 4, 1916, WA.

112   "all soaped up before," RdP to RHW, July 25, 1916, WA.

112   "the loveliest of wildflowers," HF to RHW, August 7, 1916, WA.

112   "He has no other idea," RdP to RHW, August 25, 1916, WA.

112   "keen to have his [own herd] the best" RdP to RHW, September 22, 1916, WA.

114   "fine in every way," RdP to RHW, July 1916, WA. (The honeymoon was briefly interrupted by a return to Winterthur so Harry could attend the trial of Pierre S. du Pont vs. Alfred I. du Pont.)

114   "wonderful letter for a man of 76," RdP to RHW, August 30, 1916, WA.

114   "has taken it so wonderfully," RdP to RHW, November 8, 1916, WA.

114   "keep him occupied," ibid.

115   "entered the room," RdP to RHW, October 19, 1917, WA.

115   "the second cook," RdP to RHW, November 16, 1920, WA.

115   "the kitchenmaid," RdP to RHW, September 26, 1917, WA.

115   "The whole house is run," ibid.

115   "I do hope that you will not," RW to HA, June 8, 1916, WA.

115   "really very sweet," RdP to RHW, October 1917, WA.

115   "brave and uncomplaining," RdP to RHW, December 29, 1916, WA.

116   "did you evah," RdP to RHW, January 1918, WA.

116   "I sure am fortunate," RdP to RHW, June 7, 1918, WA.

116   "Little H. is willing," RdP to RHW, October 20, 1917, WA.

116   "I am so mad I could scratch," RdP to HF, February 19, 1918, WA.

116   "After dinner we came right," RdP to RHW, April 27, 1917, WA.

118   "The Percheron stallion," RdP to RHW, July 1917, WA.

118   "the best bull has hurt," RdP to RHW, July 1916, WA.

118	"half of the cows," RdP to RHW, November 2, 1917, WA.
118	"Henry Antoine," RdP to RHW, October 29, 1917, WA.
118	"little Tommy Cat," RdP to HF, January 10, 1918, WA.
119	"Poor Louise is wretched," RdP to RHW, November 19, 1917, WA.
119	"nerve medicine," RdP to RHW, October 1918 (not exact quote), WA.
120	"Ruth is so depressed," HF to RHW, December 22, 1918, WA.
120	"divinely happy," RdP to RHW, June 24, 1919, WA.
120	"sorrow & sadness," RdP to RHW, January 29, 1920, WA.
120	"so [much] that I fear," RdP to RHW, January 27, 1920, WA.
120	"very apprehensive," RdP to RHW, May 1, 1920, WA.
120	"mental reflexes," RdP to RHW, February 10, 1920, WA.
120	"I have never told you," RdP to RHW, August 1920, WA.
120	"Now Puss if you do not wish," RdP to RHW, November 2, 1920, WA.
124	"well known nerve symptoms," RdP to HF, November 29, 1924, WA.
124	"everyone will know," RdP to RHW, November 1924, WA.
124	"so to speak a social," RdP to HF, November 29, 1924, WA.
124	"every weak point," ibid.
125	"a private sanitarium," RdP to RHW, December 6, 1924, WA.
125	"I love you more than tongue can tell," HF to RdP, December 1924, WA.
125	"Dont worry as it will be OK," HF to RdP, December 1924, WA.
125	"But oh! The famille," RdP to RHW, May 10, 1925, WA.
125	"of course, he won't have the luck," RdP to RHW, November 27, 1925, WA.
125	"Louise . . . pretty mad," RdP to RHW, June 19, 1926, WA.
125	"bounced the nurse," RdP to RHW, October 16, 1926, WA.
126	"very lonely winter," HA to his sister, Sophie Chandler (Mrs. T. P.), March 27, 1926, WA.
126	"I shall be entirely alone," HA to Marshall Bullitt, January 9, 1926, WA.
126	"level headed," RdP to RHW, undated 1925, WA.
129	"More charm to the square inch," RdP to RHW, August 1917, WA.
133	"razor & the thing you put the soap on with," HF to parents, March 22, 1896, WA.
133	"I shaved this morning," HF to parents, May 3, 1896, HML.
134	"He never could remember," JAHS, oral interview with Dana Taylor, April 5, 1973, WA.
134	"started to teach little H.," RdP to RHW, July 5, 1917, WA.
144	"I want to write to you," LdP to HF, September 18, c. 1895, WA
144	"It must be so awful," LdP to HF, May 8, 1896, WA.
144	"I do not know if Papa is elected," HF to parents, May 12, 1895, WA.

144   "Won't it be awful if Papa," LdP to HF, May 1895, WA.

144   "Goodbye darling," LdP to HF, undated [c. 1895], WA.

144   "We have the most awful old cook," LdP to HF, October 31, 1895, WA.

151   "I went to see Bertha's," LdPC to HF, June 18, 1948, WA.

153   "apple this & apple that," HF to parents, October 28, 1894, WA.

153   "black cake," HF to parents, November 8, 1896, WA.

155   "anywhere else in the house," JAHS, oral interview with Albert Feliciani, April 10, 1975, WA.

156   "interest and enchantment," Marshal Fry to HF, August 9, 1957, WA.

158   "looked perfectly lovely," HF to John and Florence Magee, January 19, 1938, WA.

159   "the dancing tent," HF to Marian Coffin, November 29, 1939, WA.

161   "I beg that you," RdP to RL, author's reminiscence.

163   "I bet it won't work," HF to JAHS, reminiscence.

163   "title" of his traveling companion, JAHS reminiscence.

163   "Equerry to H. F. du Pont," ibid.

165   "to notice everything," HF to Harlan B. Phillips, March 25, 1962, WA.

165   "a grievous struggle," du Pont, R. W., *Non Accepto*, unpublished essay, undated, WA.

165   "awful act," ibid.

165   "I forgot to tell you," HF to PdP, undated [probably 1894].

165   "with perfectionism & discipline," JAHS, oral interview with the Reverend John O'Hear, July 15, 1975, WA.

165   "real devotion," ibid.

165   "dignity & restraint," ibid.

166   "little H took a slight cold," RdP to RHW, November 25, 1921, WA.

166   "every other day colds," HF to LdP, December 1, 1938, WA.

166   "Mr. du Pont felt a chill," JAHS, oral interview with Percy Vickers, March 21, 1973, WA.

167   "guffawed" at Booth Tarkington's, RdP to RHW, March 7, 1927, WA.

167   *"enthralled,"* RdP to RHW, March 19, 1929, WA.

167   "corrupt, haunting," RdP to RHW probably March 21, 1920, WA.

167   "disgusted and fascinated," RdP to RHW, March 11, 1927, WA.

168   "dear little Ruth," Sara Delano Roosevelt to RW, 1916, WA.

168   "absolutely horrified," RdP to Marian Coffin, October 3, 1940, WA.

170   "We use the lady," JAHS, oral interview with Ruth P. McCollum, May 8, 1975, WA.

170   "I am in the greatest," HF to P. E. Guerin, Inc., December 29, 1908, WA.

170   "with the least possible delay," HF to C. L. Morlatt, June 17, 1913, WA.

170   "immediately as it is quite late enough now," HF to John W. Chapple, October 2, 1911, WA.

170   "as soon as possible," ibid.

172   "Imagine, inside your own house," RdP to author, reminiscence.

172   "socially, they were New Yorkers," JAHS, oral interview with Dr. Margaret Irving Handy, August 1, 1973, WA.

175   "This house is swell," RdP to RHW, April 11, 1931, WA.

175   "hoped to rush the house," HF to Marian Coffin, May 28, 1928, WA.

176   "Have you given my iris," HF to Marian Coffin, May 23, 1929, WA.

176   "too beautiful," RdP to RHW, October 4, 1929, WA.

176   "profligate," JAHS, oral interview with Charles F. Montgomery, May 16, 1977, WA.

176   "In the building," ibid.

176   "extravagant or wasteful," HA to HF, October 15, 1899, WA.

177   "more money than [she]," JAHS, oral interview with Dr. Margaret Irving Handy, August 1, 1973, WA.

178   "We better get the darn thing," as reported by JAHS, early 1900s.

179   "Every year," as reported to P. L. Harrison (de Brossard) about Long Island Historical Society, Southampton, N.Y., early 1960.

179   "millionaire's wife," RdP to RHW, April 18, 1931, WA.

179   "an enchanting sun-dial," HF to Marian Coffin, October 21, 1913, WA.

179   "There are two ways," JAHS, oral interview with Lloyd Hyde, May 6, 1974, WA.

180   "death blow," HF to LdPC, December 1, 1933, WA.

180   "Papa's name dragged," HF to LdPC, November 20, 1933, WA.

181   "I am absolutely broke," HF to Daniel Buckley, October 21, 1933, WA.

181   "all of the horrors," HF to LdPC, December 1, 1933, WA.

181   "shutting down half," ibid.

181   "I hope there isn't anything," JAHS, oral interview with Charles Montgomery, May 16, 1977, WA.

182   "Mr. du Pont was so surprised," ibid.

186   "lot of woodwork around," HF to Harlan B. Phillips, oral interview, April 11, 1962, p. 14, WA.

188   "omnivorous collector," JAHS, oral interview with Lloyd Hyde, May 6, 1974, WA.

188   "a few more," JAHS, oral interview with G. A. Weymouth, March 2, 1977, WA.

189   "Mr. Francis," JAHS, oral interview with Dana Taylor, April 5, 1973, WA.

190   "Mr. Hyde," JAHS, oral interview with Lloyd Hyde, May 6, 1974, WA.

190   "Will it be too late," HF to Joe Kindig, Jr., June 21, 1933, WA.

190   "I know that Ruth," HF to Charles O. Cornelius, November 23, 1932, WA.

190   his own "memorial," HF to Bertha K. Benkard, December 31, 1935, WA.

191   "There is some woodwork," HF to Thomas T. Waterman, July 31, 1935, WA.

191   "bed bugs by the million," JAHS, oral interview with Howard Lattomus, March 15, 1973, WA.

193   "wanted to have Harry's friendship," JAHS, oral interview with Lloyd Hyde, May 6, 1974, WA.

193   "the boss wore the poor woman out," JAHS, oral interview with Dana Taylor, April 5, 1973, WA.

195   "I am thinking of doing," HF to Henry D. Sleeper, June 21, 1927, WA.

196   "Whether or not my Winterthur," HF to Beverley Robinson, February 21, 1930, WA.

197   "in the way of furniture," HF to Francis P. Garvan, July 2, 1931, WA.

197   "the house is practically," HF to Marian Coffin, February 21, 1931, WA.

197   "My house here is entirely," HF to Thomas Waterman, November 7, 1932, WA.

198   "practical for living purposes," HF to LdPC, April 3, 1941, WA.

198   "had to spend," HF to Henry D. Sleeper, February 21, 1931, WA.

203   "the collection has already," HF to David Finley, May 12, 1943, WA.

204   "I ordered my steel," HF to Eugene Grace, September 1950, WA.

207   "from personal whim," JAHS, oral interview with Charles Montgomery, May 16, 1977, WA.

207   "literally clapped his hands," ibid.

207   "have a certain nimbus," Wilmarth S. Lewis, Minutes, Winterthur Board of Trustees, January 15, 1966, WA.

210   "even temperament," HA to Eugene E. du Pont, February 25, 1921, WA.

210   "absolute perfection," I. I. R. Henry to HF, May 4, 1915, WA.

211   "crankiest person around," JAHS, reminiscence.

211   "Oh, those dandelions," JAHS, oral interview with Howard Lattomus, March 15, 1973, WA.

212   "Every man has his skill," Ruth Joyce, oral interview with David S. Richard, Jr., December 20, 1989.

213   "The man had something," JAHS, oral interview with Walter O. Petroll, March 27, 1975, WA.

213   "crazy about vegetables," JAHS, oral interview with Elsie Hance, May 13, 1973, WA.

213   "Oh, man it was nice," JAHS, oral interview with William Cannon, August 10, 1973, WA.

213   "He saw the whole picture," JAHS, oral interview with Walter O. Petroll, March 27, 1975, WA.

213   "at the wrong time," ibid.

213   "Because of his insistence," ibid.

213   "He didn't postpone things," JAHS, oral interview with Charles F. Montgomery, May 16, 1977, WA.

216   "He wanted it," JAHS, oral interview with Park McCann, August 8, 1973, WA.

216   "tickled pink," ibid.

216   "He treated me like a man," ibid.

216   "You didn't dare leave," JAHS, oral interview with Dana Taylor, April 5, 1973, WA.

216   "He was an awful good man," ibid.

216   "If you broke something," JAHS, oral interview with Hendrik DeBock, June 18, 1975, WA.

216   "Everybody makes mistakes," JAHS, oral interview with George Colman, March 28, 1973, WA.

216   "Man, you couldn't keep up with him," JAHS, oral interview with Park McCann, August 8, 1973, WA.

217   "It was put in by someone," ibid.

217   "pretty near free," JAHS, oral interview with Albert Feliciani, April 10, 1975.

218   "wonderful place," JAHS, oral interview, Everett Boyce, July 15, 1974, WA.

218   "surprising place," ibid.

218   "It was wonderful to watch," JAHS, oral interview with the Reverend John O'Hear, July 15, 1975, WA.

218   "grow up," JAHS, oral interview with Averell (Mrs. Edmond) du Pont, March 1, 1973, WA.

218   "He held onto something," ibid.

218   "taste, scholarship," Yale honorary degree (LHD), conferred by President A. Whitney Griswold, June 8, 1953, WA.

218   "exquisite taste," Williams honorary degree (LHD), conferred by President James P. Baxter, June 9, 1977, WA.

218   "a living museum," University of Pennsylvania honorary degree(LHD) conferred by Dr. Gaylord P. Harnwell, January 20, 1962, WA.

218   "discerning taste," University of Delaware honorary degree (LLD) conferred by President John A. Perkins, June 13, 1954, WA.

219   "unequalled leadership," Pratt Institute doctor of fine arts degree,
       presented by Trustee Nathaniel Becker, June 4, 1965, WA.

219   "in the Field of modern industry," Sunshine University honorary Ph.D.,
       signed by A. L. Anderson, Dean, School of Industry, June 10, 1964, WA.

219   "a task well done," Horticultural Society of New York, board of directors,
       January 8, 1947, WA.

219   "guidance through the most trying," ibid.

219   "incalculable aid," New York Botanical Garden, Charles B. Harding,
       President, May 16, 1957, WA.

219   "one of the best," Garden Club of America, April 18, 1956, WA.

220   "a Museum," the National Trust for Historic Preservation, Louise du Pont
       Crowninshield Award, 1961.

221   "I arose [in Providence] at 5:30," HF to Peggy Goddard (Mrs. R. H. Ives
       Goddard), May 14, 1961, WA.

221   "The lunch after," HF to Maude Atherton (Mrs. Ray Atherton), April 27,
       1967, WA.

222   "make it look," JAHS, oral interview with Samuel E. Homsey, March 31,
       1977, WA.

224   "Somehow or other," HF to Harlan B. Phillips, March 25, 1962, WA.

225   "I speak very badly," HF to Harry M. Buten, director, Buten Museum of
       Wedgwood, Merion, Pennsylvania, August 4, 1960, WA.

225   "decorative arts," HF to Jacqueline Kennedy, March 9, 1961, WA.

225   "young and knowledgeable," HF to Jacqueline Kennedy, March 13,
       1961, WA.

225   "three thoughts in mind," ibid.

226   "I cannot wait to hear," Jacqueline Kennedy to HF, March 16, 1961, WA.

226   "if you like them," HF to Jacqueline Kennedy, April 17, 1961, WA.

226   "exhausted . . . all the furniture," HF to Jacqueline Kennedy, May 2,
       1961, WA.

226   "to tramping around the White House," Jacqueline Kennedy, to HF,
       April 28, 1961, WA.

227   "You are so efficient," Jacqueline Kennedy to HF, May 3, 1961, WA.

228   "In the East Room," HF to Jacqueline Kennedy, June 14, 1961, WA.

229   "I do not mean," HF to Jacqueline Kennedy, January 15, 1962, WA.

229   "I hope you will not wear yourself," HF to Jacqueline Kennedy,
       May 29, 1961, WA.

229   "I don't quite understand," HF to Jacqueline Kennedy, August 17, 1961, WA.

229   "I wish you would give," HF to Jacqueline Kennedy, November 2,
       1961, WA.

229   "I hope you will bear with me," HF to Jacqueline Kennedy, January 12, 1962, WA.

229   "is better. I know you would agree," Jacqueline Kennedy to HF, May 17, 1962, WA.

229   "Nothing is more elegant," Jacqueline Kennedy to HF, May 3, 1962, WA.

229   under the dryer, Jacqueline Kennedy to HF, January 20, 1962, WA.

229   "on the bumpiest plane," Jacqueline Kennedy to HF, June 8, 1962, WA.

229   "That room needs all the welcoming," ibid.

229   "the feel of a historic house," ibid.

229   "in the last half hour," HF to Jacqueline Kennedy, December 15, 1962, WA.

229   "just the right paper," ibid.

229   "quite distressed," Jacqueline Kennedy to HF, December 20, 1962, WA.

230   "Don't you think," ibid.

230   "This is the only time," ibid.

230   "It could not be helped," HF to William Elder, December 27, 1962, WA.

230   "a treasure," Jacqueline Kennedy, TV showing of White House, February 14, 1962.

230   "If you were appalled," Jacqueline Kennedy to HF, September 20, 1962, WA.

231   "a bewildered captain," Lorraine Pearce to HF, July 26, 1961, WA.

231   "There are too many people," JAHS to HF, June 23, 1961, WA.

231   "Mr. Boudin may be all right," William Elder to HF, January 15, 1963, WA.

231   "I do think," William Elder to HF, January 16, 1963, WA.

231   "did a great deal of good," William Elder to HF, January 24, 1963, WA.

231   "Don't get discouraged," HF to William Elder, January 17, 1963, WA.

232   "held him in the highest esteem," Janet Felton to RL, August 12, 1994.

232   "so sad to have missed," Jacqueline Kennedy to HF, April 5, 1962, WA.

232   "most inexhaustible chairman," Jacqueline Kennedy to HF, May 22, 1961, WA.

232   "to amaze and delight," ibid.

232   "Nothing would have been possible," Jacqueline Kennedy to HF, April 15, 1962, WA.

232   "I am so glad to say," Jacqueline Kennedy to HF, November 21, 1962, WA.

232   "loan" of an architect, HF to Jacqueline Kennedy, September 17, 1963, WA.

232   "Dear Mr. du Pont, don't you know," Jacqueline Kennedy to HF, September 26, 1963, WA.

233   "letter of friendship," HF to President and Mrs. Lyndon Johnson, undated, 1967, WA.

233   "proposed discontinuance," Committee to Save Cooper Union Museum to A. A. Houghton, Jr., July 9, 1963, WA.

234   "insubstantial . . . the rising tide of opposition," Committee to Save Cooper Union to A. A. Houghton, Jr., July 9, 1963, WA.

234   "A museum cannot suddenly," ibid.

234   "The temporary closing," Milbank, Tweed, Hadley, and McCloy, Counsel for Cooper Union for Advancement of Science and Art, to A. I. Edelman, July 16, 1963, WA.

236   "Obviously there should be," Richard P. Wunder to HF, September 9, 1963, WA.

236   "some blue sky," HF to prospective contributors to Committee to Save, November 11, 1964, WA.

237   "the goal is within," HF to Members of Committee to Save, March 1, 1965, WA.

240   "extraordinary progress," Wilmarth S. Lewis, Minutes, Winterthur Board of Trustees, January 15, 1966, WA.

240   "bloodstream of the museum world," ibid.

241   "earnest . . . purpose . . . to life," Marshall Bullitt to HF, September 20, 1924, WA.

241   "As a matter of fact," HF to Marshall Bullitt, October 8, 1924, WA.

242   "to see them, their children," HF to Robert T. Brown, April 7, 1944, WA.

244   "Knowing how I feel about," HF to RL, October 19, 1957, WA.

Acknowledgments

So many people have helped me in this endeavor that it is hard to know where to begin. Four at the outset—my husband, John Holmes, my peerless "twin," Lyn Austin, and friends Nancy and R. W. B. Lewis—were quick to see merit in the idea and have given me heart all along. Dick Lewis has been of extraordinary help in several readings of the text, and it is easy to understand his students' reverence for him.

John A. H. Sweeney, curator emeritus of the Winterthur Museum, in 1954 graduated with the first class of the Winterthur Program. His early acquaintance with my father as co-worker on many projects developed into a true friendship, which I'm happy indeed to have inherited. Uniquely equipped to provide insights both about aspects of my father's personality and about the museum, John has been my mentor every step of the way, and the fact that years ago he was inspired to capture on tape reminiscences about Henry F. du Pont from scores of associates and friends has provided me with an indispensable resource.

A more recent graduate of the Winterthur Program, Jay E. Cantor, has likewise been extraordinarily generous with his ideas, scholarly vision, and time, and I have looked to his magnificent book, *Winterthur*, for key source material and aesthetic pleasure. It is my encyclopedia.

My long-standing friend and colleague, Robert W. W. Evans, M.D., editor par excellence and a fan of the project from the outset, has gone over the script with incalculable wisdom and skill, as have two of my children, Pauline and George Lord, Jr., as well as their father, George de F. Lord, and I am greatly indebted to them all.

I also wish to give thanks to a brilliant linguist, my friend Dorothy Prelinger, especially for her labors over early correspondence of my father and grandparents—written in French and often thoroughly illegible.

Members of the Winterthur staff have been superb, beginning with Dwight P. Lanmon, director of the Winterthur Museum, Garden, and Library, who with his wife, Lorri, are my Golf Cottage neighbors. Dwight has expedited all manner of matters and commended to me as research assistant Ruth N. Joyce, of the garden staff. Gary Kulik, head of the library, provided me with essential information, and librarian Richard McKinstry and archivist Heather Clewell from the start have tirelessly unearthed and photocopied material from the daunting morass left by my father.

I am likewise indebted to librarian Neville Thompson, associate librarian Marguerite Connolly, and registration assistant Susan Newton, as well as to Patricia D. Elliott, advanced studies coordinator, and to the Winterthur photographers George Fistrovich and Herbert Crossan.

Before leaving the state of Delaware, I also wish to mention the Hagley Museum and Library, whose archivists Marjorie McNinch and Lynn Catanese have been wonderful from the beginning. Jon Williams, curator of prints and photographs, has been extremely helpful.

In a project such as this, the role of archivist—gatekeeper to the past—may be supreme, and for assistance as outstanding as that in Delaware, Douglas V. D. Brown of Groton School deserves high honors. During the past several years he has imaginatively discovered information about my father's life at boarding school, and I am touched by his interest and enthusiasm.

Thanks are due to archivists, Michael Raines of Harvard University, Dorothy Rapp of the U.S. Military Academy at West Point, Raymond Teichman of the Franklin D. Roosevelt Library at Hyde Park, Craig F. Jessup of the Roosevelt-Vanderbilt National Historical sites, also at Hyde Park, Polly Darnell and Julie P. Bressor, respectively, of the Shelburne Museum and Shelburne Farms Historical Collection in Shelburne, Vermont, Sister Maria Espiritu McCall, of the Sisters of the Blessed Sacrament in Bensalem, Pennsylvania, and A. Butikofer of Winterthur, Switzerland.

I am grateful as well to Mary Jane Mallonee, reference librarian of the

Widener University Law School in Wilmington, Delaware, Anna Malicka of the Lewis-Walpole Library in Farmington, Connecticut, and Gail Stanislow, librarian of the Brandywine River Museum in Chadds Ford, Pennsylvania.

In addition to the above, many other people have participated in this undertaking, some by providing specific information, others by dint of reading part or all of the manuscript. They are Wesley Adams, Harold d'O. Baker, Georgina Bissell, Elisabeth Blua, Mary Braga, Innis Bromfield, Thomas N. Byrne, M.D., Marion Campbell, Samuel F. Campiche, David A. Carlson, M.D., Donald J. Cohen, M.D., Madora Cooke, Janet Felton Cooper, Pauline L. Harrison de Brossard, Rose Monique de Pommereau, Emile F. du Pont, Kingsley Ervin, Albert Feliciani, Bengt Friedman, Wendell Garrett, Arthur Gordon, Ruth Harrison Grobe, James R. Hammond, Alfred and Helen Harrison, Henry F. Harrison, Alison Henning, Edna Hilley, Stanley W. Jackson, M.D., Arthur W. Joyce, Henry Lord, Margaretta Lovell, Jennifer and Bernard Mirling, the late Florence Montgomery, Barbara Oldenburg, Isabel Potter, Mary Reigeluth, Caroline Rollins, Edward Shorter, M.D., Robert W. Trivits, Rosemany Van Slyck, Anna Glen Vietor, William W. Warner, Nicholas Fox Weber, George A. Weymouth, Ellen and Robert White and Ess A. White, M.D.

Very many extra thanks are due to Nancy Tuckerman, through whom I obtained permission from Caroline Schlossberg and John F. Kennedy, Jr., to print their mother's letters.

The phrase "without whom this could not have been written" may be a cliché, but where my fantastic cohorts Ruth Joyce and Anita Jones are concerned, it approaches the literal truth. Both of them, editors at heart, are the epitome of savvy, industry, adaptability, and good humor; they have brought superb judgment to matters of style and interpretation, and have given themselves to a total involvement in this effort.

Ruth, as my research assistant, has for years immersed herself in the Delaware archives and libraries, and she helped me immeasurably with the text per se. A gifted writer and true professional, she is an ideal co-worker, with the added ability to collapse with me in helpless laughter. Anita, equally invaluable, has "typed" the entire manuscript on two different computers, and she is skilled indeed with words and their subtleties. As my neighbor in Connecticut, she has made herself available at countless impossible moments, at times all but living in my Barnhouse, or speeding there to attend to the merest semicolon.

Without the devotion to this project of Ruth Joyce and Anita Jones, it could never, as such, have materialized.

I write these acknowledgments in June 1998 in the heart of New Mexico, on George Ranney's high desert cattle ranch, a landscape entirely new to me: towering mesas above expanses of sandy earth dotted or dense with piñon pines, and junipers with driftwood-like bark. Cacti abound. The cane cholla, especially striking, unfurls magenta blossoms with yellow centers and bright yellow fruit clusters.

Enveloped by the hospitality of George and his lady, Betsy Getz, and sharing the guest house with T. Edward and Merrell Hambleton, I feel very much at home, for these are among my husband's oldest friends. I regret most deeply that John Holmes did not live to see this book published, as he had been so entirely a part of it. John's intellect, passion, and caring were immeasurable; his loss was unreconcilable.

Index

Page numbers in *italics* refer to illustrations.